BILLY GRAHAM
Evangelistic Association
Always Good News.

Dear Friend,

I am pleased to send you this copy of *Jesus in Me*, written by my sister Anne Graham Lotz. Anne is a gifted Bible teacher, bestselling author, and frequent speaker at the Billy Graham Training Center at The Cove.

Many Christians today often overlook the third person of the Trinity—the Holy Spirit. *Jesus in Me* explores the depth, beauty, and comfort of this relationship, which is offered to every believer. God's Word says the Holy Spirit is our constant companion, a *"Helper, to be with you forever"* (John 14:16, ESV). As you read this book's Biblical truths, it's my prayer that you will draw closer to the Lord—with the help of the Holy Spirit.

For more than 70 years, God has used the Billy Graham Evangelistic Association and friends like you to reach people all over the world with the Gospel. I'm so thankful for the ways He has worked—and for what He will do in the years ahead.

If you represent one of the lives the Lord has touched, we would love to hear from you. Your story has the power to impact the lives of so many others. May God richly bless you.

Sincerely,

Franklin Graham
President & CEO

If you would like to know more about our ministry, please contact us:

IN THE U.S.:
Billy Graham Evangelistic Association
1 Billy Graham Parkway
Charlotte, NC 28201-0001
BillyGraham.org
info@bgea.org
Toll-free: 1-877-247-2426

IN CANADA:
Billy Graham Evangelistic
  Association of Canada
20 Hopewell Way NE
Calgary, AB T3J 5H5
BillyGraham.ca
Toll-free: 1-888-393-0003

Praise for

Jesus in Me

"Fifteen years ago, I sat in an arena with thousands of other women as Anne Graham Lotz expounded on the person and power of the Holy Spirit. Every word was like a lit match catching fire in my soul. Since then, I've gotten an up-close, personal look at Anne's relationship with the Spirit of God. She walks with Him, listens to Him, and rests on His power to fulfill the Father's purposes for her. The truths that she has taught me—and that she now shares with you in this book—have come not just from deep study but also from the personal experience of a woman who has learned the rhythms of grace through a lifetime of faithfulness."

—PRISCILLA SHIRER, Bible teacher and author

"This book is a genuine treasury of wisdom that can be attained only through a life of walking with God and being led by His Holy Spirit. I am thrilled Anne Graham Lotz has walked this walk so that she can talk this talk for our benefit! This is about the only way to fully live the life for which we were each created. Read it and rejoice!"

—ERIC METAXAS, *New York Times* number one bestselling author of *Bonhoeffer* and *Miracles*

"One of the things I've always appreciated about Anne Graham Lotz is her passionate desire to pursue God and know Him intimately. In this recent season of suffering, Anne has learned some profound lessons and experienced the Holy Spirit as her constant companion, comforter, and friend. The result is her new book, *Jesus in Me*. I highly recommend it."

—GREG LAURIE, senior pastor of Harvest Christian Fellowship

"Most of us would give anything to be literally led through the day by the tender, firm hand of our Savior. How we'd love to hear His voice telling us clearly which way to turn and when to stop. And, oh, if we could only feel the nearness and sweetness of His presence! The good news is we *can*! In her new and most remarkable book, Anne Graham Lotz succinctly explains how the Spirit who resides within us *is* the Spirit of Jesus Himself. Hence the title *Jesus in Me*. My friend details not only how to lean on the Spirit of Jesus but also how to recognize His voice, perceive His touch, sense His nearness, and respond to His instruction. I heartily recommend this excellent book to anyone who desires a closer communion with Christ!"

—Joni Eareckson Tada, founder of Joni and Friends International
    Disability Center

"I just finished spending the day reading Anne's wonder-filled book *Jesus in Me*. It is truly a spiritual thriller—for isn't that what it is like when a child of God discovers he or she not only is indwelt by God's Spirit but also can be divinely led and empowered by His Spirit in every circumstance of life? The theology is clear in these pages, and you'll find story after story of what this Spirit-directed walk looks like in the varied trials, twists, and turns of life."

—Kay Arthur, author, Bible teacher, and cofounder of Precept
    Ministries International

"It is one thing to read a book *about* the Holy Spirit, but it is another thing altogether to read a book by an author who is *experiencing* the ongoing presence and power of the Holy Spirit. *Jesus in Me* is a living testimony that will teach you, encourage you, and inspire you to be like Christ. Regardless of where you are in your life today, God will use these transforming words to meet you at the point of your greatest need. He *is* with you always, even until the end of the earth."

—Dr. Ronnie Floyd, senior pastor of Cross Church and president
    of the National Day of Prayer

"*Jesus in Me* is a simple yet powerful book about the truth of who the Holy Spirit is and the importance of how He works in our lives. Within every page you will discover what it means to have Jesus fully alive inside you! This book is a much-needed read for the body of Christ today."

—DARRYL STRAWBERRY, evangelist and former major league
baseball player

"Anne Graham Lotz stands as one of the most anointed and gifted voices in modern-day Christianity. In her new book, *Jesus in Me,* Anne equips us with a biblically substantiated framework for a life driven, convicted, and comforted by God's precious Holy Spirit. This book will not just inspire you; it will empower you!"

—SAMUEL RODRIGUEZ, lead pastor of New Season, president of the
National Hispanic Christian Leadership Conference, author of *You
Are Next,* and executive producer of the movie *Breakthrough*

JESUS IN ME

ANNE GRAHAM LOTZ

JESUS IN ME

Experiencing *the* Holy Spirit *as a* Constant Companion

MULTNOMAH

This *Billy Graham Library Selection* special edition is
published with permission from Multnomah.

A *Billy Graham Library Selection* designates materials that are appropriate for a well-rounded collection of quality Christian literature, including both classic and contemporary reading and reference materials.

This *Billy Graham Library Selection* special edition is published with permission from Multnomah.

JESUS IN ME

Published in the United States by Multnomah, an imprint of Random House, a division of Penguin Random House LLC. Originally published in hardcover in the United States by Multnomah, an imprint of Random House, a division of Penguin Random House LLC, in 2019.

MULTNOMAH® and its mountain colophon are registered trademarks of Penguin Random House LLC.

Author is represented by Alive Literary Agency, 7680 Goddard Street, Suite 200, Colorado Springs, Colorado 80920, www.aliveliterary.com.

Paperback ISBN 978-0-525-65111-6
BGEA edition ISBN 978-1-593-28716-0

The Library of Congress has cataloged the hardcover edition as follows:
Names: Lotz, Anne Graham, 1948- author.
Title: Jesus in me : experiencing the Holy Spirit as a constant companion / Anne Graham Lotz.
  Description: Colorado Springs : Multnomah, 2019. | Includes bibliographical references.
Identifiers: LCCN 2018058173 | ISBN 9780525651048 (hardcover) | ISBN 9780525651086 (electronic)
Subjects: LCSH: Holy Spirit. | Spirituality—Christianity.
Classification: LCC BT121.3 .L68 2019 | DDC 231/.3—dc23
LC record available at https://lccn.loc.gov/2018058173

Printed in the United States of America on acid-free paper

waterbrookmultnomah.com

9 8 7 6 5 4 3 2 1

First Trade Paperback Edition

SPECIAL SALES
Most Multnomah books are available at special quantity discounts when purchased in bulk by corporations, organizations, and special-interest groups. Custom imprinting or excerpting can also be done to fit special needs. For information, please email specialmarketscms@penguinrandomhouse.com.

Dedicated to the Lonely

To them God has chosen to make
known . . . the glorious riches of
this mystery, which is *Christ in you,*
the hope of glory.

—COLOSSIANS 1:27

Contents

Contents

Experiencing the Holy Spirit as a Constant Companion

Weather permitting, early each morning that I am home, I walk and run for about two and a half miles. This has been my routine for over thirty years. As I grow older, I also grow more grateful for the physical ability to maintain this exercise. I have been consistent and committed to it, not just for the physical benefits but also because it is a stress reliever. The burdens of the day seem to be placed on hold for the thirty or forty minutes it takes to complete my route.

Over the years I have had multiple walking partners who have either moved on to other forms of exercise or dropped exercising altogether. The friend who walks with me now from time to time is a delight. While walking, we engage in energetic discussions, solve world problems, share insights into Scripture, and often end by praying for each other. Her companionship has made me aware of an interesting facet of my routine. When she walks with me, the journey does not seem nearly as long or arduous as when I walk alone. With her beside me, I seem to have more joy, more energy—and the time seems to fly by. Somehow, her presence makes my walk easier.

On the other hand, when I walk by myself, the routine seems harder, longer. My hamstrings seem tighter and unwilling to stretch for long strides. My knees ache when I pick up my pace for a jog. My breath seems more labored and shallow. My mind shifts into neutral. I find myself just trying to make it to the next bend in the trail, to the next familiar tree, to the third bridge that marks the ascent to the parking lot, to my waiting car on which I lean as I work through final stretches.

While the direction, pace, and length of the routine are the same whether I walk alone or with someone, a good companion makes a distinct difference in my overall enjoyment and well-being.

Which brings me to the walk of life. Living day after day, week after week, year after year requires effort, energy, commitment, focus, thought.

To be perfectly honest, I'm old enough to know that the path of life leads through emotional, physical, relational, and spiritual aches and pains. Some are irritating. Some disruptive. Some much more serious and even life threatening. At times I have found myself just trying to make it through this day. This month. This year. "If I can just make it to Easter break." "If I can just get to the beach for our vacation." "If I can just hang on until Christmas." There are times when I have fulfilled a commitment just to check it off my list and get on to the next thing so that I can get on to the next thing. The walk itself becomes a burden. Drudgery.

What I have needed is a walking partner. For life. Someone who would come alongside me and share every step of my journey, day in and day out. Someone in whom I could confide. Someone with whom I could discuss issues that are on my mind. Someone who would answer my questions. Help me with decisions. Listen to my complaints, my fears, my worries, my dreams. Someone I could trust. Believe. Enjoy. Someone whose very presence would bring joy. And peace. And hope. Someone who would know me. Who would understand me. Someone who would love me!

Where have I found such a walking partner? Amazingly, as a child of God, I didn't have to look around for one. I just needed to look within. Because God has given me the ultimate walking partner for life: His Spirit. And not just for life, but forever![1]

In this book I will not attempt a full, in-depth treatise on the Holy Spirit, nor will I explore all the ways He is understood or misunderstood, abused or used, sensationalized or normalized, neglected or prioritized. I will seek to share with you what I have experienced personally about this incredible divine Companion. While I do not claim that I can even begin to know all there is to know about Him, I am learning to enjoy and trust Him more and more. If anything, the more my knowledge of the Holy Spirit grows, the more I learn I still have a lot to learn! One thing I know for certain: He is not an optional extra in my Christian life. He is a divine necessity.

The indispensable necessity of the Holy Spirit has never been more evident in my life than during the writing of this book. As I began the challenge of putting words on a page, my ninety-nine-year-old father, whom I adored, went to Heaven. I was already a widow, and his homegoing left me an orphan. Six months later I was diagnosed with breast cancer, went through follow-up surgery, then began the brutal chemotherapy treatments. Through the ups and downs, the tears and joy, the grief and comfort, I have experienced the constant companionship of the Holy Spirit.

I have learned day in and day out that the Holy Spirit is all that Jesus is, though without His physical body. He is Jesus without skin. Just as Jesus is the exact representation of God the Father, the Spirit is the exact representation of Jesus's mind, will, and emotions. He is the invisible Jesus. The Holy Spirit is . . . *Jesus in me!*

Part One

Loving the Person of the Holy Spirit

Though you have not seen him, you love him.

—1 Peter 1:8

Have you ever formed ideas or opinions about someone based on what others told you? And then when you met the person for yourself, did you discover that actually he was very different from what you had been led to believe?

Recently I received an invitation to appear on a television talk show hosted by a couple who had been in the news frequently and had received quite a bit of negative publicity. Without intending to, I had absorbed some of the public's disparaging attitude. I almost declined the invitation, but when some respected advisers urged me to accept it, I did. What I discovered was almost the polar opposite of what I had been led to believe.

The couple was humble, warm, charming, thoughtful, encouraging, and supportive. They were easy to talk with, and I found my spirit resonating with theirs. To this day, I'm struck by the contrast between the public's perception of them, as well as my own preconceived opinions, and the reality of their lovely personalities and authentic testimonies.

While our perception of other people can be dramatically different from reality, the same may also be said about our perception of the Holy Spirit. Could your perception be different from the truth or even in sharp contrast to it?

I've heard the Holy Spirit spoken of as an "it," a feeling, a dove, a flame, a ghost, an emotion, or even an ecstatic experience. He is frequently referred to as the third person of the Trinity, as though He is the least of the Trinity or a postscript to the more significant Father and Son. All of which is inaccurate.

While the Holy Spirit may be symbolized by a dove or flame, while His presence may be accompanied by an emotion or feeling or ecstatic experience, He Himself is distinctly separate from those things. The Holy Spirit is not a thing but a person. His personhood is emphasized in John 16, when eleven times in eight verses, He is referred to by the personal, masculine pronouns *He, Him,* and *His.*[1]

So at the outset of our exploration of who the Holy Spirit is, we need to be clear that we are not speaking of an "it." We are speaking of a "He." He is a living person who has a mind, a will, and emotions. He is referred to as the third person of the Trinity not because He is the least but because He is the third person to be more fully revealed in Scripture.

In the Old Testament, although the Holy Spirit and God the Son—the living Word who became Jesus in the flesh—are present, it is God the Father who is primarily revealed. In the Gospels, while the Father and the Holy Spirit are certainly present, it is God the Son who is primarily revealed. Beginning with Acts and the epistles, although God the Father and God the Son are also present, it is primarily God the Holy Spirit who is revealed. In fact, the book of Acts is not about the acts of the disciples or the early church. It is a book about the acts of the Holy Spirit as He worked in and through the disciples and the early church.

If the Holy Spirit is a person with an intellect, will, and emotions, what is He really like? What is His personality? What are His responsibilities? Are you intrigued by this mysterious person? I know I have been and still am. One way we get to know Him is through His names.

In the Bible, names reveal the character of the person to whom they are given. For example, in the Old Testament, Abraham's grandson was given the name of Jacob, which means "deceiver" or "supplanter." Jacob grew up to be a man who deceived his father, Isaac. In doing so, Jacob supplanted his brother, Esau, as the heir to his father's blessing. He was well named.

Twenty years after that deception, when Jacob returned to claim his inheritance, he was blocked from doing so by the angel of the Lord, who was a visible, tangible manifestation of the Lord Himself. After an entire night of struggling, God dislocated Jacob's hip to force him to give in and give up. But instead of falling to the ground in a heap of self-pity, Jacob wound his arms around God's neck and said he would not let go until God blessed him. Right there, on the edge of the river that served as the border to the Promised Land . . . the river where they had been wrestling, God led Jacob to confess his name . . . who he was . . . the deceiver and supplanter. Then God changed Jacob's name to Israel, which means "a prince who has power with God." As a man broken, Jacob fully yielded his life to God, and he did indeed become a prince with power, the father of twelve sons who became the founding fathers of the nation that bears his name—Israel.[2]

Perhaps the most familiar example of how a name reveals someone's character is found in the name given to the Son of God. He was called Jesus, which means "Savior," "Rescuer," "Redeemer," "Deliverer"—the One who would save us from the penalty and power of sin.[3] His name accurately describes who He was . . . and who He is.

So what about the Holy Spirit? In John 16:7 Jesus gave Him a name that is often rendered "Helper" in English but is a rich word that requires several English words to effectively capture its meaning. The Amplified Bible version of the same verse indicates that the word for "Helper" could also be rendered as follows: "I tell you the truth, it is to your advantage that I go away; for if I do not go away, the Helper (Comforter, Advocate, Intercessor—Counselor, Strengthener, Standby) will not come to you; but if I go, I will send Him (the Holy Spirit) to you [to be in close fellowship with you]." In the following seven chapters, we'll consider together the personal and practical implications of each aspect of the Holy Spirit's name as listed in the Amplified Bible version of John 16:7.

One of my deepest, richest joys has been discovering by experience who the Holy Spirit is in every step of my life's journey. Each name that He has been given—Helper, Comforter, Advocate, Intercessor, Counselor, Strengthener, and Standby—reveals another aspect of His beautiful character and has provoked in me a deep love for the One who is my constant companion . . . Jesus in me. My prayer for this book is that you, too, will discover Him by personal experience as your constant companion and that the discovery will lead you to love and rely on Him more.

I

Our Helper

As my husband Danny's health deteriorated due to type 1 diabetes and its complications, I stopped traveling for the most part and embraced the joy of being his caregiver for three years. On an August afternoon, he was sitting by the pool, playing with our dog, and just relaxing in the summer sun. I stayed in the house to get some work done. Suddenly I realized it had been over an hour since I last checked on him. I ran to the window, looked toward the pool, and saw he was not there. With relief, thinking he had come in without my awareness, I ran through the house, looking for him and calling his name. No familiar voice responded. Only silence. A deep foreboding gripped my heart as I ran back to the window and saw our dog sitting by the water's edge. When I called to him, he refused to come. I flew down to the pool and found what I knew I would.

There are no words to describe my desperate cry for help as I jumped into the pool, pulled my husband to the steps, and cradled his head on my lap. Even as I called his name over and over, even as I cried out to God for help, I knew I was looking at a man who was already seeing his Lord. The expression on his face was one of strength, confidence, and utter peace.

What transpired next required all the Helper's assistance to get me through: staying on the line after my emergency call to 911, EMS arriving, medics running through the backyard and dragging Danny out of my lap, news helicopters swirling overhead, sheriff's deputies standing by the pool and guarding the property, cars filled with curious onlookers lining our street—and then the scene indelibly impressed on my mind when Danny was placed on a gurney and wheeled out of our yard as he left the house for the last time.

In His great compassion, the Helper sent visible helpers also: a chaplain with the sheriff's department who quietly stood by me as the EMS team worked on Danny, my son-in-law who put his arms around me as Danny was wheeled away, my children who came to sit with me in the small hospital ER waiting room, our doctor who appeared at Danny's bedside and urged me to put my husband on life support . . . just in case.

As I walked through the valley of the shadow that climaxed in Danny's official homegoing on the morning of August 19, 2015, I experienced moment by moment the quiet, gentle, loving presence of the Helper. Two days before our forty-ninth wedding anniversary, instead of enjoying a celebratory dinner together, I buried my beloved husband.

If I spent the rest of this book describing to you the Helper's aid and assistance to me during that time, I would still run out of pages. He poured out His help as I found myself in the position of comforting friends and family, speaking on August 21 to over one hundred men at the Bible study Danny had led, planning the service of celebration, and overseeing funeral arrangements. The incredible evidence of His supernatural help was revealed in the joy, peace, strength, and clear presence of mind that carried me through not just somehow but with absolute triumph! I will never cease to praise God for the One who "is my helper."[1]

Recently when I went through my mail, I came across a note from the wife of a man who had served with Danny on the national board of the Fellowship of Christian Athletes. Her husband had just died. She wrote that she had been his caregiver for over five years. Then she testified, "Never could I have carried the 'thankful load' without my dependence upon the Holy Spirit." And I knew exactly what she meant.

What is your testimony? Whether you are a widower or a widow like me learning to live in a new reality, or a caregiver expending your life for an ailing spouse or elderly parent or disabled child, or a parent trying to raise your children to be followers of Jesus in a wicked world, or a businessperson operating according to biblical principles of integrity, or a politician walking a tightrope between truth and political correctness, or an educator teaching values along with the curriculum, or a cancer victim trying to navigate the maze of surgical options and treatments, the Helper is available to assist, aid, or furnish you with relief. I know. Just call on Him.

2

Our Comforter

I could not have made it through the days following the heart-shattering discovery of my husband's unresponsive body in our pool without the Helper. Not only did I experience His practical, moment-by-moment assistance during the crisis, but I also experienced in a very deep way His comfort and consolation.

I have been consoled by the Holy Spirit in His role as the Comforter during times of deep grief—from the loss of two babies in miscarriage to my son's diagnosis of cancer and then the breakup of two of his marriages to the death of my beloved mother followed by the death of my father to the diagnosis of my own cancer. But nothing—*nothing*—equals the comfort He has given me since Danny's move to our Father's house.

Not only did the Comforter work within me to quiet my heart, but He also sent people to comfort me with their loving thoughtfulness and presence from the moment Danny was taken to the hospital. Both nights that Danny was on life support, our son, Jonathan, stayed with him, while our younger daughter, Rachel-Ruth, came to spend the night with me.

I knew Rachel-Ruth could not stay with me much longer because she had three young children to care for. Without my ever voicing those thoughts, my other daughter, Morrow, and her husband, Traynor, suggested they move in with me. With a mischievous smile, I looked at my son-in-law and responded,

"Maybe, but you will have to ask me, your mother-in-law, if you can live with me." With a twinkle in his eyes and a chuckle in his voice, Traynor asked, declaring it had always been his dream to live with his mother-in-law.

So Traynor and Morrow moved in with me that very day! They put all their household things in storage and for over a year lived in our two small upstairs rooms. Words fail to describe the comfort they brought to me as they quietly settled into my routine, blending it with theirs. For the fifteen months they lived in my home, we never had cross words, disagreements, or tension. Just blessing. For fifteen months I never spent the night alone in my house, which helped ease my sudden and acute loneliness in ways they will perhaps never know.

Each night, my daughter would fix dinner, then call us to the table for a wonderful meal. After dinner our devotions always focused on God's blessings. Night after night. Week after week. Month after month. Some nights, Morrow and Traynor would sense my spirit was down, and then they would get up, stand over me with their hands on me, and as Traynor traced the Hebrew letters for "YHWH" on my forehead, they prayed God's blessing over me: "The Lord bless you and keep you; the Lord make his face shine upon you and be gracious to you; the Lord turn his face toward you and give you peace."[1] And I was comforted.

I knew my daughter and son-in-law were also grieving, but I was poignantly reminded that the Holy Spirit comforts us through the love and care of those around us. They allowed themselves to be the channel of the Spirit's comfort, as God promised to "[comfort] us in all our troubles, so that we can comfort those in any trouble with the comfort we ourselves have received from God."[2]

The Holy Spirit Himself has comforted me on every level, on every day—and not only in regard to Danny. Sometimes He has used a passage of Scripture in my devotions to address some unspoken pain. Sometimes He has used another person's seemingly random comment or email or text message. Sometimes He has used a thought or insight from a book I was reading or a sermon I was listening to.

One day, after I spoke at a large church, a woman approached me rather shyly and handed me a slip of paper. When I got back to the hotel, I opened her note. On it she had drawn a picture. She said the picture best explained how the Lord had spoken to her through my message. She would have no way of knowing, but she was addressing the very issue I had been struggling with, and I knew the Holy Spirit was comforting me through her pencil sketch, which I still have in my Bible.

The Comforter seemed to pull out all the stops when my father moved to Heaven in February 2018. I received the news by telephone when I was in the presence of a dear friend. She immediately wrapped her arms around me and prayed as we both wept. From that moment forward, I was comforted by my family who surrounded me and by hundreds of friends who left so many voice mails and sent so many text messages to my cell phone that I had to silence it.

I'll never forget riding in the motorcade as we escorted Daddy the 120 miles from Asheville, near our family home, where he had been living, to Charlotte, North Carolina, his childhood hometown, where he would be buried. The route had been previously published, and the people of North Carolina poured out to pay their respects. For the entire route, any cars not already lined up beside the road pulled over and stopped—on both sides of the interstate. Tens of thousands of people stood beside the road, waving homemade signs, holding up Bibles or crosses with one hand while the other was placed over their hearts, or solemnly waving. I saw a mother holding a newborn, a father pushing his young daughter's wheelchair as close to the road as he could get, a rabbi blowing a shofar, fire engines with the American flag draped from their ladders on every overpass . . . all conveying that they shared in my family's grief. For that moment in time, it was as though the whole world had stopped to mourn and weep with us. And I was comforted.

Could it be that you have missed the comfort of the Comforter because it has come indirectly through someone or something else? Like Mary Magdalene at the empty tomb, are your tears blinding you to the presence of Jesus right there beside you?[3] Right there *within* you? My prayer is that He will use these words to comfort you as you experience the constant companionship of the Holy Spirit. Ask Him to open your eyes to the nearness of the One who is, in fact, Jesus in you.

3

Our Advocate

Have you ever needed an advocate? Someone who could plead your cause and give you favor in the eyes of your boss? Or parent? Or mother-in-law? Or committee chairman? One of the names given to the work of the Holy Spirit is that of Advocate.

My husband and I needed the Advocate to plead our cause during a time of public humiliation when we were, in essence, removed from the church where we had been members for fifteen years. My husband had been chairman of the board of deacons, the head of the men's fellowship, and the teacher of the largest Sunday school class in the church. But things began to unravel when the senior pastor retired and Danny was placed on the search committee for a new pastor. Danny took a firm, uncompromising position to uphold the inerrancy of Scripture, while all the other committee members, with one exception, rejected it. During a Sunday morning business meeting, he was publicly removed from the committee to the sound of applause filling the sanctuary.

Several weeks after my husband was removed from the search committee, deacons also voted to remove my Bible class of five hundred women from the church premises. Their fear was that, during the interim between pastors, the presence of my class would influence the congregation in a way they found unacceptable. In the days that followed, the local newspaper carried multiple stories giving details of Billy Graham's daughter being thrown out of a Baptist church. While I refrained from public criticism of the church or anyone in it, I privately prayed for the Advocate to step up and defend me. He did! One year later, in that same newspaper that had carried the humiliating accounts of our removal, a full two-page profile effectively exonerated me and my class from any wrongdoing.[1]

If you have traveled with a mission team or worked on a church staff or been involved in ministry outside your home, you may also have experienced strained or even broken relationships. We don't expect such hurtful issues to arise within the Christian community. Yet sadly they do all too often. Instead of becoming angry, bitter, or resentful, this is a time to turn to the Advocate and ask Him to plead your cause.

The Advocate knows what He is doing. And He has done some amazing things. We see Him at work in the shadows of the Old Testament. He gave Joseph favor with Potiphar until he was put in charge of everything that Potiphar owned; then favor with the prison warden, who put him in charge of the entire prison; then favor with Pharaoh himself, who placed him as second-in-command in Egypt, where Joseph saved the world—including his own family—during severe famine.[2] We see the Advocate at work when Nehemiah, the Persian king's cupbearer, was given favor to return to Jerusalem and rebuild the walls after years of Babylonian captivity and exile.[3] And again when Queen Esther was given favor with the king, thus positioning her to save her people from annihilation.[4]

We also, of course, see Him at work in the New Testament. When the early church sent out the first two missionaries, they chose Paul and Barnabas, who in turn chose to take a young assistant with them, John Mark. But early in the journey, John Mark left them and went home to Jerusalem.[5] When Paul and Barnabas returned sometime later, they gave a thrilling report of the impact of the gospel in the Gentile world to their sending church in Antioch and to the council in Jerusalem. After a time of preaching and teaching in Antioch, Paul felt led to go on another mission trip. Barnabas agreed to go but wanted to take John Mark. Paul sharply disagreed because the young man had deserted them on their first trip, failing to complete his assignment. "They had such a sharp disagreement that they parted company."[6] Paul and Barnabas went their separate ways, with Paul taking Silas, and Barnabas taking John Mark. While the blessing was that the missionary effort doubled from one team to two, it was obvious that the Advocate's intervention was needed to reconcile these Christian brothers and ministry partners for their own sakes as well as to prevent a rift from developing in the early church.

While the Bible doesn't give us details, we know that at the end of Paul's life, one of the very last requests he made before his execution was to ask Timothy, "Get Mark and bring him with you, because he is helpful to me in my ministry."[7] Obviously the Advocate had worked effectively to plead John Mark's cause to the extent that he and Paul had become trusted ministry coworkers.

In what way do you need Someone to defend you? Jesus promised, "I will ask the Father, and he will give you another Advocate, who will never leave you."[8] Whether your situation involves a misunderstanding with your neighbor, or a disagreement within your church, or tension in your home, or slander in your school, or gossip in your office, the Holy Spirit is available to defend you and plead your cause. Always. Ask Him. He's never lost a case.

Our Intercessor

Whereas the Holy Spirit in His role as advocate pleads your cause and defends you, as an intercessor He actively works between you and others to reconcile differences. An intercessor is a mediator, and the Holy Spirit stands ready to serve as your go-between when relationships are strained or broken.

Every parent needs an intercessor! I certainly have—more times than I can count.

Our three children all loved attending Baylor University in Waco, Texas. The education was superb; the focus, Christ centered; and the social life, full of zest and fun. Danny and I had only one concern: the school was a twenty-four-hour one-way drive from our home in North Carolina. I consoled myself by saying it was really just a six-hour plane ride, but then, who can afford frequent plane flights? So we were able to count on seeing our children only twice a year while they were in school—over Christmas and summer breaks.

The second year our younger daughter, Rachel-Ruth, was at Baylor, she called home to discuss the classes she was signing up for in the spring semester. For the life of me, I can't remember now what they were, but I clearly remember we had a strong disagreement. The conversation ended with Rachel-Ruth hanging up on me. When I called back, there was no answer. Repeatedly. This was when the Intercessor stepped in.

By divine coincidence my schedule included a speaking commitment in Dallas within the month of that phone conversation with Rachel-Ruth. When I accepted the invitation, I had no way of knowing it would place me close to Rachel-Ruth at the very time I would need a face-to-face meeting with her. But, of course, the Holy Spirit had known, so He had made the arrangements. After fulfilling my responsibilities in Dallas, I got into a car and drove to Waco, then showed up at Rachel-Ruth's door. She threw her arms around my neck and said she was sorry for the separation that had come between us. Then we both wept as we talked the situation through until it was resolved. I knew the Intercessor had worked in both of our hearts—softening mine to more sympathetically listen to her reasoning for her course load and convicting hers to be more respectful in her tone as she explained her desires. In the end the Intercessor helped resolve and reconcile what had been a strained relationship.

One wonderful aspect of the Holy Spirit is that if He indwells you and indwells the person with whom you have a strained or broken relationship, you can pray and stir Him up within both of you. Ask Him to work in your heart and the other person's heart to bring you together.

I recently talked with a friend, Patti, about how she and her husband, John, applied this principle to their relationship with their daughter, Mandi, and her husband, Scott.[1] Early in Mandi's dating relationship with Scott, she began withdrawing from family functions and gatherings, and she withdrew most noticeably from Patti and John. Their very close family bond seemed to be lost almost overnight, without warning or explanation. Mandi became completely absorbed by her relationship with Scott along with some new friends who seemed to encourage the distancing, leaving Patti and John feeling confused and alienated from their daughter.

The situation deteriorated further when Mandi and Scott became engaged. They rushed into the marriage, dismissive of the traditional biblical parental blessing. After their wedding they had minimal contact with the family.

Patti and John spent many tear-filled nights in agony over the "loss" of their beautiful daughter. They knew they were in a spiritual battle and were keenly aware the Enemy had targeted their family, seeking to destroy the cherished relationships.

Patti and John allowed their broken hearts to press them to their knees, where they prayed unceasingly that the Intercessor would intervene on their behalf. He did. An illness that ended in the loss of a beloved family member prompted more frequent communication between Mandi and her parents. Subsequently, the Holy Spirit began to stir in all of them a desire for reconnection.

Several years later, the arrival of Mandi and Scott's first baby gave everyone an overwhelming desire for what God intends the family to be. Soon after, the Intercessor moved in Scott's heart and inspired him to have a one-on-one conversation with John. They openly discussed the painful beginning of their relationship, which allowed for a more genuine relationship to blossom. Patti and John now find much joy in their role as doting grandparents, as well as being an integral part of their daughter's life.

Although they will always need the Intercessor's involvement, the healing has begun, the family unit has been restored, and the hearts of everyone continue to overflow with praise and gratitude to the One who made it all possible.

Even as I share with you these stories of the Intercessor's healing touch, I confess that I have had strained or broken relationships over the years that have not been resolved or reconciled, even though I have prayed earnestly. Still I am confident that the lack of resolution is not because the Intercessor has been inactive. I wonder whether it's more likely that some of those involved, including myself, have hardened their hearts to His activity. This is one reason it seems wise to pray with King David, "Search me, O God, and know my heart; test me and know my anxious thoughts. See if there is any offensive way in me, and lead me in the way everlasting."[2] I also know that some wounds take time to heal and some broken things take time to mend.[3] So I continue to pray for my heart, and those of others, to submit to the Intercessor's active involvement.

If you have a relationship that is strained or shattered, frayed or fractured, battered or broken, pray. Ask the Intercessor to search and soften your heart as He gets actively involved. He will. I know.

5

Our Counselor

As a young girl, I read the Old Testament story of Solomon, who was the heir to his father David's throne. Following David's death, Solomon was overcome not only with grief but also with the weight of responsibility that was now his. The young king went up to the tent of meeting to seek the Lord through an extravagant sacrifice. God responded to Solomon's desperation and invited him to ask for whatever he wanted.

Solomon didn't ask for fame, fortune, or even favor with the people. Instead, Solomon said, "Give me wisdom and knowledge, that I may lead this people, for who is able to govern this great people of yours?"[1] In response, God poured out His blessing on Solomon and granted him an abundance of wisdom and knowledge that would be unmatched by any earthly king before or after him.[2]

I was deeply impressed by Solomon's request. If he could ask God to give him wisdom, then why couldn't I do the same? So I began praying for God's wisdom. Continually. Consistently. And I believe God has answered my prayer in proportion as I have opened my heart, mind, and life to the One who is the counselor. As I look back, I can see with the clarity of hindsight that the Counselor has given me not just advice but sound wisdom again and again for small and large decisions as He has taken responsibility to manage my entire life.

I have never been more grateful for the Counselor's guidance than I was when I was informed by my doctor that I may have breast cancer. I had gone to her for a separate medical issue when she found a mass that she felt was suspicious. I initially dismissed her concern because no one in my very large family had ever had breast cancer, except for one cousin about forty years ago. But I agreed to go for a diagnostic mammogram and an ultrasound. I can't explain how, but the Helper prepared me by letting me know in advance what the diagnosis would be.

Sure enough. The tests both clearly revealed that I had cancer. When the radiologist showed me the results on the screen, while I was shocked, I was not in the least traumatized. He turned to face me, looked me right in the eyes, and said, "Mrs. Lotz, are you sure you are okay?" To which I replied, "Yes. I'm fine. God is in control of my life." And I knew with certainty that He was. And is. And will be. When the doctor walked out, the technician took both of my hands and prayed a prayer of healing over me, then walked me to my car. I knew the Comforter was using that sweet young woman to reassure me of His loving care.

But the diagnosis plunged me into a deep dependency on the Counselor, as I was now caught up in a whole new world of options and decisions that would shape my journey through cancer treatment. The first decision I had to make was how and when to tell my children, their spouses, and my grandchildren.

I immediately went home from the radiologist, and instead of calling friends and family, I turned to the Counselor. I knew my family would all be coming for lunch three days later, on Sunday, as we remembered together the same day three years earlier when we had gathered around my husband and released him from life support. Anticipating a day already filled with emotion, I could hardly bear to think of adding the burden of my news to their tender hearts. As I prayed, the Counselor didn't just whisper; He seemed to speak loudly to me from Deuteronomy 29:29: "The secret things belong to the LORD our God, but the things revealed belong to us and to our children." I knew that the news of this cancer that had been revealed was to be shared with my children, their spouses, and my grandchildren.

Following our Sunday lunch, I pulled out my Bible. Instead of leading them in a time of devotional thought, as is our custom, I shared how God was moving in my life. As a mother, I've never been so grateful as I was when I saw every one of them respond with rock-solid faith. Of course there were tears, but all were confident that God had given us a blessing in disguise. Like eagles who ride the winds of a storm, we were going to spread our wings of faith and soar!

With Morrow taking the lead, they encircled me and laid hands on me. My son, Jonathan, lay facedown on the floor with his big hands wrapped around each of my ankles. Rachel-Ruth prayed a warrior's prayer against the Enemy. Then one by one, from the youngest to the oldest, my dear family prayed for God's will to be done and for His glory to be revealed as together we traveled through this "valley of the shadow of death."[3] And I had a profound sense that there was a smile on our Father's face, and tears in His eyes, as He bent down to catch every syllable of their prayers.

The following Friday the doctor whose initial exam had discovered the mass sent me to a surgeon. I checked with my primary-care doctor, who confirmed the surgeon was excellent. I registered at the clinic, filled out pages of information, and met with the surgeon, who then performed a biopsy. Several factors unsettled me, but I brushed my concerns aside, knowing the pathology report that would come back in a few days would determine many things. But Sunday night I could not sleep. I seemed to have lost the deep peace I had experienced since my diagnosis. I was restless and agitated. About four in the morning, I asked the Lord why my spirit was so upset. The Counselor seemed to impress me with the thought that the surgeon I had seen was not the right one for me. That insight plunged me into a desperate cry to the Counselor. Where was I to go? How would I find the surgeon of God's choosing for such a critical and immediate need?

When morning came, my devotional reading included Isaiah 30:21: "Whether you turn to the right or to the left, your ears will hear a voice behind you, saying, 'This is the way; walk in it.'" I knew that the Counselor would whisper His directions to me, which He did almost immediately. My daughter Rachel-Ruth called early to check on me. Both she and Morrow had gone with me to the surgeon. I shared with her what I felt the Spirit had said, but I didn't know what to do. She reminded me that on that very day I was to have lunch with my sister-in-law, Vicki Lotz, and Sylvia Hatchell, the head women's basketball coach at the University of North Carolina. Sylvia was four years past her own tremendous battle with advanced leukemia. When Vicki had arranged this lunch date at the end of May, the only time the three of us had free on our calendars was this day, August 27. I knew that lunch with Sylvia and Vicki would be a divine appointment. And it was!

I went to lunch, not knowing quite how to tell them without adding a layer of gloom to what was supposed to be a fun time with friends. What would I say? Toward the end of the meal, the conversation touched on Sylvia's health. She was and is doing remarkably well. I asked whether she had been pleased with her treatment, and she had replied, "Oh yes. It was the best." I knew God had opened the door for me to reveal my diagnosis, so I did. My sister-in-law's eyes filled with tears, but Sylvia, the dynamic, type A coach that she is, took her cell phone, jumped up from the table, and the next thing I knew, I was scheduled for appointments at the UNC Lineberger Comprehensive Cancer Center, where she had been treated for her leukemia. Vicki then led the three of us in prayer. I left lunch filled with peace once again, confident the Counselor had given me His wisdom and direction.

During the week that followed our lunch, I went back to the first surgeon to get the pathology report. She was kind and informative. I let her know I was getting a second opinion from UNC, which I did. As Morrow, Rachel-Ruth, and I compared the two cancer centers and surgeons, we knew that the Counselor was leading me to UNC.

The Counselor's wisdom for these early decisions greatly encouraged me, and I became more and more confident that He would guide me in every step of this cancer journey.

I have reached the point, not just in my cancer journey but also in my journey of faith, that every major decision, especially ones that involve others, needs to be confirmed by Scripture to ensure that I am indeed hearing the voice of the

Holy Spirit. While I can never be absolutely certain I have heard the Spirit accurately, as I take Him at His word and act on it by faith, the decision is confirmed by circumstances that follow and by the confirmation within my own spirit.

Have I ever made wrong, unwise decisions? Oh my, yes! The unwise ones seem to loom so large in my memory that if I'm not careful, I can feel swept downward in a death spiral of self-flagellation. Especially because I know better than to make a decision without dependence on the Counselor.

Can God redeem the messes that are the consequences of our unwise choices? Yes, He can! Absolutely! But we still have to endure the pain and suffering and sometimes tangled web of complications that such choices inflict. I have endured many sleepless nights, sobbing into my pillow, because of my unwise choices that have harmed those I love.

The worst choice I ever made was the day I came home from having been at my office all morning and saw my husband sitting happily by the pool, playing with our dog. My daughter had just come in and reported that her dad wanted to stay outside. I decided to leave him a little longer so I could get some work done. While he was capable of coming in on his own by using his walker, the effort was difficult for him, and I knew he would need my encouragement and help. But instead of heeding the subtle prompting of the Counselor to let Danny know I was available to help bring him inside, I chose to leave him there. That decision will haunt me for the rest of my life. Because he never came in again.

But even that unwise decision has borne fruit because I have learned the painful lesson of forgiving myself. If God has said, *Anne, I forgive you,* and He has, then who am I to say, "Thank You, God, but I can't forgive myself"? Are my standards higher than His? So I have simply had to bow my head and allow His grace to wash over me, absolving me of guilt. And I have seemed to hear the gentle whisper of the Spirit: *Anne, Danny's time was in My hands. His days were determined. I set limits on his life that he could not exceed. August 19, 2015, was his time.*[4]

What else have I learned from the right and the wrong choices? The wise and the unwise decisions? I have learned, and am still learning, to lean hard on the Counselor. The writer of Proverbs encourages us, "Trust in the LORD with all your heart and lean not on your own understanding; in all your ways acknowledge him, and he will make your paths straight."[5] I must lean on Him in utter dependency as I intentionally, specifically, and personally ask for His counsel, claiming His promise: "If any of you lacks wisdom, he should ask God, who gives generously to all without finding fault, and it will be given to him."[6]

The best adviser, the best business manager, the best life coach, is the Counselor. He is readily available. 24-7. Without charge. But we must turn to Him. If we want to live lives that truly work best, you and I cannot go our own way, or follow our own logic, or somehow conclude that we know best, or decide that if we follow the Spirit's leading, we'll somehow end up with less than if we do it our way, or think that getting what we want will make us happier than what He wants, or think that we don't need Him for this small decision, or _____ (you fill in the blank).

What do you need the Counselor for right now? Could it be that, like me, you need Him to absolve you of guilt for one or more wrong decisions? Do you need to forgive yourself? Or offer forgiveness to someone else for that person's wrong decisions?

Are you also confronting cancer and the related choices of doctors, surgery, treatments, and follow-up? Or maybe you need wisdom not for healthcare but for pending business decisions. Marriage. Career. Education. Do you need direction? Discretion? Discernment? Deliverance? Talk to your Counselor. Pour out your heart. Be honest. Transparent. *Lean hard on the One who is Jesus in you.*

6

Our Strengthener

When I was a young girl growing up in western North Carolina,
almost every Sunday afternoon my family would hike to the ridge. I found it
interesting that the trees either stood tall and strong or were lying broken on the
ground. When I pointed this out to my mother, she explained that it was because the trees on the ridge had no protection from the fierce wind that swept
through, howling so loudly at times it sounded like a freight train passing by.
She said that, with nothing to break the wind's force, the trees either grew strong
enough to resist the pressure or toppled to the ground.

Life is somewhat like the trees on the ridge. When the winds howl, bearing
down with intensity during times of pressure or persecution, suffering or sickness, trouble or turmoil, disease or disaster, attack or agony, either we can fold
up in a fetal position, whimpering in self-pity, or we can get a grip on the Holy
Spirit, who, in a unique way, strengthens us on the inside as we lean on Him. As
Paul testified, the Strengthener is most effective when we are at our weakest,
because that's when we are the most dependent on His strength.[1]

Often we feel the weakest when we face strong winds of opposition, persecution, or some other issue that is overwhelming. But these winds are our opportunity to be strengthened under pressure.

This strength that grows under pressure is illustrated in the Old Testament story of Joseph. He was a handsome, somewhat spoiled young man—the

favorite of his father, Jacob. In a jealous rage, his brothers finally got fed up and sold Joseph to a passing caravan of Ishmaelites.[2] He ended up on the slave block in Egypt, where he was bought by Potiphar, the captain of Pharaoh's guard.

After serving Potiphar faithfully, Joseph was sexually harassed by Potiphar's wife. When he forcefully rejected her attempts to seduce him and fled from her presence, she accused him of attempted rape. He was thrown into prison, where he languished, forgotten by all except God.[3]

The Bible gives us interesting insight into one possible reason God allowed Joseph to be enslaved and imprisoned for thirteen years through no fault of his own. Joseph had been a loyal, obedient son to Jacob, only to be sold by his brothers. He had been an honest business manager of Potiphar's affairs, only to be falsely accused by Potiphar's wife. Yet God allowed the winds to howl until they were so fierce, Joseph must have been tempted to succumb, give up, and break under the pressure. Instead, the literal translation of Psalm 105:18 relates the following: "They have afflicted with fetters his feet, iron hath entered his soul."[4] We can almost visualize the Strengthener at work in the dungeons of Egypt.

When Joseph finally emerged from prison in a supernatural deliverance, he was strong in his character, focused in his faith, and totally undistracted by the treasures and temptations around him as he sought to live for the glory of God and the salvation of others.[5]

Multiple times God has told me He would strengthen me through the howling winds of hardship. In Jeremiah He clearly warned me that people would fight against me but that He would make me an iron pillar.[6] Through Isaiah He told me that people would rage against me and oppose me but that I was not to be afraid because He would strengthen me.[7] He encouraged me from Revelation that if I would endure patiently and with humility, He would make me "a pillar in the temple of my God."[8]

These promises came back to my mind during a recent experience with gale-force winds. I was honored to be invited by a member of the Legislative Council of Telangana State in India to address the second annual National Day of Prayer, to be held on the parade grounds in the capital city of Hyderabad. Having been to India four times previously, I knew this would be a difficult assignment, but I felt the Counselor advising me that this was from Him.

The winds of resistance began to swirl almost as soon as I accepted the invitation. Because my Indian hosts had advertised my coming through billboards, churches, and websites, enemies of the gospel networked with one another to threaten, intimidate, and ultimately try to prevent me from speaking in India. The focus of the resistance was the visa I had applied for, which the Hindu extremists attacked as being invalid. However, I knew it wasn't.

The negative pushback prompted some people to be concerned for my safety. One respected friend urged me to tell the organizers that the struggle was too great, that the prospect was too dangerous, and that God was closing the door. My friend's concern was valid, as the government in India has become hostile to any religion other than Hinduism. Persecution of the Christian church is escalating.

To be honest, if God had closed the door, I would have been somewhat relieved. I knew the trip itself would be grueling, the time change would flip my day and night, and the effort to speak to multiple audiences through translation was an enormous challenge under any circumstances but especially so one week after Christmas when I was very tired from all the celebration and activities. But I rejected that line of reasoning, as God had not closed the door. The invitation was still valid, I had given my word that I would go, and I was committed. I could literally feel the Holy Spirit strengthening my resolve.

Just two weeks before I was to leave for India, the visa came through. But the winds of resistance picked up once more on the day of my departure, which found me in the doctor's office with a random, unexpected medical issue. I returned home around noon to pack, planning to leave for the airport at four fifteen. This would give me and those traveling with me the required two hours before catching the international flight to London at six thirty.

Around three thirty in the afternoon, I received an email from my assistant informing me that the Indian Embassy was strongly urging me not to go to Hyderabad. I called the number of the official who had been communicating with my assistant and spoke with a man who restated that I was not to leave for India at that time. He gave no valid reason, just that it would not be safe for me to go. I felt I was being subtly threatened. I replied that if I didn't leave for India within the hour, I would not arrive in time to speak at the National Day of Prayer. When I hung up, I called one of my father's associates who lives in India, woke him up in the middle of the night his time, and told him what was happening. He immediately said that it was a scam and that as long as my visa was not revoked in writing, I was good to go.

I looked up the telephone number of the Indian Embassy in Washington, DC, and asked my daughter to call them to verify whether the man I had spoken with was legitimate. When she called, she discovered that the man was a member of the Embassy staff and that the Embassy was strongly advising me not to travel to India on that day. Again, no reason was given. It was interesting to me that the more resistance I faced, the more the Spirit strengthened my resolve to press through.

It was now about four thirty, later than the time I had wanted to leave for the airport. My laptop computer was open, and my eye was caught by an email from the Indian Embassy saying my visa had been revoked! I stared at it in disbelief. There it was—in writing! I called my father's associate in India, who burst into tears. With both of us weeping, he began to pray, speaking words of worship and praise of the One who is in ultimate control, but his prayer held desperation also. When I hung up the phone, I looked at those in the room and inquired in a choking voice, "How is it that sometimes the Enemy seems stronger than the Lord?"

At that moment, I was aware that the resistance was producing in me a strength of resolve that I had not had previously. I articulated what I was feeling—that I knew with certainty God had called me to go to India at that time, on that day. What I didn't understand was how the door then could possibly be closed.

I informed those who were to travel with me that we were not going. We came up with a plan B, which was to record a video of the message and send it electronically. At five fifteen my daughter's cell phone rang. It was the Indian Embassy calling to say I could go to India after all! She asked the caller to repeat what she said, and the woman clearly stated, "Tell your mother she can go to India." But was it too late? I almost agreed with the hiss of the serpent in my ear—*Don't go. You won't catch the flight. Plus, it's a very hard trip, too hard for someone your age.* I rejected that temptation with a strength of will I knew was not my own. I firmly decided to try to make the flight, and if I didn't, I would know I had done everything humanly possible to catch it.

We grabbed our bags, dragged them as quickly as we could out the door, threw them in the back of the SUV my daughter was driving, put on our seat belts, and—nothing happened. The car was dead. The motor didn't even turn over! I told everyone we would have to somehow pile into my small car, and we jumped out. When we went to get our luggage out of the SUV, the tailgate would not open. The vehicle's electrical system had totally shut down. So we dragged our bags over the back seat and threw them in my car—sitting on them and holding them on our laps as we raced to the airport.

We arrived at the check-in desk of the airline just forty-five minutes before the flight to London was to leave. The desk clerk checked my passport and visa, tagged my bags, then turned to my travel companion and asked for her visa. While she frantically searched, I threw up arrow prayers as I called my assistant to ask whether she knew where the visa was. She replied she didn't know because she had not been involved at that level in my companion's arrangements, but after a pause, she said she thought it was an e-visa. We looked carefully through our travel documents, and there it was! Even the desk clerk let out an enormous sigh of relief.

We ran through security and made it onto the plane just before the door closed.

As I sat on the plane with my heart beating out of my chest, my thoughts swirling in every direction, I knew with deep conviction that I was exactly where God wanted me to be. The more the Enemy tried to stop me, the more the Strengthener worked within me. My expectations were high to see what God was going to do, because the Enemy seemed so afraid. Deep within I sensed a rock-solid confidence that I was on assignment.

We arrived in Hyderabad twenty-four hours later. I had a smooth transition through customs and was given the coveted stamp in my passport that let everyone know I was officially and safely in! I was warmly greeted by local officials and pastors, then whisked away to the hotel. On the way, I was told once again how dangerous it was to give the gospel and that I needed to be very careful not to speak against other religions. My reply was that it had not occurred to me to speak against other religions but that I had not traveled all the way to India to leave out the gospel.

When we arrived at the hotel, we were graciously welcomed and shown to our rooms. I made time for a cup of coffee with one of the men who had been so helpful in the planning. Once again, I was respectfully warned not to offend the authorities.

The National Day of Prayer was scheduled to take place in the evening on the day immediately following my arrival. On that day, I went to a local restaurant for lunch. The Indian woman who had been assigned to help us received a cell phone call, which she took away from the table. When she returned, the look on her face told me something was up, so I asked whether everything was all right. She responded, "Actually, no. You are being asked not to speak tonight at the National Day of Prayer. Just bring a greeting." I felt the presence of the Strengthener when I looked at her and replied, "I didn't come to India to bring a greeting. I came to give a message, and I will."

As we drove to the meeting that night, I was told that the home minister, who is Hindu, was coming with members of the Indian Judiciary. They had the power to arrest and deport me on the spot. I wasn't deterred in the least. Instead, like Joseph in the Old Testament, I was strengthened with iron in my soul.

With the home minister and other dignitaries sitting behind me, I delivered the message I believe God had given to me, urging the people to pray for India as Daniel had prayed for Judah.[9] The audience that stretched out in front of me came from all over the nation and was estimated by the police to be a half-million people. I did my best to explain that anyone could pray but that only those who had a covenant relationship with God were guaranteed an answer. Then I laid out how they could establish a covenant relationship with God . . . and gave the gospel.

I was not deported. In fact, I spoke three more times while I was in Hyderabad: once to church pastors and leaders, once to 450 rural churches who combined services so that I could speak to about ten thousand of their members, and once to about eight thousand women. Each time, I had to overcome warnings, rebukes, or other types of pressure to compromise the messages. Yet when I gave the invitations at the last two large meetings, so many hands were raised and so many people stood to indicate they were claiming Jesus as their Savior that it looked as if everyone in the audiences of thousands was making that commitment. In the end God's Word went forth, the gospel was proclaimed, and I believe He was glorified as many people responded to the truth and were saved.

Before leaving Hyderabad, I met with the legislative council member who had originally invited me to come. He expressed amazement that all the many, seemingly insurmountable obstacles had been overcome. With a face that shone with the light of Heaven's joy, he patted his chest over the area of his heart and said in broken English, "My phone has not stopped ringing. Pastors are calling me to say that the church in India has been revived!"

After I boarded the plane to leave Hyderabad early in the morning, I looked out the window as the lights of the city were coming on. They were just dots in the darkness. And the Helper, Comforter, Advocate, Intercessor, Counselor, and Strengthener seemed to whisper to my heart, *Anne, that's what we've done. We have put holes in the darkness.*

I was filled with praise for the Strengthener, who had given me the power to endure and to overcome the Enemy's resistance. While my body was wiped out and weak from sleepless nights and unfamiliar food, while I looked forward to going home and being surrounded by my family, I knew I was leaving part of my heart with those dear leaders below, who had the responsibility of continuing to turn on the Light. As the plane climbed higher into the sky, my prayer ascended also—prayer for the Holy Spirit to pour Himself out on the great nation of India, igniting real revival in the hearts of His people.

Reflecting on my own experience makes me wonder about you. What strong, howling winds of adversity are sweeping through your life? Is the Enemy hissing in your ear, suggesting that you've been forgotten by God? Overlooked or unloved by Him? That in some way He is not pleased with you and that the wind is His way of punishing you? Or that it's evidence you are not in God's will or in His place of blessing?

Instead, could it be that the wind is the Strengthener at work in your life? Think about it . . .

7

Our Standby

As difficult as the assignment to India was, it wasn't a crisis. The resistance and obstacles seemed to unfold as the journey proceeded. On the other hand, sometimes we face emergencies that plunge us into sudden, desperate need.

Have you ever experienced such a crisis? Something totally unexpected, unwanted, and disastrous that suddenly exploded in your life? Was it when you went to the doctor for your annual checkup, only to be diagnosed with a dreaded disease? Was it when your spouse walked away . . . left . . . just dropped out of your life and your marriage with no warning? Was it when your employer announced he no longer needed your services and, after faithfully working until almost retirement age, you suddenly found yourself out of work and out of a pension? Was it when you received a phone call from the police, who said your son had been picked up for selling drugs?[1]

Crises are crises because they are sudden, unexpected, disastrous emergencies.

One of the most intriguing aspects of the Holy Spirit's name in the Amplified Bible version of John 16:7 is Standby. This conveys the revelation that the Holy Spirit can be relied on either for regular use or for an emergency. When we find ourselves in the midst of a crisis, the Standby is ever present to help us. His

41

role is confirmed and underscored by Psalm 46:1: "God is our refuge and strength, an ever-present help in trouble."

One such emergency is indelibly etched on my mind. Several years ago I was driving from my father's house, where I had been visiting for several days, to my own home, where I lived with my husband. It was a beautiful, cloudless day with virtually no traffic on Interstate 40. About an hour and a half into the four-hour drive, as I was cruising at seventy miles per hour, I spotted a lone car up ahead going slowly in the right-hand lane. I moved my car into the passing lane so I could maintain my speed. As I pulled up within about fifty feet of the car, without warning it suddenly turned sharply to the left. There was no way I could avoid hitting it broadside! I slammed on my brakes, turned my steering wheel hard left in order to avoid smashing into the driver's door—and then things got crazy.

While I did avoid hitting the driver, I crashed into the front of her car, not just once but again and again. The speed of the collision caused both cars to spin around and around, smashing into each other like bumper cars at the fair. Crunching metal, breaking glass, jolting impact . . . all was surreal.

Fighting the strong pull of the car to flip, I was able to wrestle it out of its crazy spinning motion, only to find myself careening straight across the highway and headed for the drop-off beside the road. The knuckles on both of my hands were white as I tightly gripped the steering wheel. I applied the brakes once again. This time the car responded. I was able to guide it to the shoulder of the road and stop. I sat very still. What happened next was a phenomenon I'll never forget. I heard loud cheering! High-fiving! Voices were shouting, *Anne! Wow! That was an incredible piece of driving! Great job!* Except no one was in the car. No one was around me. I sat there, listening, until a knock on my car window brought me back to reality. A passing driver who had witnessed the accident was peering in the window to see whether I was okay. But I couldn't speak. I heard him remark to the driver of the other car, "I think she's in shock," which made me smile. He had no idea! The real shock wore off as the voices began to fade. And I was left to cope with the aftermath.

I had prayed for safety and protection before leaving my father's house, which has been a lifelong habit before taking a road trip. I'm grateful I had pre-prayed because the accident erupted so suddenly there was no time for conscious prayer at that moment. All I could manage was a heart scream. *Help!* The absolutely wonderful thing about the Holy Spirit is that He is always standing by to do just that.

And the Standby came through in every way. It was below freezing outside, yet two other drivers who had been passing by stood by my car until the highway patrolman came to file a report. The woman who had been driving the other car explained she had gone to sleep at the wheel—two miles from her home! While her car also was smashed beyond recognition, she walked away to tell about it!

Looking back, I'm confident that my prayer before leaving my father's house had been answered. There is no doubt in my mind that the voices I heard in my car immediately after the accident were from an angelic team the Standby had assigned to take care of me. This experience underscored a serious lesson, that the only way to prepare for an emergency is to be pre-prayered. A crisis leaves no time to establish a relationship with God, no time to get right with Him, no time to learn how to pray. It leaves . . . no time. Period. A crisis just erupts without warning! So it's critically important to establish a personal relationship with God through faith in Jesus Christ . . . now. To make sure that relationship is free of any sin that might cloud it or put distance between God and us . . . now. To establish a prayer life . . . now. *Now.* Before the crisis erupts. Then when it does, you and I can count on the Holy Spirit to be our Standby. He may not keep us from the emergency, but He will be with us in it and bring us through it.

One of the most comforting stories that confirms Jesus stands by us in our crises is found in Mark's gospel.[2] After having fed five thousand people with five loaves and two fish, Jesus had put His disciples in a boat and sent them to Bethsaida. During the evening, a sudden storm descended on the Sea of Galilee. Mark recorded that Jesus "saw the disciples straining at the oars, because the wind was against them. About the fourth watch of the night he went out to them."[3]

Think about it. The disciples were exactly where Jesus had put them. They were in His will when the storm arose. But He was standing by. He saw them, He went to them, and He brought them through the crisis in such a way that they were all strengthened in their faith.

What unexpected emergency has erupted in your life? How are you handling it? Are you emotionally flailing about as you find yourself swamped by the waves of fear? Are you spiritually spiraling down in confusion, wondering what you could have done wrong to deserve this? Are you physically exhausted from lack of sleep and from straining to find a way out? Then it's time to cry out to the One who is standing by. Stop doubting His presence. Ask Him to give you comfort through His Word. Invite Him into your situation. Give Him absolute freedom and authority to take charge. Trust Him to bring you through. He will. And your faith in Him will be stronger as a result.

Part Two

Enjoying the Presence of the Holy Spirit

You will fill me with joy in your presence.

—Psalm 16:11

H ow many things have been around us for a long time that we simply have not noticed?

Like the bagel lever on my toaster. I recently went online to find another toaster because the one I've had for about twenty years no longer toasted both sides of the bread. When reading the reviews of the brand I was interested in, I came across one purchaser who was pleased that the model she selected toasted one side of her bagel while leaving the other side warm and chewy. I jumped up to see whether that could be why my toaster was toasting only one side of my bread. Sure enough. My toaster had a bagel feature that was turned on. When I turned it off and put in a slice of bread, both sides toasted evenly. I had to laugh, even as I felt foolish for not having noticed the bagel feature that had been there as long as I had owned the toaster.

While toasters hold nowhere near the significance of the Holy Spirit, could it be that many of us have never really noticed Him either? Maybe we've never been taught to notice Him.

As I've already shared, I grew up in the mountains of western North Carolina. Some of my memories are unpleasant, such as missing my father during his long and frequent absences, fighting with my siblings, and grieving over pets who died. But most of my memories are filled with warmth, love, and fun that included hiking with my family to the ridge behind the house, enjoying Chinese meals complete with chopsticks, playing Bible games with my grandparents, and taking my dog, Peter, to the new McDonald's on Tunnel Road in Asheville for a hamburger—for him—without onions or the pickle.

One thing I don't remember is anything about the Holy Spirit. Even though Jesus was beloved, obeyed, and served by my parents and grandparents and even though Jesus was central to my family, I don't remember being taught about the Holy Spirit. Which has made me wonder whether you would say the same thing.

What have you learned or been taught about the Holy Spirit? The only recollection I have of any mention of the Holy Spirit is from church—and we went to church every Sunday. Except that He wasn't called the Holy Spirit. He was called the Holy Ghost. Every Sunday without exception, after the offering was taken, four elders with dignified bearing would walk in synchronized step down the center aisle to lay the gifts that had been collected on the communion table. As they solemnly marched, the congregation chanted a singsong refrain:

Glory be to the Father and to the Son and to the Holy Ghost.
As it was in the beginning, is now, and ever shall be,
World without end.
Amen. Amen.

At the end of the church service, again without exception, the pastor would pronounce the benediction, indicating in my small child's mind that now we could go home and have a delicious Sunday lunch. So I wasn't very attentive or curious about the way he concluded with a benediction. I was vaguely aware that he always pronounced the final prayer in the name of the Father, in the name of the Son, and in the name of the Holy Ghost. Amen.

It was not until years later when I was teaching a weekly Bible class that I learned the amazing truth of who the Holy Spirit is. I was twenty-nine years old, in my second year of Bible teaching, and doing my best to convey insights into the gospel of John for the five hundred women who sat before me each Wednesday. In hindsight, I was like the blind leading the blind. The only reason I knew more than they did was that I had studiously crammed during the week leading up to the lecture.

The week before February 22, 1978, I was cramming as usual in preparation to teach John 14 to my class. And there it was! Jesus told His disciples, "I will ask the Father, and he will give you another Counselor to be with you forever—the

Spirit of truth. The world cannot accept him, because it neither sees him nor knows him. But you know him, for he lives with you and will be in you."[1]

Several thoughts came to me in quick succession . . .

. . . That the Spirit was another counselor.

. . . That the Spirit was a distinct person from Jesus but just like Him.

. . . That the Spirit would come from the Father.

. . . That the Spirit was *with* the disciples at that time but would be *in* them at a future time.

Like a time-delayed video of a flower bud opening into full bloom, the revelation seemed to unfold gradually. The Spirit would be "another" counselor. So who was the first counselor, who would make the Spirit *another* one? Jesus! The Spirit would be exactly like Jesus yet another distinct person. He would come down from God. Even as Jesus had come down from God in human form, the Spirit would come down from God in spirit form. Jesus clearly identified the Counselor as the Holy Spirit.[2] The disciples already knew Him because Jesus was filled with the Spirit. They were with Jesus; therefore, they were already with the Spirit. But Jesus was announcing that a day would come when they would no longer be with the Spirit because the Spirit would be sent to actually indwell them.

What an amazing, wonderful discovery that still thrills me! It is more than worthwhile to give Him our attention so we can get to know Him, love Him, and enjoy the presence of the One who is Jesus in me—and in you.

His Presence in Eternity

It was Christmas Eve 1968. Three astronauts were on board the *Apollo 8* spacecraft as it orbited the moon in the first-ever mission of its kind. With cameras transmitting the view from the window of the space capsule, the astronauts' experience was shared with the world in the most-watched television broadcast of that time. The crew of three, Bill Anders, Jim Lovell, and Frank Borman, said they had a message for all the people back on Earth. With the barren gray lunar landscape below them and planet Earth dangling like a blue marble in the blackness of space in the far distance beyond them, tens of millions of people watched and listened to the crackly voices of the astronauts transmitted by radio frequency from outer space. Each took a turn reading Genesis 1:1–10 from the King James Version of the Bible . . . [1]

In the beginning God created the heaven and the earth.

And the earth was without form, and void; and darkness was upon the face of the deep. And the Spirit of God moved upon the face of the waters.

And God said, Let there be light: and there was light.

And God saw the light, that it was good: and God divided the light from the darkness.

And God called the light Day, and the darkness he called Night. And the evening and the morning were the first day.

And God said, Let there be a firmament in the midst of the waters, and let it divide the waters from the waters.

And God made the firmament, and divided the waters which were under the firmament from the waters which were above the firmament: and it was so.

And God called the firmament Heaven. And the evening and the morning were the second day.

And God said, Let the waters under the heaven be gathered together unto one place, and let the dry land appear: and it was so.

And God called the dry land Earth; and the gathering together of the waters called he Seas: and God saw that it was good.

I will forever applaud those three men who led the entire world in an incredibly powerful, unparalleled moment of worship. I wonder, though, how many people listened to the Bible's timeless description of Creation but missed the presence of the Holy Spirit described in the second verse? "The earth was without form, and void; and darkness was upon the face of the deep. And the Spirit of God moved upon the face of the waters." The truth hidden in plain sight is that the Holy Spirit was already present at Creation. Where did He come from? The answer: He didn't. He always has been, and He always will be. The verse plainly states He is the Spirit of God, and thus, He is eternal. He had no beginning and He will have no end.

As an eternal person, the Spirit of God has always been present for all time and in all places. In fact, there is no place in the entire universe where He has not, is not, or will not always be fully present.[2]

While the Bible doesn't use the word *Trinity* to refer to the Father, Son, and Holy Spirit, many passages in Scripture reference all three persons of the Godhead. While the first three verses of Genesis give us a subtle glimpse into this mystery, verses 26 and 27 are startling as they change pronouns from the plural as God speaks—"Let us make man in our image, in our likeness"—to the singular—"God created man in his own image, in the image of God he created him"—indicating that God is one God yet more than one.

All three persons of the Godhead are clearly designated in the Great Commission as the One in whose name Jesus commanded us to baptize and make disciples: "Go and make disciples of all nations, baptizing them in the name of the Father and of the Son and of the Holy Spirit."[3]

As the apostle Peter opened his first letter to the churches in Asia Minor, he wrote that the believers there could rest assured that all three persons of the Trinity were involved in their salvation as well as their subsequent spiritual growth. He revealed that they "have been chosen according to the foreknowledge of God the Father, through the sanctifying work of the Spirit, for obedience to Jesus Christ."[4]

Another clear picture of this mystery can be seen at the baptism of Jesus. Matthew bore witness that the persons of the Trinity (the names of whom I've italicized) were present: "As soon as Jesus was baptized, he went up out of the water. At that moment heaven was opened, and he saw the *Spirit* of *God* descending like a dove[5] and lighting on him. And a voice from heaven said, 'This is my *Son*, whom I love; with him I am well pleased.' "[6]

I don't understand the mystery of the Trinity, nor can I explain it.[7] It's been said that if our God were small enough for us to understand, He wouldn't be big enough to save us. So I simply bow my heart before Him in worshipful adoration of the Father, who loved me so much that even though He knew I would sin, He planned for my redemption, then sent His Son as the atoning sacrifice for my sin. I love the Son, who, when the Father sent Him, got up from Heaven's throne, took off His glory robes, came all the way down to earth, went all the way to the cross, then rose up from the dead to open Heaven for me. And I am learning to love and enjoy the companionship of the dear Holy Spirit, who is Jesus within me, every moment of every day. Praise God, I don't have to understand Him in order to experience and enjoy His presence.

I urge you to take a few moments now to worship and enjoy Him. If you have access to YouTube, you might listen to the audio of the astronauts reading Genesis 1 in the vastness of space . . .[8] or take note of a beautiful sunrise or sunset . . . or the full moon on a frosty autumn night . . . or the smell of freshly mowed grass after a summer rain . . . or the sound of waves crashing onshore . . . or the feel of a newborn baby's soft hand . . . or the sight of fluffy white clouds scurrying across a cobalt-blue sky . . . or _____ (fill in the blank).

Just make time to worship and adore the One who was present in the beginning, hovering over our planet, energizing it to be transformed into a place of beauty.

His Presence in History

The Holy Spirit, who is present in eternity, has also been present in time and space throughout human history.

If we have any familiarity with the Holy Spirit at all, our knowledge may be primarily based on the New Testament. But we find tantalizing glimpses of His presence throughout the Old Testament.

THE HOLY SPIRIT IN THE OLD TESTAMENT

An interesting contrast to note regarding how the Holy Spirit related to God's people in the Old Testament and then in the New Testament is perhaps best observed through the use of prepositions. Because in the Old Testament He came *upon* certain people to empower and equip them for certain tasks. When the task was completed or when the Spirit no longer could use the person, He would remove Himself. He seemed to come and go with no permanent attachment.[1]

His Presence Coming upon Individuals

The following examples in the Old Testament give a sampling of why His presence came upon a person:

- He equipped workers with necessary skills to build the tent of meeting.[2]
- He gave wisdom to Israel's elders so they could help Moses judge the people.[3]
- He gave Gideon favor in the eyes of God's people and the courage to defeat the enemy.[4]
- He gave physical strength to Samson.[5]
- He gave King David detailed plans for the temple that his son Solomon would build.[6]
- He anointed Isaiah to preach.[7]
- He lifted Ezekiel up out of his circumstances and placed him where God wanted him to be.[8]

One of the most notable examples in the Old Testament of the Holy Spirit's presence coming *upon* someone is that of Saul, the son of Kish. When the prophet Samuel anointed Saul as the one God had chosen to be the first king of Israel, "the Spirit of God came upon him in power,"[9] enabling him to transition from being a keeper of donkeys to being a leader of a nation. The presence of the Spirit of God upon Saul was evident as he became a valiant warrior who delivered Israel from some of her fiercest enemies.

One day God spoke to King Saul through the prophet Samuel, commanding him to utterly destroy one enemy in particular, the Amalekites. Saul obeyed but only partially. Instead of destroying everything as God had said, he looted some of the best plunder for himself and for his men.[10] The consequences were disastrous. God rejected Saul as king and removed the Holy Spirit from him.[11]

Saul continued to reign as king of Israel but without the presence of God's Spirit. As a result, he lost a measure of his sanity; he was helpless before the enemy's greatest fighter, the giant Goliath; he was humiliated by a young shepherd boy who gained victory over Goliath and thus the entire Philistine army with a slingshot; his national popularity was transferred to the boy who had slain Goliath; and he was ultimately defeated in battle, where he lost his life.[12]

His Presence Coming upon David

When the Spirit was removed from Saul, almost simultaneously He came *upon* the young shepherd boy, David, when Samuel anointed him the second king of Israel.[13] But the presence of the Holy Spirit was no guarantee of a smooth ride or a problem-free life. It has been estimated that fifteen to twenty years passed from the time David was anointed until he actually took possession of the throne. Years and years of fighting battles, running from Saul, engaging in guerilla warfare, and developing a band of mighty men who, in time, would be the leaders of his elite army.[14] Yet in the midst of all the difficulties and disappointments, the Bible describes David as a man after God's own heart.[15] Every king thereafter was measured by the standard that David set.

The prayers and songs that David wrote in Psalms were truly inspired by the Spirit of God, evidenced by the fact that they have a permanent place in God's Word. David's psalms reveal his heartfelt love for the Lord and his absolute trust in Him. They have been used as models for the prayers of God's people for generations. David's articulate words seem to express our own despair, anguish, fear, hope, anger, joy, and trust.

Without Psalms we would be spiritually impoverished. Think of the familiar lines that David penned when out in the fields, keeping watch over his father's sheep, watching a spectacular sunrise or sunset: "The heavens declare the glory of God; the skies proclaim the work of his hands." Or leading his sheep out to pasture, meditating on "The LORD is my shepherd, I shall not be in want." Was it when the Philistines came against him that he wrote, "The LORD is my light and my salvation—whom shall I fear?" When he reached one of the lowest points of his life, he revealed from firsthand experience, "The LORD is close to the brokenhearted and saves those who are crushed in spirit." Running from his enemies, hiding in the caves and the rocks, he prayed, "In you, O LORD, I have taken refuge; let me never be put to shame; deliver me in your righteousness. Turn your ear to me, come quickly to my rescue; be my rock of refuge, a strong fortress to save me."[16]

David's spiritual sensitivity and maturity were remarkable. He was a man's man, a leader's leader, a king whose greater Son would one day sit on his throne forever.[17] All of which makes David's downfall even more devastating.

Several years after David was securely enthroned, at a time when kings went off to war, David stayed home. He was complacent, at ease, off guard, dangerously vulnerable to temptation. It came in the form of a beautiful woman who was bathing in full view as the king gazed over the city from the roof of his palace. After inquiring, he was told she was the wife of one of his own mighty men, Uriah, who at that moment was fighting David's enemies. David sent for her, slept with her, impregnated her, manipulated circumstances to arrange for Uriah to be killed, then took her as his wife.[18] What an astounding free fall that sends a warning that reverberates down through the centuries. If David could plummet to the depths of sin and disgrace, it could happen to anyone. Especially when we are spiritually complacent, at ease, off guard, and have time on our hands. That's the time to be on guard!

As horrific as David's moral collapse was, he seemed to brush it aside. The woman bore him a son, and for a time, everything on the surface seemed good. But underneath the facade, his spirit was in agony as he lost his peace and spiraled downward into a state of physical, emotional, and spiritual weakness. He gave sober insight into his condition as a warning to all unrepentant sinners when he confessed in Psalm 32, "When I kept silent, my bones wasted away through my groaning all day long. For day and night your hand was heavy upon me; my strength was sapped as in the heat of summer."[19] While he may have put on a good front, day and night he was miserable and barely able to cope with his load of guilt.

God had mercy on David and did not leave him to wallow in his guilt or wither away in his anguish. He sent His spokesperson, Nathan, to confront him.[20] David's sin was finally out in the open. To his credit, he did not deny what he had done, make excuses, or blame others. With a face that must have burned with shame and a heart that was shattered, he manned up. He replied to Nathan's blistering indictment, "I have sinned against the LORD."[21]

If you, too, have had a sickening knot in the pit of your stomach that comes from well-deserved guilt from which you can get no relief, echo David's words as your own prayer: "I know my transgressions, and my sin is always before me. Against you, you only, have I sinned and done what is evil in your sight."[22] God is merciful and forgiving to those who come to Him in true repentance. Don't play games with the labels you give your sin, to make it seem less sinful. Call it what it is. It's fornication, not safe sex. It's adultery, not an affair of the heart. It's lying, not exaggeration. It's murder, not a right to choose. It's stealing a person's reputation, not gossip. It's slander, not a pious prayer request. God promises that if you and I honestly, sincerely, humbly confess our sin—call it out for what it is in His eyes—He will forgive and cleanse us.[23]

Three thousand years after David's deeply moving prayer of confession in Psalm 51, his words are still used by penitent sinners as they seek God's forgiveness and mercy, because "the sacrifices of God are a broken spirit; a broken and contrite heart, O God, you will not despise."[24] Praise God! God receives anyone and everyone who comes to Him with a humble, contrite heart.

But notice David's heart-stopping plea in verse 11: "Do not cast me from your presence or take your Holy Spirit from me." David knew the Holy Spirit could be given and the Holy Spirit could be taken away. He had seen firsthand what happened to Saul when God's Spirit was removed. He knew he did not deserve the continued presence of the Holy Spirit, so he specifically cried out to God to give him what he did not deserve.

God, who is gracious to sinners, responded to David's honest confession and heartfelt plea. While He allowed David to experience the consequences of his horrific actions, the Spirit of God was not removed but remained on his life.

I can't help but wonder whether you, too, have succumbed to the temptation that led to David's downfall. Were you tempted to go outside your marriage for sexual pleasure, and you did? Or maybe you succumbed to the temptation to follow the crowd around you and pursue sexual experiences before marriage? Or are you addicted to pornography, needing more and more deviant images to satisfy your craving that has become insatiable? Or maybe you gave in to the temptation to overspend, overindulge, overeat, overdrink . . . to lie, cheat, steal, bribe, betray, abuse . . . to _____ (you fill in the blank). While you have adopted the world's attitude that it's okay and everyone does it, is your load of guilt heavy underneath? Robbing you of real happiness? Have you come to hate yourself and the web of sin and deceit you have woven that now traps you, yet you cover up with a casual, carefree countenance?

Do you, like David, fear losing your salvation? Do you live with a fake smile pasted on your face to cover up the emptiness you feel inside? Are you convinced that your sin and guilt disqualify you from the supreme privilege of having God's Spirit in your life? That you are not worthy of Him? In the Old Testament, that would have been probable. But everything dramatically changed following the death, resurrection, and ascension of Jesus to Heaven. Our relationship to the Holy Spirit permanently changed two thousand years ago on the Feast of Pentecost when He entered history in a radical new way.

The Holy Spirit in the New Testament

Right before the death of Jesus on the cross, after supper on the same Thursday evening He was betrayed, He began to prepare His disciples for His departure. In an upstairs room somewhere close to the temple in Jerusalem, as night was falling, He poured truth into His small band of beloved, handpicked followers. He taught them about humility in service as He washed their feet, including the feet of Judas before He dismissed him from the table. Jesus then taught the eleven remaining disciples about Heaven, the place He called His Father's house, which He was going to get ready for them, telling them plainly how they could get there; about the persecution they would face because of their association with Him; and about fulfilling His Father's demand for much eternal fruit if they would abide in Him as a branch abides in the vine.[25]

The faces of the eleven men must have drained of color as they began to take in what He was saying. He was getting ready to leave! With wide-eyed consternation, they also began to understand that He expected them to continue His ministry in His physical absence! On the inside they must have been screaming in protest, *No! No! No! We can't possibly carry on without You. Don't leave us! Please!*

Seeing their expressions of protest and grief, Jesus quickly reassured them, "I will not leave you as orphans; I will come to you. . . . But I tell you the truth: It is for your good that I am going away. Unless I go away, the Counselor will not come to you; but if I go, I will send him to you."[26] How astounding! What Jesus declared stops me and grips my thoughts. He said it would be to the disciples' advantage for Him—Jesus—*to go away.* How could that possibly be? What could be better than having Jesus physically present with them? Apparently, having the Holy Spirit would be better! Again and again that evening, He revealed He would come to them in the form of the Holy Spirit, whom the Father would send to them.

Given that the Holy Spirit has been present since before time began and that He was present throughout the Old Testament, coming upon certain people to equip them for the responsibility God had placed upon them, how would this coming of the Holy Spirit be different? What was Jesus referring to?

His Coming at Pentecost

Jesus was referring to a day as historically significant as the day He was born in Bethlehem, as the day He was crucified on Calvary, as the day He was raised from the grave, and as the day He ascended back into Heaven. He was referring to a day fifty days after His death and resurrection and ten days after His ascension, when the Father would send down the Holy Spirit, not to come *upon* His people but to actually come *into* them.

Following His resurrection, Jesus continued to heighten the expectation of His disciples for the unique advent of the third person of the Trinity. He had given them a temporary measure of His Spirit to help them in His absence before Pentecost; He had instructed them not to leave Jerusalem until the Spirit was given; and He had encouraged them by revealing that when the Holy Spirit came, He would give them the power to carry on His ministry throughout the world.[27]

But then, after Jesus ascended into Heaven, nothing happened. For ten days, one hundred and twenty of His followers met for prayer in an upstairs room that was very likely the same room where the disciples had gathered with Him for supper the night He was betrayed. While we are told, "They all joined together constantly in prayer,"[28] we are not told what they prayed or how they prayed. But it's safe to assume they were praying fervently, sincerely, almost desperately—without ceasing—for Jesus to keep His promise and come to them in Spirit form. What we know for sure is that their prayers were answered on the day of the Feast of Pentecost.

From the description given in Acts 2, as the morning of the feast day unfolded, His followers were in the upstairs room sitting together. Perhaps they were praying or reading Scripture or discussing the last instructions they had received from Jesus. At nine in the morning, without warning, there was the sound of a violent wind. The trees were not bending, clothing was not billowing, and curtains hanging in the open windows were not moving. It was just the sound of a hurricane-force wind. Before they could react to what they heard, they were electrified by what they saw: on each person's head appeared a flame! Then they were each filled with an intense awareness of the presence of Jesus. In fact, He had never felt so close. They must have felt wrapped in Him! Saturated in Him! Filled with Him! Without any doubt, they knew Jesus had come to them just as He said He would. But His presence was now in them in the person of the invisible Holy Spirit. The Father had kept His promise! And without any conscious effort, the enormous relief . . . the ecstatic joy . . . the electric thrill that they experienced rose up from their hearts and poured out of their lips in a symphony of praise![29]

In their state of euphoria, the followers of Jesus must have moved to the nearby temple area. They were quickly surrounded by thousands of people who had converged on the city to celebrate the Feast of Pentecost. The Holy Spirit's supernatural presence was revealed when the curious onlookers determined that the disciples were speaking in each listeners' own language! "Utterly amazed, they asked: 'Are not all these men who are speaking Galileans? Then how is it that each of us hears them in his own native language? . . . What does this mean?'"[30]

Backed by the other disciples, Peter assumed the leadership responsibility, stood up, and addressed the onlookers with authority. He told them plainly that in fulfillment of Scripture, God had poured out His Spirit. And then, in the first public, verbal presentation of the gospel, he boldly described the life, the death, the resurrection, and the ascension of Jesus to which he and the other disciples were eyewitnesses.[31] He concluded by declaring that Jesus, "exalted to the right hand of God . . . has received from the Father the promised Holy Spirit and has poured out what you now see and hear."[32]

Then Peter proclaimed truth . . .

. . . to some of the very people who had stood by and done nothing while Jesus suffered the worst crime ever perpetrated in human history.

. . . to some of the very people who had actively participated in the mob demanding "Crucify him!"[33]

. . . to some of the very men who had nailed Jesus to the cross.[34]

Peter shouted for all to hear, "Let all Israel be assured of this: God has made this Jesus, whom you crucified, both Lord and Christ [Messiah]."[35]

Amazingly, the crowd did not erupt in a riot or rush Peter in a rage nor drag him off to be stoned. Instead, they were cut to the heart and asked what they could do. Peter's response marked a pivot in history: "Repent and be baptized, every one of you, in the name of Jesus Christ for the forgiveness of your sins. And you will receive the gift of the Holy Spirit."[36] About three thousand people responded! Repented! And received the Holy Spirit! On that historic day, the church was born!

So, dear sinner. What have you done that you feel puts you beyond the realm of God's forgiveness and redemption?

If He could forgive the very people who had stood by and done nothing when Jesus was arrested, tried, tortured, then crucified,

. . . if He could forgive the very people who had consented to His death and delivered Him for execution,

. . . if He could forgive the very people who had gathered at the governor's judgment hall and shouted "Crucify him!"

. . . if He could forgive the very Romans who had carried out the death sentence and nailed Jesus to the cross,

. . . if He could forgive the very same crowd of people that was guilty of the worst crime ever perpetrated in human history past, present, or future,

why do you think He won't forgive you? Like those in the crowd on the temple steps, simply cry out to Him. Throw yourself on His mercy. If you lack words, perhaps the following will help:

Merciful God,

I cry out to You. Now. I know I'm a sinner. I have rationalized my sin, defended it, excused it, denied it, but I cannot rid myself of the guilt. While I put on a confident air in public, on the inside I'm ashamed . . . empty . . . hopeless. But I've come to the end of pretending. I'm so very tired of being tired of carrying this burden of guilt. My sin keeps coming to mind. I long to be free . . . genuine . . . real . . . with nothing to hide. Before You and before others. I know I don't deserve Your attention, much less forgiveness, but within me now is a small spark of hope. If You could forgive those who crucified Jesus, then would You also forgive me? You have said that You will not despise a broken, contrite heart.[37] *So please, God of King David, do not despise or reject my cry.*

I confess to You my _____ (fill in the blank).

I'm so sorry. Like David, I know I have sinned against You, not just against myself or others. Cleanse me within. I long to experience freedom from guilt and freedom from the fear of Your judgment. Create in me a pure heart. I invite You to enter my life as I surrender to Your full authority. Redeem me. Use me. For Your glory.

The specific words aren't as important as the cry in your heart and the sincerity of your faith as you turn to God, and God alone, for forgiveness and redemption. He will forgive you. He will redeem you. That's why He sent His only Son. His very name—Jesus—means He will save you from your sin.[38] But in addition, because you are living on this side of Pentecost, it gets even better.

His Presence in Humanity

Back at the beginning of time, Adam and Eve had perfect bodies, perfect jobs, perfect health, perfect resources, perfect relationships, a perfect environment—yet they were still dissatisfied. They wanted the one thing they'd been told they could not have. They disobeyed God and took it. This moral and spiritual failure initiated all sin. Sin entered not only their lives but also the life of every person born into the human race since, except for Jesus.

After God pronounced judgment on our first parents and before He removed them from His presence, He killed, or sacrificed, an animal and clothed them in its skin.[1] I've wondered whether there were tears in His eyes and flowing down His divine face as He did so, because He knew that it was a temporary fix. He knew that the permanent remedy for the sin of the world—the only way people would ever be brought back into a personal, right relationship with Himself—would be through the shed blood of the Lamb, His own Son, which would take place thousands of years later.

God made it very clear that without the shedding of blood, there would be no forgiveness.[2] While I don't fully understand why a blood sacrifice was, and still is, required, a Puritan writer put it this way in his prayer:

Before thy cross I kneel and see
 the heinousness of my sin,

my iniquity that caused thee to be 'made a curse',
   the evil that excites the severity of divine wrath.

Show me the enormity of my guilt by
   the crown of thorns,
   the pierced hands and feet,
   the bruised body,
   the dying cries.

Thy blood is the blood of incarnate God,
   its worth infinite, its value beyond all thought.
Infinite must be the evil and guilt
   that demands such a price.[3]

Praise God for the precious blood of the Lamb! Because if there is no for-giveness, there could be no right relationship with God.

In the meantime, after Adam and Eve sinned and before the Cross, God set up a system that required every sinner to come to Him through a blood sacrifice. When the law was given in the days of Moses, the manner of sacrifice was clari-fied. The law stated that when someone sinned, he was required to bring a sacri-fice to the tent of meeting in the midst of the Israelites' wilderness encampment.[4] Later the designated place would be the temple in Jerusalem. The sin offering required varied from a bull to a goat to a lamb to a dove or a pigeon for the very poor. But the principle was the same for each large animal killed: the sinner was required to place his hand on the offering. It was as though his sin traveled down his arm, passing through his hand onto the animal. The sinner then took a knife and killed the animal so it was clear that the sinner was responsible for the ani-mal's death. The priest then would take the blood, sprinkle it on the altar, and atonement was made for the person's sin, absolving the sinner of guilt and rec-onciling him to a holy God.

Hundreds of years would go by, millions of animals would be slain, oceans of blood would be shed, yet when sinners walked away from the sacrifice, they had no lasting assurance that their sins were forgiven. Their unease was rooted in simple logic. How could the blood of bulls, goats, and lambs really make atonement for sin?[5] But they went through the sacrificial system by faith, as it pointed to something—Someone—they didn't fully understand. From our perspective, we know that sacrificial system was pointing to Jesus.

In the Old Testament, truly penitent sinners who sacrificed in obedience to God's Word were given, as it were, IOU notes by God guaranteeing that one day they would be forgiven of any and all sin. Then came the momentous day when a rather ordinary-looking man walked beside the Jordan River. He caught the attention of John the Baptist, the first spokesperson for God in over four hundred years to arrive on the scene in Israel. John's God-given, prophetic role was to prepare the way for the Messiah by calling the people to repentance. The people went out by the hundreds to hear him and to respond by being baptized as a sign they were willing to repent, to turn away from their sin. On this day, with the crowds hanging on every word he uttered, John shouted, "*Look!*" Then he pointed to Jesus of Nazareth as the Lamb of God, who would take away the sin of the world.[6]

Three years later that same man, Jesus of Nazareth, who had been identified as God's Lamb, would be bound by nails to the altar of the cross and sacrificed by God for the sin of the world. Past sin. Present sin. Future sin. All sin was atoned for through the shed blood of Jesus Christ. And all those IOU notes were paid in full!

How thankful I am that today sinners don't have to go to a designated place and slaughter a designated animal, with blood spurting everywhere. Instead, we go to the altar of the cross and grasp the Lamb of God with our hands of faith. As we confess our sin, it's as though the guilt of our sin is transferred to God's Lamb. We acknowledge that even if no one else had ever sinned, our sin alone would have required His death, and we tell Him we are sorry and we are willing to turn away from sin. As a result, our sin is atoned for by His blood; we are forgiven and brought into a right relationship and fellowship with God and given eternal life.[7]

Praise God! If you cried out to Him using the prayer in the previous chapter—or any other prayer of repentance—you are forgiven. You are redeemed. Your heart has been cleansed. You have entered into a right relationship with God through your faith in His Son, Jesus Christ. You have peace with a holy God! Take a moment now to just say, "Thank You! Thank You! *Thank You* for hearing my cry, forgiving my sin, and redeeming my life!"

THE HOLY SPIRIT'S PRESENCE WITHIN

The Cross stands in the center of time. Before the Cross, people were forgiven of their sin and brought into fellowship with God as they looked forward to a future Savior, exercising their faith by participating in the sacrificial system as God required. Today people are forgiven of their sin and brought into fellowship with God as they look back to the Cross, exercising their faith by claiming Jesus as God's Lamb sacrificed for their sin.

However, on this side of the Cross, our salvation experience has an added dimension. We now also have the indwelling of the Holy Spirit. This is the dramatic difference that Pentecost has made. The Holy Spirit no longer just comes *upon* certain select people. The Holy Spirit now comes *into* anyone and everyone who places faith in Jesus Christ.

Which means that anyone and everyone can be forgiven. Anyone and everyone can come into a right relationship with God. Anyone and everyone can be restored to fellowship with God. Anyone and everyone can be born again. We can start over. And best of all, anyone and everyone can enjoy the presence of Jesus living within. Even you. Even me. Hallelujah! What a Savior!

This astounding, supernatural miracle is illustrated by the experience of the Virgin Mary. She was a young girl, living in the small mountain village of Nazareth. We assume she was like any other girl in her town—poor, somewhat uneducated, yet with the small hopes and dreams of all teenage girls in her village to one day be a wife with a home and children of her own. But she also must have been unlike others in her innocence, purity, godliness, and desire for the things of God. She may even have clung to a deep desire for the Messiah to come in her lifetime. While she knew from the familiar prophecy of Micah 5:2 He would not come from Nazareth and therefore she would have had no expectation of her own involvement with Him, she could dream.[8]

When she reached the marriageable age of approximately thirteen or fourteen, she was betrothed to an upright man named Joseph. Once she entered into the betrothal, she was considered married to Joseph in every way except sexual intimacy. The betrothal would last for approximately one year, during which time they lived separately. Joseph would then use this time to prepare a home that they would share after the formal wedding ceremony. For years, for centuries, according to Jewish tradition, this had been the way of her people. Everything about Mary's betrothal was normal . . . traditional . . . customary . . . *until the angel came.*

What was Mary doing on that history-splitting, life-altering day? Was she winnowing wheat? Harvesting grapes? Milking a cow? Making cheese? Baking bread? Drawing water? Was she just going about her everyday responsibilities when God invaded her life? I suspect Mary had never seen an angel before, yet it wasn't his appearance that troubled and frightened her. It was how he greeted her. "Greetings, you who are highly favored! The Lord is with you."[9] Seeing her expression, the angel immediately sought to put her at ease by telling her not to be afraid. But what he then revealed must have thrust her into the stratosphere of bewildered amazement: "Mary, you have found favor with God. You will be with child and give birth to a son, and you are to give him the name Jesus. He will be great and will be called the Son of the Most High. The Lord God will give him the throne of his father David, and he will reign over the house of Jacob forever; his kingdom will never end."[10]

It is forever to Mary's credit that she didn't drop down in a dead faint or run away in panic or laugh hysterically at something so absurd. Instead, with great poise and sincerity, she inquired, "How will this be . . . since I am a virgin?"[11]

Consider carefully the angel's response, because his explanation to Mary of what would happen to her physically parallels what happens to you and me spiritually when we receive Jesus Christ by faith. The angel answered her question in this way: "The Holy Spirit will come upon you, and the power of the Most High will overshadow you. So the holy one to be born will be called the Son of God. . . . For nothing is impossible with God."[12]

In spite of the stunning news . . .

. . . in spite of the fact this would immediately turn her life upside down and inside out

. . . in spite of the fact she knew she would face public humiliation

. . . in spite of the probability of Joseph's rejection

. . . in spite of the immediate destruction of all her own hopes, plans, and dreams

. . . in spite of everything this would cost her,

Mary immediately submitted to what she recognized as God's will for her when she responded, "I am the Lord's servant. . . . May it be to me as you have said."[13]

At that moment, Mary fully embraced what God had for her, which was radically different from anything she had ever thought of for herself. Her faith in God's word as it was told to her by the angel, and her submission to God's will as she let go of her life to embrace His, resulted in the miraculous conception of the physical life of Jesus within her.

And this is the similarity between Mary's experience and ours:

When you and I place our faith in God's Word, which says . . .

. . . that we are all sinners

. . . that physical, spiritual, and eternal death are the wages of sin

. . . that God sent His only Son, Jesus, to die on the cross so that whoever places faith in Him would not perish but have everlasting life

. . . that the blood of Jesus is sufficient to atone for any sin and all sin

. . . that if we confess our sin, God will be faithful to cleanse us and forgive us

When we place our faith in God's Word, which says . . .

. . . that He will give us eternal life, which is not only Heaven when we die but also a personal, right relationship with God now

When we place our faith in God's Word, which says . . .

. . . that we will have the right to become God's child, born supernaturally into His family, if we believe on the name of the Lord Jesus Christ and receive Him into our hearts

When we place our faith in God's Word, which says . . .

. . . that if we hear the word of truth, which is the gospel as I have just related, and believe it as it applies to us

. . . that if we claim Jesus as our personal Savior and Lord, grasping the Lamb of God with our hands of faith, confessing our sin and guilt, believing that they are now transferred to Him and that we are cleansed with His blood, at that very moment, we conceive spiritually the life of Jesus within us in the person of the Holy Spirit. And that's a miracle![14]

The Bible describes this as the miracle of rebirth.[15] Because when His life is conceived within you, you become a new creation on the inside.[16] Although you will always have your old, sin-infected mind, emotions, and will until you join Jesus in glory, you now have His mind to think His thoughts, His emotions to love those you don't even like, and His will to do the right thing even though you have a strong tendency to do the wrong thing.

THE HOLY SPIRIT'S PERMANENT PRESENCE

As we've seen, from the Day of Pentecost to this present day, anyone and everyone who is willing to turn from sin and publicly confess faith in Jesus as Lord, Savior, and Messiah is forgiven of any and all sin.[17] Not only that, but forgiven sinners enter into a right relationship with God while personally receiving the

Holy Spirit, who doesn't just come *upon* them but comes *into* them.[18] Forever! Unlike King Saul, He will never leave you. And unlike King David, you need never, ever fear losing the Holy Spirit. He will never forsake you.[19]

Once you are truly born again, you can never be unborn. Think about it. If you did nothing to earn your salvation or the gift of the Holy Spirit, what could you do to unearn them? And if God has given you eternal life but in some way you could lose it, then it would be temporary, not eternal.

I was a young girl of about nine years of age when I first experienced the joy of knowing that Jesus is mine and I am His. I don't recall the exact year, but I do remember the day. It was Good Friday. For several years in a row, a silent movie titled *King of Kings* was shown on television in celebration of Easter. My mother would gather my siblings and me to watch the special presentation as a family, using it to impress on us the serious meaning of the events depicted.

On the Good Friday of the year in question, for some reason I don't remember watching the movie with my family. It may be they were distracted by other things so I watched it by myself, or it could be we watched it all together yet it seemed as though its message was for me alone. When the scene of the cross came up before my eyes, even though I had viewed it repeatedly in the past, on that particular day I knew with certainty that Jesus had died for me. When the movie ended, I slipped upstairs to my bedroom, knelt beside my bed, and told Jesus that I knew He had died for my sin. I told Him I was sorry. I asked Him to forgive me and cleanse me with His blood. I asked Him to be my Savior. I remember thinking I wanted Him to be glad He had made that sacrifice . . . that all the pain and suffering and blood and torture and humiliation and agony I had seen portrayed on the screen had been worth it from His viewpoint because of one little girl's response. And then I invited Him, with tears streaming down my cheeks, to come into my heart. And I am convinced that on that day Jesus did come into my heart, in the person of the Holy Spirit.

While I didn't understand, or really even know, about the Holy Spirit, I did know something was different. I remember as I quietly walked down the stairs to tell my mother what I had done that I felt cleaner. Lighter. As though an unseen load had been lifted. And the load that I now know was a burden of guilt, which simply comes with the territory of being a sinner, even if the sinner was only nine years of age, has never returned. And the Holy Spirit has never left.

One vitally important blessing of the Holy Spirit's presence within me is that I'm not alone and never will be. After living with my husband for forty-nine years, the abrupt transition into singleness has been something I wasn't prepared for. My precious children eased me into widowhood by their hovering presence. As I shared with you earlier, my younger daughter stayed with me while Danny was on life support. The day he was removed, my older daughter, Morrow, and her husband, Traynor, moved into my house and lived with me for the next fifteen months.

But the time finally arrived for Morrow and Traynor to move out and into a beautiful home of their own. With tender thoughtfulness they did so gradually, saving most of the move for when I was with Daddy for Thanksgiving. When I returned from Thanksgiving, I walked into an empty house. Truly empty. For the first time since Danny had moved to Heaven. As I walked through the door, enveloped in silence and stillness, I sensed the presence of the Spirit of God. As I still do.

When I return from a trip and there is no one to meet me at the door, I'm not alone.

When I sit down to dinner for one, I'm not alone.

When I curl up in a chair to read beside the fire on Sunday afternoon, I'm not alone.

When the doorbell rings unexpectedly at two in the morning, I'm not alone.[20]

When I snuggle down at night in the same bed I shared with my husband for forty-nine years, I know I am not alone.

Yet I long for a stronger faith that sees the invisible, hears the inaudible, comprehends the incomprehensible! A faith that is strong enough to carry me through all the challenges of singleness. A faith that sees me through to the end of this cancer journey. A faith that is strong enough to pass down to my children, grandchildren, and beyond. A faith that is strong enough to be contagious to those around me. Faith in the continuous, 24-7 presence of the invisible Jesus in me. Faith that enjoys the presence of the Holy Spirit, who is from the beginning, sent down as a gift from Heaven, to live in me. Forever!

Do you, too, long for faith that really works? Faith that will see you through lonely hours of bereavement? Faith that will be strong in the face of adversity? Faith that remains unshaken when practical circumstances are shattered? Faith that shines like a light in the darkness, pointing others to Jesus? Then fully embrace the Holy Spirit with absolute, total, unreserved trust, and begin experiencing His constant presence . . . on the inside.

Part Three

RELYING ON THE POWER OF THE HOLY SPIRIT

You will receive power when the Holy
Spirit comes on you.

—ACTS 1:8

Danny Lotz and I were married on September 2, 1966, in the same mountain chapel where my parents had been married twenty-three years earlier and in which I had been raised. On any given Sunday during my childhood, my family and I could be found sitting toward the front on the right-hand side of Montreat Presbyterian Church. It's the same chapel where I was baptized and where I shared my first public testimony. A myriad of meaningful memories flood my mind whenever I think of all that has transpired within those old mica-flecked stone walls.

Our wedding took place in the evening on a beautiful Labor Day weekend, and it was all that I could have dreamed. The old stone and wood-paneled chapel was filled with flowers that banked the front wall, cascaded from the rafters, and elegantly draped the end of each pew. The aisle was lined with the same long white cloth that my parents had walked over when they were married.

As I stood beside Daddy with my arm looped through his, waiting to walk down to the front of the chapel, where I would say my vows, he whispered words of encouragement in my ear. I could see my tall soon-to-be husband standing at the front, waiting, grinning from ear to ear. As the groomsmen and bridesmaids took their places, the music paused. With as dramatic a flourish as the old organ could manage, the wedding march began, and Daddy and I began to slowly make our way down the aisle.

My father-in-law, a pastor from New York City, presided over the first part of the ceremony, asking, "Who gives this woman to be married to this man?" My father answered in his loud, confident preaching voice, "Her mother and I do." Then he kissed my cheek, placed my hand in Danny's, stepped around to face us, and completed the ceremony by leading us through our vows of commitment to each other. In that brief ceremony, I became a wife. And I knew I had made a commitment for a lifetime.

Within twenty-four hours, that commitment was challenged in a way that is humorous today but was miserable then.

The morning after the wedding, we were scheduled to catch a plane out of Atlanta that would take us to San Diego, where we would spend the remainder of our honeymoon. After a quick breakfast, we got into Danny's baby-blue Oldsmobile Starfire convertible and headed south on Interstate 85 toward Atlanta.

An hour or so into the drive, I noticed the gas gauge was hovering near empty. In a sweet tone of voice, I mentioned it to Danny. He brushed it off and said all was well. About ten minutes later I looked over, and the needle was now pointed straight at the *E*. Not wanting to appear strong willed or dominant on my very first day as his wife, I said as pleasantly as I could, "Danny, darling, don't you think we should go ahead and stop for gas? The needle is now pointing toward empty." Again his reply was that the needle wasn't very accurate and that everything was fine.

Within minutes, we felt the car jerk, heard the engine cough, and then everything went silent as Danny guided the gliding car to the shoulder of the highway. We had run out of gas! To make matters worse, this particular section of the interstate was like a no-man's-land. Neither of us could remember when we had last passed a gas station.

My tall, handsome, tanned, athletic, brand-new husband said, "Anne, it's no problem. I'll go find some gas. You stay here." Then he rolled up the windows, locked the doors to keep me safe, and trotted off down the highway. Now I had multiple problems. The car had no gas. My husband was gone. It was at least ninety degrees outside. And we had parked beside a section of land that smelled as though every sewer in the county emptied into it, ensuring I would keep the windows closed!

Forty-five minutes later I saw a tow truck coming from the opposite direction with its lights flashing. It did a U-turn, then pulled up behind the car. Out jumped my husband with a can of gas. He quickly poured the gas into the car's tank, thanked the tow-truck driver, waved as the truck drove off, opened the door, turned the key in the ignition, and nothing happened. He tried it again. Nothing! The battery was dead!

To his credit, my new husband put the best possible spin on things when he reassured me, "Anne, it's okay. Now I know where the gas station is." With that, he rolled up the windows, locked the doors, and ran off down the highway. Again. This time I waited about thirty minutes before I saw the flashing lights of the truck coming toward me. The truck swung around so that it was nose to nose with the car. Danny jumped out and, with the help of the tow-truck operator, opened the hood, attached cables to the batteries in his car and the truck, then slid into the driver's seat and turned the key in the ignition. This time the engine revved.

As the tow truck was disengaging, a passing car slammed on its brakes, pulled over to the side of the road, then reversed to where we were still parked. All four doors of the car burst open at once, and out jumped Danny's older brother, Sam, and three of his friends, who were returning to Atlanta from the wedding.

With a look of consternation, Sam exclaimed, "Danny, what's going on?" So Danny told him. Then Sam, Danny's bachelor brother, asked with a big grin, "How's married life?" To which my husband enthusiastically replied, "Great, Sam! You should try it!" I was glad Sam hadn't asked me. I was nauseated from the smell of the swamp beside the road, soaking wet from having been locked in a car in the sweltering heat, and if someone had offered me an annulment, I would have taken it on the spot!

On that first day of marriage, I learned a simple but valuable life lesson: no one can run on empty. You and I can't run on empty in a car or in a marriage or in life. Which is why God has given us His Holy Spirit. He is the "fuel"—the power—that enables us to live the Christian life.

Although you have said your vows of commitment to the Lord Jesus and have therefore entered into a personal relationship with Him, do you find yourself running on empty? Are you trying harder to be a "good Christian," putting more and more effort into pleasing God, only to find the desired result elusive? Do you find yourself just going through the motions? Are you attending church and Bible studies, but increasingly you're living behind a facade, pretending to be more spiritual than you really are? With a fake smile on your lips and the "proper" words on your tongue, are you just trying to make it one more week . . . one more day . . . one more hour . . . one more step? Hoping against hope no one notices? Is your mind gripped by the thought *I can't do this. I'm just not cut out to live the Christian life*?

Don't be discouraged. There is hope! The One who is within you will enable you to live out the vows you have made. The key is learning to rely on His power.

His Power to Transform

The power of the Holy Spirit is impossible to humanly measure, because it's the power of God Himself. Other than the cross, resurrection, ascension, and return of Jesus, there is surely no greater display of His power in all the Bible than that which we read in the opening verses of Genesis 1—the same verses that were read by the *Apollo 8* astronauts.

The second verse of Genesis 1 describes planet Earth as being formless— without any shape, empty of any substance or meaning, devoid of any light, and covered with water in a fluid, unstable condition. It was, in essence, good for nothing. Just a waste of space . . . a blob dangling in the darkness . . . until the Spirit of God began to hover over it. While the planet was in that useless, meaningless state, the Holy Spirit began to pulsate and energize it until it was ready to respond to the command of God: "Let there be light."[1] When the command was given, amazingly, the light came on!

All the way through Genesis 1, we read the pattern that as the Spirit of God continued to hover over the planet and the word of God continued to go forth, day by day by day changes took place. On the second day the waters were divided so that Earth was given dimension with a sky and room to breathe. On the third day God's word called forth a foundation, and dry ground appeared. To the dry ground, God added seed-bearing plants and trees. On the fourth day the planet that had been aimless with no direction was given the light of the sun by day and the moon and stars by night to serve as signals and seasons. On the fifth day the seas were filled with fish and the air was filled with birds as the planet became animated.

On the sixth day the land was filled with all kinds of animals and creatures. It was then that God said, "Let us [note the plural implying that God the Father; God the Son, who is the living Word; and God the Spirit were speaking as one] make man in our image, in our likeness. . . . So God created man in his [singular] own image, in the image of God he created him."[2] So God did! Male and female were created, and the human race began.

When God evaluated the result of all that He had made, He pronounced His satisfaction and saw that it was very good, in dramatic contrast with the way the planet was described in Genesis 1:2 when it was formless, empty, and dark.[3]

The very same power of the Holy Spirit that transformed planet Earth in the beginning is available to transform human life today. Sometimes the transformation He brings about is sudden and dramatic. Sometimes it takes place more gradually over days, months, and even years. But His power to do so remains undiminished and undiluted. It's the same today as it was at the beginning of time. Totally capable. Fully sufficient. Completely adequate.

Transformation Anticipated

The evidence of the Holy Spirit's power to transform is clearly seen in the life of one of Jesus's disciples. Simon Peter was a fisherman who had a tendency to say and do the wrong thing at the wrong time. While he was a strongly committed follower of Jesus, his discipleship was marred by failure after failure. Like you and me, he struggled to keep his vows.

Simon's relationship with Jesus began when his brother, Andrew, exclaimed, "We have found the Messiah."[4] He must have shrugged, wondering how in the world his brother would know whether he did find the Messiah. But he dutifully followed Andrew and was introduced to Jesus. The Savior looked at him and saw not who he was but who he would become.[5] Jesus changed his name from

Simon to Peter to reflect the transformation he would experience through the power of the Holy Spirit. But Simon Peter then returned to fishing. Apparently, he wasn't that impressed.

Several days later Simon Peter and Andrew were washing their fishing nets when they saw a large gathering of people along the lakeshore. Jesus was in the center of the crowd, trying to teach. As Andrew, Simon Peter, and the other fishermen watched the commotion, Jesus walked toward Peter, then climbed into his empty boat! He asked Peter to push out a little distance from the shoreline; then Jesus began to preach, using Peter's boat as a floating pulpit. When He finished teaching, He turned to Peter and said, in essence, "Let's go fishing!" Peter protested by saying he had fished all night and had caught nothing. The fish weren't biting. Seeing what must have been a confident, expectant expression on Jesus's face, he stopped resisting and agreed to try again: "Because you say so . . ."[6]

When Simon Peter followed Jesus's instructions and fished His way, he caught so many fish that his net began to break. A second boat pulled up beside Peter's to help him haul in the fish, but the catch was so large, both boats began to sink! Peter's reaction revealed he now agreed with Andrew. Jesus was surely more than just a man. Peter fell on his knees and begged Jesus to get out of his life. Peter had never felt so dirty and sinful and unworthy. He knew he was in the presence of God and was terrified.

Jesus quickly reassured him, telling him not to be afraid. That from that day forward, he would be changed from a fisher of fish to a fisher of men. In anticipation of that promised transformation, Peter dropped his nets, got out of his boat, and left everything to follow Jesus.[7]

TRANSFORMATION NEEDED

While Peter followed Jesus with no hesitation or reservation, he stumbled badly as he tried to live out his commitment. One day Jesus inquired of His twelve closest followers what other people were saying about Him. They shared the rumors they had heard—that He was John the Baptist or Elijah or Jeremiah or one of the other prophets who had come back from the dead. With a penetrating look, in order to clarify their focus and strengthen their faith, Jesus cut through the rumors and led them straight to the truth when He asked, "Who do you say I am?"[8]

Peter's leadership was on full display, as well as his keen intelligence, when he answered for the other eleven men, "You are the Christ, the Son of the living God."[9] The praise his confession evoked from Jesus must have brought a flush to his face and a thrill to his heart: "Blessed are you, Simon son of Jonah, for this was not revealed to you by man, but by my Father in heaven."[10] Peter had soared to the very pinnacle of faith. Then, just as quickly, he plummeted to the depths of failure.

Shortly after Peter's confession of faith, Jesus confided in His disciples that soon He would suffer, be killed, then rise from the dead. Peter—who had just confessed that Jesus was the Son of God . . . God in the flesh . . . God in human form—had the audacity to take Jesus aside and contradict Him. How astounding that he had the audacity to rebuke Jesus! He adamantly declared, "Never, Lord! . . . This shall never happen to you!"[11] I can only imagine the face of the Son of God with eyes of blazing fire, commanding Peter, "Get behind me, Satan! You are a stumbling block to me; you do not have in mind the things of God, but the things of men."[12]

After such a stinging rebuke, it would be logical to assume that Peter would never again contradict his Lord. But we find him doing so on the very night Jesus was betrayed by Judas. Jesus warned that all the disciples would abandon Him when He was struck down. But Peter thought he knew better and declared, "Even if all fall away on account of you, I never will." When Jesus turned to him and revealed that Peter would deny all association with Him three times that night, Peter emphatically argued, "Even if I have to die with you, I will never disown you."[13] But before the cock crowed, he denied three times that he even knew Jesus.[14]

There were other dramatic moments of failure, such as when Peter got out of the boat, went to walk on the surface of the lake as he saw Jesus doing, then sank in the waves.[15] Such as when he was alone with Jesus, James, and John on a high mountain and saw Jesus transfigured in His glory as the Son of God. As if that wasn't phenomenal enough, he then saw Moses and Elijah appear to talk with Jesus! It's hard to imagine being able to even whisper when gazing at such a supernatural scene, but Peter gushed, out loud, that they needed to build three tabernacles, one for Jesus, one for Moses, and one for Elijah. His blurted comment was ludicrous for many reasons, not the least of which was his implication that Jesus be treated as though He was simply a man, just one of the prophets like the others. On this occasion, God the Father leaned out of Heaven and told Peter to be quiet and instead listen to His Son.[16]

Each of these scenes tells us that while Peter was fully committed to being a disciple, he struggled with a pattern of failure. His spirit was obviously willing, but his flesh was weak.[17] He needed the transforming power of the Holy Spirit.

Has your experience been like Peter's? For every step forward in your Christian life, you seem to take two steps backward. Have you repeatedly lapsed into your old way of thinking? Your old way of talking? Your old way of doing things? Your old way of viewing things? While you know you are saved . . . you know you are a follower of Jesus Christ . . . you don't always act like it. Are you so inconsistent as you try to live out your vows that you feel like giving up? Have you convinced yourself that you're just not cut out to be a "good Christian"? If it's any encouragement, sooner or later almost every Christian comes to this moment of crisis.

This end-of-your-rope, beat-your-head-against-a-brick-wall feeling of frustration as you struggle with a pattern of failure is like trying to cut down a large tree with a chain saw without first yanking the starter rope to fire up the engine and activate its power. The repeated failures can actually be blessings in disguise, as they bring you to the end of yourself. Finally you come to the point where you acknowledge you need more than your own willpower. More than your own choices. More than your own anything.

You need the transforming power of the Spirit of God.

TRANSFORMATION EXPERIENCED

For Peter, everything changed at Pentecost when the Holy Spirit was poured into him and the other disciples. At that life-altering moment, God's power was activated in Peter. The difference was dramatic and immediately evident. Whereas before Pentecost he had been so afraid of the opinions of others, including those of a little servant girl, that he had denied knowing his Lord, following Pentecost he boldly—and publicly—proclaimed Jesus as Israel's Messiah, the sinner's Savior, the risen Lord, and the unique Son of God. Using the Old Testament Scriptures, he articulated the gospel with clarity and relevance. Thousands responded to Peter's thunderous declaration by repenting of their sin and claiming Jesus as Messiah, Lord, and Savior.[18]

Could Peter's boldness have been produced by an emotional reaction to Pentecost and not the genuine power of the Holy Spirit? Possibly, except as the emotion waned, Peter's courage would have too. Instead, he continued to live and preach with jaw-dropping authority and power.

Not long after Pentecost, Peter and another disciple, John, were going up to the temple to pray. They entered through the Beautiful Gate, where a forty-year-old man who had been lame his entire life begged them for money. If he had been there for years, as the text implies, and if Peter and John had walked through that gate as they surely had on numerous occasions, how had they not noticed him before? Or had they noticed him but known they didn't have any power in themselves to help him so had walked on by, time after time? But this time was different. This time, instead of turning the other way, as we often do when confronted with the needy because we also know we don't have the power in ourselves to help them, Peter and John stopped and looked at the man. Then Peter demanded, "Look at us!" Fully expecting to be given a coin or two, the man looked up at them. Instead of giving him money, Peter explained, "Silver or gold I do not have, but what I have I give you. In the name of Jesus Christ of Nazareth, walk."[19] It takes no imagination to visualize the thrilling reaction of the formerly disabled beggar! He began walking, then jumping, then running as he entered the temple area with Peter and John.

Because the man had been a common sight as he lay begging at the gate almost every day of his life, he was immediately recognized, and a crowd began to gather. Quizzical amazement and exclamations of wonder erupted. Once again, Peter seized the opportunity to boldly explain the gospel, asking the curious onlookers, "Men of Israel, why does this surprise you? Why do you stare at us as if by our own power or godliness we had made this man walk?"[20] Then Peter proceeded to tell them about Jesus. He offered proof from Scripture that He was indeed the Messiah. He then drove home the critical need for his listeners to respond by challenging them to turn from their wicked ways and place their faith in Him.

When thousands more people responded to Peter's appeal, temple priests, the captain of the temple guard, and religious experts became exceedingly alarmed. They surely had thought that by executing Jesus of Nazareth, they had silenced His followers and teaching once and for all. Yet here were former cowards boldly declaring His name and message. Not only were their words making an impact, but who could argue with the miracles that accompanied the preaching? So the authorities fell back on what they thought would be an effective deterrent. They had Peter and John arrested, then thrown into prison. But the next morning when Peter and John were brought before Israel's rulers, elders, and teachers of the law—the same men who had placed Jesus on trial, found Him guilty of blasphemy, and turned Him over to the Roman governor for execution—these men received a stunning shock!

Peter had denied Jesus when confronted by the curiosity of a little servant girl, so how would he handle his own face-to-face interrogation by the most powerful religious leaders in Israel, who already had proven themselves to be enemies of Jesus? It would be understandable if Peter had softened his remarks. Or if he had turned to John and said, "You've got this." Instead, while looking at their haughty, accusatory faces, Peter, filled with the Holy Spirit and thus filled with His power, said to them, "Rulers and elders of the people! If we are being called to account today for an act of kindness shown to a cripple and are asked how he was healed, then know this. . . . It is by the name of Jesus Christ of Nazareth, whom you crucified but whom God raised from the dead, that this man stands before you healed. . . . Salvation is found in no one else."[21]

The religious leaders were blown away! Confounded! What had come over Peter? Why wasn't he properly afraid of them, subservient, intimidated, cowed by them? As they privately conferred with one another, they concluded that the only explanation for the difference in Peter was that he had been with Jesus. Then this hostile, murderous group of religious leaders, who had the legal authority to severely punish Peter and John, called them back in. They forcefully charged the disciples not to speak or teach again in the name of Jesus.

In Peter's response to their charge, we can almost see the invisible Holy Spirit hovering over him, energizing and emboldening him, surging in and through him as Peter laid down the gauntlet: "Judge for yourselves whether it is right in God's sight to obey you rather than God. For we cannot help speaking about what we have seen and heard."[22] The leaders were dumbfounded! When had they ever been so boldly defied? When had anyone ever dared speak the truth to their faces? If they had taken the time to reflect, they would have remembered a man who had stood before them about two months earlier in quietness and confidence. A man so dignified and authoritative that they'd had the uneasy feeling they were the ones on trial, not Him. While we don't know whether any of them experienced déjà vu, they sputtered and threatened. In the end they released Peter and John. They couldn't risk angering the crowds of people who were praising God, caught up in this miraculous evidence of the power of Jesus's name.

When Peter and John returned to the growing fellowship of Jesus followers and reported all that had taken place, everyone broke out in praise and prayer. "After they prayed, the place where they were meeting was shaken. And they were all filled with the Holy Spirit and spoke the word of God boldly."[23] Like a chain saw when the cord is pulled, the church roared to life!

Peter's testimony is exhibit A of the power of the Holy Spirit to transform weakness into strength, fearfulness into courage, timidity into boldness, impulsiveness into self-control, foolishness into wisdom, and a pattern of failure into resounding, eternal success!

What is your testimony? If you were honest, would you say you've been trying hard to live the Christian life but it seems about as effective as trying to cut down a tree with a chain saw that's not powered up? And if you were really honest, would you like to tell God that being a Christian just doesn't work for you? I wonder whether the problem isn't with the Christian life as it has been designed to be lived. Could it be that the problem is with you?

While you have the power of the Holy Spirit within you, the cooperation of your full surrender, obedience, and faith is required to activate it. Maybe it's time for you to "pull the cord."

12

His Power to Transform
You and Me

While the evidence of the Holy Spirit's transforming power in my life has not been as dramatic as in Peter's life, it's still there for others to see. I've been changed . . .

. . . from someone who was so afraid to speak in front of people that I got physically sick before standing at a podium to someone who can walk onto a platform without fear.

. . . from someone who was so shy I wouldn't even go shopping by myself to someone who can sit in front of a television camera and answer an interviewer's questions.

. . . from someone who hesitated to give my opinion if I thought it was different from that of others to someone who has presented the gospel to Hindus, Jews, and Muslims.

. . . from someone who felt bound in a small house with small children to someone who counted it life's greatest privilege to stay home and take care of my husband.

. . . from someone who was so consumed with worry that I had multiple stomach issues to someone who has learned to rest in the Father's will and trust Him—especially when I don't understand.

While the Holy Spirit has made multiple changes in my life, they did not happen all at once. The changes have been more like the changes that took place in Genesis 1 with planet Earth. They've been gradual, progressive, day by day as I've grown in my faith, deepened in my relationship with Jesus, surrendered more and more to His absolute authority, and increasingly learned to rely on the Holy Spirit's power. It's been said that "the conversion of a soul is the miracle of a moment, the manufacture of a saint is the task of a lifetime."[1] While the changes that take place are through the Holy Spirit's presence and power, our cooperation is required as we activate His power by choices we make.

Even a casual observer can plainly see the dramatic difference in Peter's life, and it's obvious that the change was brought about not just by the indwelling presence of the Holy Spirit but by something more. Repeatedly Scripture says that he was filled with the Holy Spirit.[2] Our burning questions then become, What is the filling of the Holy Spirit, and how can we experience it? It's imperative that we find out, since it's not an option in the Christian life. We are commanded to be filled with the Holy Spirit.[3]

While there may be more theological and complex answers to the primary question of what the filling of the Holy Spirit is, a simple analogy may help explain: I may invite you to come into my home but then make sure the rooms you enter are limited to ones that are presentable. I would welcome you into my living room or dining room or sunroom. But I would be mortified if you glimpsed, much less entered, my laundry room, which is always a wreck. I would not want you to step into my bedroom and bath, which I consider private and off limits. And I know I wouldn't want you to go upstairs since I rarely do, and therefore it is seldom dusted or vacuumed. In other words, you are welcome to come into my home, but you're not free to be "at home." To roam around. To look or go wherever you want.

The same can be true in a spiritual sense. We can invite Jesus in the person of the Holy Spirit to come into our lives but then tell Him, more or less, to stand right there. By the door. Or in the areas open to the public. We can refuse Him access or control of sensitive areas that we would like to keep private. Or areas cluttered with old, dusty memories of bitterness or resentment or unforgiveness. Or "rooms" filled with piles of the dirty laundry of sin that we don't want to confront.

If we want to experience the fullness of the Holy Spirit's transforming power, then we must first be willing to throw open the door of every area of our lives and invite Him to fill us with Himself.

CONFESSION OF OUR SIN

Let's start with the pile of dirty laundry—the sin that we need to deal with but often lack courage to confront. One important aspect of the Holy Spirit's filling is this: He can fill a small vessel or a large one, an old vessel or a young one, a poor vessel or a rich one, an educated vessel or an ignorant one, a beautiful vessel or a plain one, but as a holy and perfect God, He can't fill a dirty one. Our sin presents a blockage.

In order to be filled with the Holy Spirit, you and I need to keep short accounts with Him, confessing our sin as soon as it comes to our attention, then asking for cleansing.

To be filled with the Holy Spirit is a daily, continuous process that in some ways is similar to the daunting task of cleaning out my two-car garage. I keep one side of the garage cleared so that I can pull my car into it. But the other side is a convenient place to deposit larger items I can't get into the attic or pieces of furniture I'm holding for my children or bags of fertilizer that haven't been spread or lawn mowers, spreaders, yard tools, flowerpots, paint cans, and anything else I don't want in the house. From time to time it becomes so cluttered that I have difficulty even walking through it. When my son, Jonathan, asked me one year recently what I wanted for Christmas, I told him I wanted one day of his time to come and help me clean out the garage. He showed up in January to tackle the mess. He opened both garage doors to let in the light and fresh air, then started with the first thing he came to and worked his way from front to back. He dealt with some things by neatly stacking and storing them. But most other things he threw away. When he finished, he swept up, and both sides of the garage were clean and orderly. Every time he has come home since, he has checked the garage to make sure I'm not filling it back up with things that need to be thrown out.

Our hearts and lives can be like my garage. The thought of cleaning them up can be overwhelming. Rather than tackling everything at once, you and I need to open the "door" and let in the light of God's truth. Bring in the fresh air through prayer. Then start with the first thing that comes to your attention. Ask the Holy Spirit to help you sort out each thing you come to, some of which may need to be dealt with and some of which may need to be totally removed. The Holy Spirit will help you sweep your heart and life clean, then fill it with Himself. He will constantly be checking to make sure you remain clean so you can be filled with Him. He will let you know if He sees you cluttering up your heart again, as He has done for me on multiple occasions.

One year I was shopping for a Christmas gift for one of my daughters. I knew she wanted a particular pair of pajamas. When I went to the intimate-apparel section of the local department store, I found exactly the style I was looking for but not the size. Then I found a clever solution. If I took the top of one pair and matched it with the bottom of another pair, I had what I was looking for. I looked around to make sure no one was watching before I slipped the pajama top off one hanger and placed it with the pajama bottom on another hanger. I held my breath as I went to check out, afraid the sales clerk would notice that I had rearranged the items. But she didn't. She rang up my purchase, I paid for it, and then I walked out of the store satisfied that I had gotten a gift I knew my daughter would love.

My pleasure didn't last long enough even for the drive out of the parking garage. I became so increasingly miserable I could hardly continue to drive. I knew I had stolen a pair of pajamas. There! I said it. I stole something. In re-arranging the pajamas, I used deception to purchase something that the store had not offered for sale. It was late afternoon, and I knew I had to get home to prepare dinner for my family. I could not go back to the store that night. So I had to wrestle with the shame and the guilt for an entire night. I assure you I could not pray. I didn't want to read my Bible. I was a mess.

The next morning, I was waiting outside the department store for the doors to open at ten. When they did, I walked straight to the intimate-apparel section, looked around, and spotted the same sales lady. Before I could give myself the opportunity to duck my head and back out, I walked straight up to her, clutching the bag with the pajamas in one hand and the receipt in my other hand. Looking her in the eye was extremely difficult. But I did. I told her what I had done, apologized, and asked whether I could return the pajamas. The deer-caught-in-the-headlights look on her face told me either she didn't understand what I had just said or never in her life had anyone confessed something similar to her. She didn't say anything. She just shrugged and did the paperwork for the return. I walked out of the department store without the pajamas my daughter wanted but with a light heart, a clean conscience, and an awareness that the Holy Spirit was keeping my life free of "clutter."

When I sin, the Holy Spirit disciplines me with conviction, shame, and guilt until I feel I'm smothered spiritually. Almost unable to think clearly or take a deep breath, I'm aware that my sin has grieved and hurt Him.[4] Someone once said He is the most uncomfortable comforter they know! That has certainly been my experience.

I once lied to my next-door neighbor in what had been just a casual conversation. I cannot remember now what the lie was. I remember being miserable with the Holy Spirit's conviction until I picked up the phone, called and told her I lied, said I was sorry, and asked for her forgiveness. She graciously responded that she thought nothing of it. While she may have brushed aside my lie, my humble confession had an impact. First of all, it had an impact on me. It was so painful it served to be a strong deterrent to repeating the same sin. But it also had an impact on my neighbor. She observed my sincere desire to be right with God, and as a result, she wanted to get right with Him too. In time, she came to my Bible class and placed her faith in Jesus. Her life was changed, and mine was changed also, as it helped correct any tendency to misspeak or spin the truth.

Is there a sin that the Holy Spirit is prompting you to correct? (In appendix C found at the back of this book, I have provided a list of sins that may help you get started in confronting and confessing your own.) The pain, embarrassment, or outright humiliation may seem like a high price to pay, but it's highly effective. What you receive for the "payment" is an increasing fullness of the Spirit.

SURRENDER TO HIS SUPREMACY

In order to be filled with the Holy Spirit, the rooms of our lives need to be not only cleansed but also filled as we give Him unrestricted access to every nook and cranny, every dark recess, every memory, every ambition, every relationship, every attitude, every habit, every thought, every action in our lives. Every area is placed under His supreme authority.

One of the best definitions of the filling of the Holy Spirit was given by a great Bible teacher that I heard years ago. Alan Redpath was a well-spoken, dignified British preacher who authored over a dozen books and who served as the pastor of Duke Street Baptist Church in London and later The Moody Church in Chicago. In a message I heard him give to a group of Bible Study Fellowship teaching leaders, Dr. Redpath succinctly defined the filling of the Holy Spirit as moment-by-moment surrender to the moment-by-moment control of the Holy Spirit. I have never forgotten it.

Dr. Redpath's definition implies, of course, that there is not one filling that lasts a lifetime. The filling of the Holy Spirit is a little bit like the Atlantic Ocean flowing into the Mediterranean. As the Mediterranean Sea evaporates, the Atlantic flows into it, keeping it full. The same is true of the filling of the Holy Spirit in our lives.

When you and I receive Jesus into our hearts and lives, He comes into us in the person of the Holy Spirit, as we have already seen. And because the Holy Spirit is a person, when He comes to indwell us, we have all the Holy Spirit we will ever have. In other words, the newest believer has as much of the Holy Spirit as the oldest believer has, because we don't get a person in pieces. Yet regrettably, He seems to get us in pieces. We surrender to Him our Sunday mornings when we are in church but not our Monday mornings when we go to the office. We surrender to Him our Wednesday nights when we go to Bible study but not our Saturday nights when we go out with our friends. We surrender to Him our family but not our business. Our entertainment but not our eating. Our ministry but not our marriage. Our past but not our future. And so it goes . . .

Think about it. Ask yourself whether it's worth the cost to withhold some area of life from the Holy Spirit. Because His power in your life is activated in direct proportion to the degree you surrender and fully rely on Him.

The Bible records that the Jesus followers of the early church experienced multiple fillings. But it is interesting to note that while they were described by others as being filled with the Holy Spirit, they did not make this claim about themselves.[5] Perhaps the reason is that people who are filled with the Holy Spirit are so totally focused on Jesus and so absorbed by their concern for others that they lack any self-consciousness.

This gives me pause. I wonder, What do others say about me? What do others say about you? Has anyone ever described you as a Spirit-filled person? What do you and I need to do to make sure we have surrendered every part of our lives so we can be filled with the Spirit?

Take time now to conduct an inventory of your life. What have you surrendered? And what have you not surrendered? Perhaps the following checklist will help. Have you surrendered your . . .

. . . eating, exercise or lack of it, entertainment?

. . . career, church, children?

. . . marriage, ministry, memories?

. . . money, motives, methods?

. . . pleasures, pastimes, pain?

. . . fears, family, failures?

. . . health, habits, hopes?

. . . dreams, decisions, doubts?

. . . reputation, relationships, reading?

. . . stress, success, sickness?

. . . attitude, ambition, authority?

. . . past, present, future?

Go back through the list again. This time more slowly. Ask the Holy Spirit to pinpoint anything and everything you have not surrendered to His absolute authority; then just do it. Now. Make the conscious decision to let go of the control of your life in any of these areas or other areas that He brings to mind. Then deliberately yield authority to Him. Don't be afraid to surrender everything. Don't worry that you will lose out or miss out, that you will be less happy or less satisfied, that you won't have as much pleasure or fulfillment. Actually, full surrender is the pathway to the fully blessed, Spirit-filled life. (In appendix B found at the back of this book, I have outlined the steps we can take to allow the Holy Spirit freedom to fill us without hindrance.)

The decision to surrender may be difficult because it is so contrary to our own pride and sense of self-sufficiency. The enemy of our souls will also work hard to resist the decision. He knows that once we make it, God will flood us with indescribable peace and joy, pouring out one blessing after another. And in the process, we "are being transformed into his likeness with ever-increasing glory, which comes from the Lord, who is the Spirit."[6]

When I led Just Give Me Jesus revivals, I challenged the thousands of people gathered in the arenas to surrender everything to Jesus. And if, at that moment, they were willing to make that choice, I invited them to stand, hold up their white flag of surrender, which could be anything from a tissue to a piece of notebook paper to a baby's diaper, and sing the words of an old, familiar hymn as a prayer. I want to give you the same challenge now. Don't be afraid. Use the words of that same hymn as your own prayer:

All to Jesus I surrender,
   All to him I freely give;
I will ever love and trust him,
   In his presence daily live.

All to Jesus I surrender,
   Humbly at his feet I bow,
Worldly pleasures all forsaken,
   Take me, Jesus, take me now.

All to Jesus I surrender,
   Make me, Saviour, wholly thine;
Let me feel the Holy Spirit,
   Truly know that thou art mine.

All to Jesus I surrender,
   Lord, I give myself to thee;
Fill me with thy love and power,
   Let thy blessing fall on me.

I surrender all, I surrender all,
   All to thee, my blessed Saviour,
   I surrender all.[7]

Amen.

If that is sincerely your prayer, then praise God. Praise God! He will take your surrender seriously. In many ways, your life has just begun. Because the power of the Holy Spirit is more than adequate to fill you to overflowing with Himself.[8] He will give you one blessing after another while transforming you into a person who reflects the beauty of Jesus, who is in you.[9]

3

His Power to Transform Others

Looking back at the first-century church, the only explanation for the impact that it made on the entire world in one generation is the Holy Spirit. The task assigned to the disciples was really a mission impossible. For the most part, the disciples were an uneducated, untrained, eclectic band of men from a rural, nondescript area of the world. How could they convince anyone that Jesus of Nazareth was relevant? How could they convince Jewish scholars, who knew the Scriptures, prophecies, and ceremonies, that this same Jesus was the long-awaited Messiah? How could they convince the Jewish public, who repeated every day, "Hear, O Israel: The LORD our God, the LORD is one,"[1] that Jesus of Nazareth was God in the flesh, the redeemer of Israel? How could they convince the Roman world, which worshipped many gods, that there was one true, living God and His name is Jesus? How was it possible that by AD 380 the disciples had been so successful that Christianity was named the official religion of the Roman Empire?

How can you and I convince anyone that a man who lived two thousand years ago—who was subjected to a criminal execution as a blasphemer—is relevant today? How can we convince anyone of the truth . . .

"For God . . ." Which god is that? We all worship our own gods.

"so loved the world that he gave his one and only Son . . ." One Son? Aren't we all God's children?

"that whoever believes in him . . ." That sounds exclusive and intolerant to me.

"shall not perish . . ." Perish? Judgment? Hell? How medieval.

"but have eternal life . . ."[2] I don't believe there is life after death. I think we just all snuff out in the end.

How can you convince others that they need Jesus when they are younger than you are? They are glued to their iPhones, wearing earbuds, hiding in their hoodies, and they don't even seem to speak your language.

How can you convince others that they need Jesus when they are older than you are? They seem to know it all, have heard it all, and have managed to get by this far in life without Him, thank you.

How can you convince others that they need Jesus when they are your peers? They are working hard, living for the weekends or for that dream vacation. Maybe they will consider Jesus when they are established in their careers . . . or when they finally get their kids off to school . . . or when their kids get married . . . or when their spouses retire . . . you know, when it's more convenient.

How can you convince people who are richer than you are that they need Jesus? They have everything they need and most of what they want.

How can you convince people who are poorer than you are that they need Jesus? What do you know about gnawing hunger and real need?

How can you convince people who are smarter than you are that they need Jesus? They seem to know it all. And besides, their self-confidence is intimidating, and they ask questions you can't answer.

How can you convince people who are really hurting . . . grieving . . . that there is Someone who loves them? They shrug, look away, and mumble, "Then where was He when such and such happened? Why didn't He stop it? Why does He let the innocent suffer?"

How does anyone convince anyone else of the truth? Is it by logic? Eloquence? Reasoning? Charm? Wit? Sympathy? How can we convince another person to see the invisible? To hear the inaudible? To understand the incomprehensible?

We can't! No one can. Jesus clearly explained that it's not our responsibility to convince people when He told His disciples, speaking of the Holy Spirit, "When he comes, he will convict the world of guilt in regard to sin and righteousness and judgment. . . . When he, the Spirit of truth, comes, he will guide you into all truth."[3]

You and I have not been commanded to be successful as we tell others about Jesus. We have not been commanded to lead others to place their faith in Him. We are commanded simply to be faithful in declaring the truth. Praise God! The burden of responsibility belongs to the Holy Spirit when it comes to convincing others of the truth of their own sin and need for a Savior.

Not Transformed by Our Might

I've had the privilege of sharing the truth with many people over the years, some in one-on-one encounters and some in larger groups. One of my sweetest memories is of a beautiful older woman, a dear friend who attended my Bible study class. Elizabeth is always impeccably dressed, perfectly coiffed, charming in speech, and elegantly dignified. She is a genuine southern lady. I shared the gospel with her on many occasions, but she always took offense. She bristled at the suggestion that she needed to be born again. She insisted she was a Christian. She went to church, her husband taught Sunday school, she believed Jesus was God's Son . . . but she was unsure whether He was the only way to God. She had lots of questions about the Bible, and she was defensive of people who followed other religions. Out of my love for her, I tried and tried and tried to convince her of the truth—that she needed to be born again.

One day we were sitting on my front patio, and I asked her point blank whether she had ever confessed her sin, told God she was sorry, and asked Him to forgive her and cleanse her with the blood of Jesus. Could she pinpoint a time when she had opened her heart and invited Him to come in as not only her Savior but also her Lord? I underscored from our recent Bible study lesson that Jesus said she must be born again if she was to see the kingdom of Heaven.[4] To my dismay, this elegant lady, who always showed perfect self-control, was so offended that she rose up, got into her car, and left my house! For the rest of the day, I beat myself up for having pushed her too hard, even as I kept praying for her.

Several days later Elizabeth called and asked whether she could drop by. Of course, I said yes, then began to be apprehensive about her visit. Was she returning to read me the riot act? Had she come up with fresh ammunition to use in her arguments against the gospel as it applied to her? When I heard the doorbell ring that morning, I invited Elizabeth into my home and, with more than a little apprehension, sat with her in the living room. She proceeded to tell me that after she had stormed out the week before, she had attended a social function that same day. Another friend who was in the same Bible class walked up, and Elizabeth, still incensed over our conversation, poured out her anger and frustration. This friend looked her right in the eye and said, "Elizabeth, why don't you do what Anne said and see if it makes a difference? Why don't you just pray, confess your sin, and ask Jesus to forgive you and come into your heart? It can't hurt."

Elizabeth's expression was warm and her eyes were sparkling as she related to me what happened next. That same evening, she and her husband drove to the beach for a few days of R & R. It was late at night, and Elizabeth was riding in the back seat of the car so she could rest as her husband drove. Her friend's words spoken at the party came to mind, and she thought them through. She decided right there, with her husband oblivious in the front seat, to take her friend's suggestion and do what I had said. She prayed, confessed her sin, asked for forgiveness, then invited Jesus to come live in her heart. I'll never forget her exclamation of wondrous joy as she said, "Anne, I felt like a load had been lifted! A burden I didn't know I was carrying was suddenly gone! Anne, *I know* I have been born again!" And she was!

I've observed the difference that Jesus, in the person of the indwelling Holy Spirit, has made in Elizabeth's life. She still has questions, as her mind is inquisitive, but she no longer argues. Instead, she receives the answers. She has become a strong woman of prayer who leads others into God's presence, and she actively shares her faith.

Once again, I'm reminded that it's "'not by might nor by power, but by my Spirit,' says the LORD Almighty."[5] All my words were as nothing until Elizabeth herself turned to the Lord. And I'm convinced that while my words and those of others prompted her, the only reason she did was that the Holy Spirit actually drew her to Himself.

Another example of the Holy Spirit's convicting power is in the life of a guy I'll call Joe. He was born and raised in a religious home by strict parents. They seemed to know nothing of God's love, grace, and forgiveness, and therefore, Joe didn't either. For eight years his next-door neighbor not only physically and verbally abused Joe but also introduced him to pornography. As a result, Joe was convinced he was unworthy, unlovable, and did not fit in. He never divulged the abuse or the addiction. He simply set a life's course trying to escape the condemning voices in his head.

Joe tried to escape his mental and emotional conflict by chasing after girls. Then sports. Then money. Lots of it. Then drugs. Alcohol. A palatial home. Fancy cars. Designer clothes. Travel to exotic destinations. He soared to number one in profitability and number two in sales within his company. But nothing could erase his shame.

As the pressures at work became bigger and the demands greater, he turned to cocaine. He spent one thousand dollars per week to feed his habit, smoked three to four packs of cigarettes a day, and drank a pint of liquor every night just to try to get to sleep. He started gambling.

Joe eventually checked himself into four different rehab clinics, without success. He married his girlfriend after she became pregnant, but she then took the baby and left him. He was fired, his fancy cars were repossessed, and he was left broke. He had snorted a quarter of a million dollars in cocaine and had nothing left except mountains of debt. He owed the IRS, credit-card companies, and drug dealers. He filed for bankruptcy, then pawned everything he had to buy more drugs. He stole from friends and ran from the law and the drug dealers.

Joe ended up homeless. Hopeless. Penniless. Alone. Suicidal. The voices in his head, telling him he was unworthy and unlovable, began to scream louder and louder.

Then the Holy Spirit stepped in.

Joe ran into Ed, a guy he had partied with at work. Ed told Joe that he wasn't partying anymore because God had changed his life. Joe dismissed him. For another year he continued running from life and stealing to pay for his habit. Then he bumped into Ed again. When Ed invited him to church, Joe went, and for the first time in his life, he heard the gospel. He went back to church. Then back again. On the third visit, Joe walked forward at the time of invitation and surrendered his life to Jesus. Joe repented.

Three months later Joe was clean and sober. He had stopped smoking and doing cocaine, with no desire to do either. The chains of addiction were gone. Over time he developed accountability partners, paid back everyone he owed, restored his relationships with his ex-wife's family and his son. He was not restored to his old job, but God opened a door at another company, where he is doing well.

The only explanation for the dramatic turnaround in Joe's life is the power of the Holy Spirit. Jesus set him free. He discovered that he was not unlovable or worthless since Jesus had given His life for him. And he discovered that his identity was in what Jesus thought of him, not in what his neighbor had told him.

But Transformed by His Power

Whom do you know who needs to change? A disobedient teenager who is showing early signs of real rebellion? A classmate who is binge drinking? A coworker whose obscene language poisons the office environment? A church leader who exerts authority without compassion? A sibling who is hooked on pornography? An unmarried sister who is visiting an abortion clinic—for the third time? A parent looking for thrills during a midlife crisis?

How many times have you warned the person about the need to change?

Have you called, texted, emailed, spoken to the person, trying to lay out the dire consequences of the path he or she has chosen—all to no avail? Have you become angry and frustrated to the point that your relationship is strained and perhaps now even broken? Has your genuine love and concern been perceived as self-righteous, judgmental criticism?

Without realizing it, we can find ourselves trying to play the role of the Holy Spirit in the lives of others. Especially in the lives of our adult children, their spouses, or our grandchildren. It's one thing to offer advice or counsel, but it's another thing to try to convict them of sin. It doesn't work. I know. I've tried. When I've sought to convict others of wrong behavior, I've ended up not helping them but straining our relationship to the point that they won't listen to anything I have to say.

It's a huge relief to know that it's not my job to convict anyone else of sin. That's the Holy Spirit's job. Which leaves me free to love people just as they are. Yes, I can counsel and advise if they are open to it. Yes, I can speak the truth in love. Yes, I can point out the potential consequences of their sin. But in the end the most effective thing I can do is to pray for them with a heart full of love. Because the power to transform is His alone.

The apostle Paul cared so much about others that, following his own salvation experience, he devoted his life not only to bringing others to salvation through faith in Jesus Christ but also to helping grow them up into mature faith and godliness. He wept over them, preached to them, bragged on them, but in the end he entrusted them to the One who was the guardian of their souls.

Who, like Paul, are you weeping over? Witnessing to? Devoted to help grow into maturity in their faith? Sometimes it's hard to even know how to pray for those we care so much about. Write down their names. Then use the words of Paul's beautiful and heartfelt prayer for the Ephesian believers as you pray for those you are desperate to see change:

"I pray that out of his glorious riches he may strengthen you with power through his Spirit in your inner being, so that Christ may dwell in your hearts through faith. And I pray that you, being rooted and established in love, may have power, together with all the saints, to grasp how wide and long and high and deep is the love of Christ, and to know this love that surpasses knowledge—that you may be filled to the measure of all the fullness of God."[6]

Part Four

EMBRACING THE PURPOSE OF THE HOLY SPIRIT

We, who with unveiled faces all reflect the
Lord's glory, are being transformed into his
likeness with ever-increasing glory, which
comes from the Lord, who is the Spirit.

—2 CORINTHIANS 3:18

L ike me, have you sometimes thought of priorities in the same way you think of New Year's resolutions? A list might look something like this:

- Lose weight
- Start exercising
- Drink less Diet Coke
- Drink more water
- Eat less sugar
- Read more books
- Go to bed earlier
- Get up earlier

Like using a shotgun to shoot a fly, hoping that at least one of the hundreds of bits of bird shot will hit it, we make resolutions hoping to keep at least one of them so we will be better off at the end of the year. The reality is that we rarely keep any of them for the next month, much less the next twelve months.

Regrettably, many of us conduct our lives according to this same philosophy. We lack clarity in prioritizing our days because we have no clearly defined purpose in life. This leaves us to simply react to life's challenges and opportunities. In the end we find ourselves with a life that is at best scattered like bird shot with few worthwhile things to show for it or at worst wasted and devoid of eternal significance. What we all need is a clearly defined overall purpose to live for.

What is your life's purpose? To be honest, when I was younger, I never thought much about where my life was headed. My goal was simply to make it through the school year so I could go on to the next school year. I was motivated to do the best I could, but I really just wanted to graduate so I could put that level of education behind me. I never had a strong desire to go higher. Before long, Danny Lotz entered my life and swept me off into marriage.

I'm not sure when the feeling of emptiness began to gnaw deep down inside. I do remember lying in bed, gazing out the window late at night with my husband quietly sleeping beside me. I looked up at the star-studded sky and felt a longing for something more. It was a yearning that was not completely satisfied by the birth of our first child or the Sunday night Bible study we offered in our home for university athletes or the Thursday morning Bible study I shared with several other young women my age. Actually, the routine of responsibility—making the bed, fixing breakfast, washing the dishes, going to work, doing the laundry, fixing supper, washing the dishes, crawling in bed, going to sleep, then repeating the entire litany of responsibility the next day—just intensified my yearning.

Looking back, I know that the yearning in the deep well of my being was a yearning for a life of significance, for a cause to live for that was bigger than myself. It was a yearning for purpose.

What about you? Has the purpose for which you've been living continued to challenge and fulfill you? Or have you, too, sensed a restless emptiness deep within? Have you longed to live for something more? Bigger? Greater? If you have, then maybe we can be encouraged by the fact that many people like us long for significance, as evidenced by the wildly popular bestselling book *The Purpose Driven Life*, in which the author, Rick Warren, zeroes in on a question that is almost universally asked: What on earth am I here for?

This yearning for significance can also be seen in the crazy popularity of selfies and Snapchat, Instagram, and Facebook. People do outlandish things that a previous generation would consider embarrassing and unacceptable. They strip, curse, march, demonstrate, and clamor in general for recognition and popularity and notoriety. Why? Where does that desire for something greater come from? Why are we stirred to yearn for a life that is more than ordinary?

There may be two answers: One is that we are created in the image of God, with a capacity to know Him in a personal, permanent relationship, for the purpose of bringing Him glory. Until that purpose is fulfilled, we will be empty, deeply dissatisfied, and unfulfilled as we continually try to fill the void with substitutes.[1]

But what about those of us who have established a personal, permanent relationship with God through faith in Jesus Christ? Why are some of us also restless and dissatisfied, yearning for something greater? The only viable answer seems to be the Holy Spirit, who begins to work in us a desire to live for a purpose greater than ourselves.

Years ago I experienced the pure delight of attending an outdoor symphony in Vienna, Austria. A friend and I sat on folding chairs arranged in a semicircle around the stage of a small acoustic shell. It was fascinating to watch the musicians take their places, then listen to the discordant notes of them tuning their instruments. After a few moments, everyone grew quiet. In an atmosphere pregnant with anticipation, a small man stepped up on the stage, then raised a baton in his right hand. When he moved the baton, waving and pointing and directing the musicians in front of him, the sound was exquisite. While I'm no connoisseur, I knew that without the conductor we may have heard sounds but not the incredibly beautiful waltzes of Johann Strauss that filled the park.

In some ways, our lives are like a symphony. And the Holy Spirit is the conductor. He is the one who brings forth the beautiful music of a life that glorifies God. Like the conductor pointing his baton, the Holy Spirit quickens us, guides us, ignites us, shapes us, and equips us until our lives resound with the glory of the Lord.[2]

He Quickens Us

When I was newly married, looking up at the night sky and longing for something more to life, I believe the Holy Spirit was hovering over my heart and mind to stir up within me spiritual life, much as He did when He hovered over planet Earth in the beginning to bring it to physical life. I believe He energized my spirit and quickened my desire to break out of a mundane, mediocre faith and pursue God. There is no other reason for the strong stirring I still feel to this day to bring God glory by fulfilling His unique will for my life. My father put it this way: "The only explanation for Anne is the Holy Spirit." And I believe Daddy was right.

In order to transform us into the image of Jesus Christ so that we bring Him glory by increasingly reflecting His image and character, the Holy Spirit energizes, or quickens, us into spiritual life.[1]

HE QUICKENS US INTO LIFE

The Holy Spirit quickened us when we were unsaved, unbelieving, outside the family of God in order to bring us to the point we recognized we were sinners, renounced our sin, came to the cross, and claimed Jesus as our Savior and Lord. Our rebirth is a result of His quickening miracle in our lives.[2] As a young girl, I knew without a doubt that He had quickened me into spiritual life when I confessed my sin, asked for forgiveness, invited Jesus into my heart as my Savior, and surrendered my life to Him as my Lord. I knew I had been born again into God's family. I knew I had His life within me.

While this spiritual quickening of the Holy Spirit is difficult to describe, it is similar to the physical quickening a woman experiences when she carries a baby. I'll never forget, after having gone through months of infertility and then having had two miscarriages, what it was like not only to be told I was pregnant once again but also then to carry the baby long enough to actually feel movement within me. Any woman who has ever carried a child knows the thrill of feeling that first tiny flutter within that confirms all that the doctor has been saying—a baby is on board! There is no doubt in her mind that life is growing within her.

He Quickens Us into Growth

Once we are born again and we are assured of His life within us, the Spirit continues to quicken us, or stimulate us, to grow into maturity in our faith.

Our awareness of the Spirit's quickening within may begin with a tiny flutter. Just a small desire, a small spark of faith, a small choice. Jesus explained it this way: "It is the spirit that quickeneth; the flesh profiteth nothing: the words that I speak unto you, they are spirit, and they are life."[3] In my experience the quickening of spiritual life has come in tandem with the reading and studying of God's Word.

This is what I experienced as a young mother with three small children. The Spirit had already been quickening me by stirring up within a desire to be a better wife and mother. I had observed my own mother's patience and godliness as she raised five of us without my father's day-to-day involvement, and I wanted what she had. I rightly concluded that her inner strength and beauty came from time she spent with the Lord in prayer and Bible reading. While I wanted the same, I lacked the will to make those disciplines a consistent habit. Looking back, I know it was the Holy Spirit who planted that desire in my heart, then stirred it up until I acted on it.

When I was first told of Bible Study Fellowship, I recognized it as the possible answer to my own need. When no one else agreed to start the class and teach it, I stepped into that role. I knew if I taught it, the preparation for the weekly lecture would force me to stay in the Scriptures. I was right. It did. As a result, I believe over time I became a better wife and mother—not on the level of my mother but certainly better than I would have been without the accountability of leading the class.

The first year I taught, we were assigned the book of Genesis. While I loved every insight and application we gleaned from the first eleven chapters, my life's goal took shape beginning with chapter 12. As I studied the life of Abraham, he seemed to walk out of the pages of my Bible and into my life. I saw him as an ordinary man who lived an extraordinary life of significance primarily because he followed God in obedient faith one step at a time, for the rest of his life. He was not perfect. He failed miserably at times. But Abraham never quit. He never went back to his old way of life. The result was not only that Abraham and his descendants were richly blessed in a covenant relationship with God but also that Abraham established a friendship with God.

Abraham didn't say God was his friend. God said three times in Scripture that Abraham was His friend.[4] That was impressive to me, inspiring. If I told you I was a friend of the queen of England, you might smirk, thinking at the very least that I was exaggerating. But if the queen said that Anne Lotz was her friend, that would be different.

So right then, after I had been teaching for only a few months, I knew that was my desire. I wanted, and still want, a relationship with God that one day He will describe as a friendship. My reasoning was that if Abraham could know God in a relationship that God described as a friendship, then why couldn't I?

While no human being with finite mind will ever be able to grasp the height, the depth, the width, the length of who God is, I made the decision to know Him and grow in that knowledge. I want to know Him better today than I did yesterday. Better tomorrow than I do today.

As I reflected on what it means to know God, I thought of those in the Bible who knew Him and I decided I wanted to know Him as they did. I wanted to know Him like . . .

. . . Noah, as his Refuge from the storm and his Salvation from judgment.

. . . Abraham, as his Friend.

. . . Hagar, as the God who sees me.

. . . Moses, as the Liberator and Bondage Breaker, the One who makes a way when there is no way.

. . . Joshua, as the Captain of the Lord's hosts.

. . . Elijah, as the Fire Giver, the Rain Maker, and the still, small Voice.

. . . David, as the Shepherd.

. . . Isaiah, as the Lord of glory seated on the throne.

. . . Meshach, Shadrach, Abednego, as the Son of God in the fire with them.

. . . Daniel, as the One who shuts lions' mouths.

. . . Mary, as a baby in His humanity.

. . . Mary, Martha, and Lazarus, as the Resurrection and the Life.

. . . Peter, as the Forgiver and Restorer.

. . . Paul, as the Redeemer who has power to transform.

. . . John, as the King of kings and Lord of lords, who reigns forever and ever.

Why can't you and I know God as they did? If God is the same yesterday, today, and forever—and the Bible says that He is—then He hasn't changed.[5] So if we don't know Him as the people did in the Bible, nothing is wrong with God, but there is something wrong with us.

When I came to that realization, I set out to pursue friendship with God one step at a time, for the rest of my life.[6] The only legitimate explanation for having come to that decision in the first place, then sticking with it over a lifetime, is the quickening of the Holy Spirit. He has given me an insatiable desire to grow in my faith and in my relationship with God—to know, love, obey, and serve God. While that desire has launched me on a lifelong journey, it has also led me to the very thing I sought: a life of significance . . . a life that makes a positive, eternal difference in the lives of others . . . a life that brings Him glory in the process of day-to-day living as I pursue the goal of growing in my faith and in my knowledge of Him.

What about you? If you are sure you are saved and therefore know that you have a personal, permanent relationship with God, have you stopped short of the privilege of getting to know Him? Really know Him? How well do you know His character? Do you know what He wants? What pleases Him? What His plans are? The extent of His power? What He thinks about you and your family? Have you experienced the fulfillment of His promises?

What goals have you set in order to fulfill your life's purpose? As we will see in more detail in the next chapter, our lives' purpose overall is to glorify God and enjoy Him in the process. In other words, we are to live so that when others see us or hear us or know us, they will be drawn to God and want to know Him too.[7] To achieve that purpose, we need to apply it to our specific roles. I am now, literally, a widow and an orphan. I want others to observe what Jesus would be like if He were also a widow and an orphan and bring God glory by the way I live out my roles. I am also a mother and a grandmother. I want to live in such a way that when others observe me as a mother and a grandmother, they are able to see what Jesus would be like if He were a mother to my children and a grandmother to my grandchildren—with the goal that they would want to know Him for themselves. If you are a doctor, then your goal is to show people what Jesus would be like if He were a doctor so they would want to know Him for themselves. If you are a teacher, your goal is to show people what Jesus would be like if He were a teacher so they would want to know Him for themselves. If you are an attorney, your goal is to show people what Jesus would be like if He were an attorney so they would want to know Him for themselves. If you are a cook, a politician, a fast-food worker, a postal worker, a nurse, a realtor, a janitor . . . whatever you are, your goal is to draw people to Jesus by what you do and say . . .

by who you are . . . so that they want to know Him for themselves. Achieving that goal helps fulfill your life's purpose of bringing glory to God!

HE QUICKENS US FOR SERVICE

While all the above is true, you and I also have a specific role to fill as it regards our lives' purpose and significance.[8] It involves service.

When we have grown in our relationship with the Father to the point where we love Him with all our hearts, minds, souls, and strength—when we experience the deep joy, abiding peace, and overwhelming gratitude of knowing that we are members of His family and that His heavenly home is our inheritance— then it stands to reason that we will be motivated to live in such a way that we seek to pay back the supreme debt of love we owe Him.[9]

Love is not just a noun. It's a verb. And the Holy Spirit quickens, or stimulates, our love for God to such a degree that we want to do something for Him. That's what service is. Service is not something we have to do. It's something we want to do. It's an overflow of our love and worship of the One we are coming to know. The apostle Paul expressed it this way: "God has poured out his love into our hearts by the Holy Spirit, whom he has given us. . . ."[10] "It is God who works in you to will and to act according to his good purpose."[11]

One way to discover the specific service God has for you to do is to look back on your life. What has God placed in your storeroom of experience?[12] God is not whimsical. He is very intentional in what He allows into our lives, so consider carefully. If your parents were abusive or alcoholics, could it be that He wants to use and redeem your suffering as a means of helping others who come from a similar background? If you have been through a divorce or cancer or bankruptcy or some similar disaster, could it be that God has prepared you to minister to others who have been through a comparable experience? If you've been homeless or the CEO of a *Fortune* 500 company, could it be that God wants to use you to reach others who are in the same position?

Do you see? This makes life so exciting! Nothing is wasted! Your entire life's experience is worthwhile and can be used to make an eternal impact in the life of someone else. The Holy Spirit can so flood us with God's grace that we are quickened to look beyond ourselves—our own pain and suffering or our own happiness and success—to reach out and help someone else.

I experienced this in a powerful way when I was diagnosed with cancer. I immediately felt a deep peace and a tremendous sense of expectancy that never left me. One reason, besides the prayers of thousands of people for me, was that the Holy Spirit quickened me to look beyond myself and see tens of thousands of people who were suffering in a similar way. People who perhaps doubted His love and His presence and His blessing because of what they were going through. I felt honored—privileged—to suffer with them, if for no other reason than to reassure them of His love, His presence, His blessing, His undivided devotion, His constant companionship.

In part 3 I shared with you the story of Joe, who, after thirteen years of addiction to cocaine and alcohol, having suffered all the physical, practical, emotional, and professional consequences of his sinful lifestyle, was redeemed by Jesus and transformed by the power of the Holy Spirit. But his story doesn't end there. Joe began to reach out to people who were like he had been. He started feeding the homeless. He began a recovery ministry for others who struggled with substance abuse as well as their own mental tapes that told them they were worthless and insignificant. He got involved in prison ministry. As a result, Joe has discovered a greater purpose for his life than he had ever thought possible. A purpose that has taken him back onto city streets and into prisons in order to share the hope and freedom he has found through the forgiveness and grace of Jesus Christ.

As I sat down to write Joe's story, he shared with me that on a recent visit to the prison, an inmate had confessed to him that he had killed his wife and the boyfriend she was having an affair with. Joe then shared with this inmate his own experience following his conversion and transformation by the power of the

Holy Spirit. Joe had married for the second time. This time he was determined to be a godly, Christlike husband to a woman he was devoted to. He served her as he would have served the Lord, not only providing for her every need but also doing his best to make her life easier by taking on the mundane housekeeping chores. For fifteen years things seemed ideal as they served the Lord together. And then one day she moved out and moved in with another man she had been playing tennis with. He did all he could to win her back, but two years later they were divorced. In his own words, "I drew closer to God during that time. I didn't run. I didn't try to escape. By His grace and mercy, I was just able to stay put in that pain. But God was there."

As Joe shared with the prison inmate the story of his own painful experience, the great big guy fell into his arms and cried like a baby—then gave his own heart to Jesus. And in bringing life to another who had been hurt in much the same way he had been hurt, Joe experienced God's purpose for his life in a fresh way. He once again had firsthand evidence that the Holy Spirit can use the broken pieces of our lives to bring blessing and life to others—and ultimately glory to God!

Take a moment to reflect. What's in the storehouse of your life's experience? How can you use it to accomplish your life's purpose of bringing glory to God by drawing on it to help someone else? Who would benefit from knowing about God's faithfulness to redeem you and bring you through? Think about it. Is the Holy Spirit even now quickening you to embrace His purpose by using your experiences, as difficult and challenging as they may be, to help achieve it?

He Guides Us

To avoid an undirected or misdirected life, leadership institutes and career seminars explain that we need to determine what our purpose is and set goals to accomplish that purpose. Then the priorities we establish are the steps we use to achieve the goals and ultimately fulfill the purpose. Applying this as followers of Jesus Christ, we need to determine our lives' overall purpose, set clearly defined goals that will help us accomplish it, then establish priorities that will enable us to achieve the goals we have set.

We need personal, consistent guidance to keep us focused.

When I was a girl growing up in the mountains, early summer was heralded by the appearance of the indigo bunting, a small cobalt-blue bird with black wings. He would perch on top of the maple tree just outside the rail fence that bordered our front lawn. The unmistakable sound of his lilting song would echo across Little Piney Cove. When I heard it, I would run for my father's binoculars, which he kept in a large brown leather bag in his study. I would take the binoculars out of the bag very carefully, go to the front porch, press the eyepieces against my face, then aim in the direction of the bird's song. But everything was blurred . . . mountains, trees, rail fence, and grass. So I would turn the little ring between the eyepieces, and as I did, everything would come into sharp focus. There he would be, swaying on top of the maple tree, his beak lifted toward the sky, warbling his heart out.

In a similar way, as we choose to fix our eyes on Jesus, pursue righteousness, live by the truth, and fulfill God's purpose for our lives, the Holy Spirit will guide us, sharpening our focus in the midst of life's distractions and confusion.

If you have made this choice, on what have you focused your entire life? If you were honest, would you say your focus is multifaceted? A little blurred by multiple responsibilities and demands? Is your life's overall purpose to be good? To be holy as He is holy? To be filled with the Holy Spirit? To lead others to faith in Jesus Christ? To maintain your faith through the trials of life? To learn to pray powerfully? To make it into Heaven with an abundance of rewards to lay at His feet? While those can be terrific goals, none of them is sufficient as an overall purpose worth living for. It may be time to ask the Holy Spirit to turn the "ring" and sharpen your focus.

Before I was baptized at the age of nine in Montreat Presbyterian Church, I had to memorize the Westminster Shorter Catechism. I didn't realize until years later that the Holy Spirit would use it to guide me to my life's purpose, but He did. He brought the purpose into focus in the only question and answer that I can actually remember: "What is the chief end of man? Man's chief end is to glorify God, and to enjoy him forever."[1] I didn't grasp the importance of that pithy statement at the time, but now I understand that it pinpoints our purpose— our "chief end"—as followers of Jesus: It's to glorify God. Pure and simple. In all we do. In all we say. In who we are.

And that overall purpose brings everything in life into sharp focus. It's actually the same purpose for which Jesus lived and died.

FOCUSED ON GLORIFYING THE FATHER

In the magnificent prayer Jesus prayed on the night of His betrayal in John 17, He clearly stated His life's purpose: "I have brought you glory on earth." His purpose was to glorify His Father, revealing Him in all He said and did to the extent that others were drawn to worship Him and be reconciled to Him.

If His life's purpose was to glorify God, what was His goal that enabled

Him to fulfill His purpose? He plainly revealed that it was "completing the work you gave me to do."[2] Completing the work His Father had for Him involved seeking God's will through prayer, then submission and obedience to it every moment of every day.

This brings us to His priorities. If Jesus was going to achieve the goal of finishing His Father's work, it would not be an accident. It would not be a coincidence. It would not be good luck. It would be because He was intentional. Focused. To achieve His goal of finishing His Father's work and therefore accomplishing His greater purpose of bringing glory to God, He had to set specific priorities. We can observe all this playing out early in His ministry.

Jesus and His disciples were walking from Judea in the south up to Galilee in the north. One route led through the Transjordan area. While there was another route, many Jews avoided traveling that way because it led through the territory of the despised Samaritans. Yet the Bible clearly states, "He had to go through Samaria."[3] Keeping in mind that His overall purpose was to bring glory to God, the strong implication is on that particular day He had a specific goal. Accomplishing that goal required setting the priority of going through Samaria.

Sure enough, at Jacob's well in Sychar, Jesus met a Samaritan woman who had a desperate heart's cry for the living God. Following His conversation with her, she ran into town to tell others that she had met Someone who had told her everything she had ever done.[4]

The disciples had returned with food, but Jesus explained, "I have food to eat that you know nothing about."[5] Astonished, the disciples wondered where He had been able to find something to eat in the middle of nowhere. Jesus plainly told them, "My food . . . is to do the will of him who sent me and to finish his work."[6] Clearly, He wasn't speaking of lunch. He was speaking of His life's goal, which was not to eat or to sleep or to rest or to enjoy life or to be popular or to be famous or to live up to the expectations of others or anything at all other than doing and finishing the work God had given Him to do. Why? Because in finishing His Father's work, His Father would be glorified, and that was His overall purpose.

FOCUSED WITH STEADFAST RESOLUTION

Note the clarity of Jesus's purpose coming into focus as it dictated His goal and determined His priorities. Amazing, isn't it? We gain insight into what was required in order for Jesus to achieve His life's purpose and accomplish His life's goal when we read in Isaiah's prophecy about the Messiah, "Therefore have I set my face like flint."[7] What was required was a steadfast resolution to fulfill His purpose, an unwavering focus on His goal, and a faithful commitment to set daily priorities and persevere at all costs until the day He ascended back into Heaven.

Let's try to put this in perspective. Jesus had left all He had known in Heaven in order to come to earth to do His Father's will. As the Son of God, Creator of everything, Jesus had lived for all eternity surrounded by the glorious presence of the Father and the Holy Spirit. From the very beginning of time and space, He had received the adoration of the universe. But He got up from Heaven's throne, took off His glory robes, and came to earth to be born in a stable, surrounded by filth, poverty, and threats on His tiny life. During His earthly ministry, He never had a home to call His own or a place where He could lay His head. Instead of being adored, He was betrayed, blasphemed, despised, and rejected. In the end He was crucified. But He rose from the dead to save anyone and everyone who comes to Him, offering them forgiveness of sin and giving them, instead of judgment and hell, eternal life and Heaven. Through the sacrifice of His own life, He is able to bring us to a deep conviction of our own sin, confession, and reconciliation with Himself.[8]

His Father was glorified, His goal of finishing His work was accomplished, and the priorities that He had established enabled Him to complete everything God had for Him. Lest there be any doubt, He put an exclamation point to all the above when from the cross He shouted, "It is finished."[9] Praise God! Jesus then put back on His glory robes not only as the Son of God but additionally as the Son of Man. He would never have accomplished and achieved all that He did if He had lost focus, even for a moment. The writer to the Hebrews described it best: "Let us fix our eyes on Jesus [stay focused], the author and perfecter of our faith, who for the joy set before him endured the cross, scorning its shame, and sat down at the right hand of the throne of God."[10]

Think with me for a moment as I ask you once again: On what are you focused? What is your life's purpose that determines your goals and priorities? If your purpose is to be physically fit and healthy, what happens when you are diagnosed with cancer? If you live for your children or spouse, what happens when they walk away and disavow you? If you live to make as much money as you can, what happens when the stock market crashes and you lose a lifetime of savings? If you live for your reputation, what happens when you are slandered? If you live for your career, what happens when you lose your job?

What happens if your purpose is to speak, travel, write books, give interviews, conduct seminars, record video and audio, lead an organizational team, then health dictates you step away from it all and stay home? This is not just a rhetorical challenge. This was my reality. When diagnosed with breast cancer, which involved follow-up surgery, chemotherapy, and radiation, I had to step aside from ministry. All speaking, traveling, media involvement, seminars, videos—anything and everything that required a schedule and commitments outside my home. If those activities had been my purpose, then I would have been devastated. But I wasn't. Not even close. The truly blessed realization was that stepping aside in no way interfered with my life's purpose. I didn't resent it, fight it, hate it, struggle with it, weep over it, complain about it, or feel sorry for myself. Not at all! I just relaxed and embraced the new journey God placed me on, knowing that He would give me many unique opportunities to bring Him glory. That alone is my life's purpose.

What about you? If your life's overall purpose is to bring glory to God, you, too, can accomplish that purpose whether you are healthy or struggling with a disease, whether you have a happy, loyal family or you are disowned, whether you are a billionaire or on welfare, whether you have a sterling reputation or it's been stolen from you, whether you climb to the top of the career ladder or drop to the lowest rung. It doesn't matter. You and I can bring God glory in whatever state we find ourselves. And that is a purpose worth living for.

If your life's purpose is anything else or less or different or what you falsely assume is more, then at the very least your life is spiritually blurry, out of focus. At worst you are at risk of either wasting your life, from Heaven's perspective, or messing up in a devastating way. Like a falling row of dominoes, your life's purpose determines your goals that determine your priorities.

Jesus promised that "the Holy Spirit will guide you into all truth."[11] So ask Him to guide your focus until it's laser-like in steadfast resolution to bring God glory in all you say and do. Then relax. Regardless of whatever life may bring your way, embrace the Spirit's purpose.

He Ignites Us

As we embark on our journey of faith, not only does the Holy Spirit within quicken us . . . stimulate us . . . stir us up . . . and then guide us to focus on our lives' overall purpose of bringing God glory, but He also sets us on fire to fulfill that purpose. Because the Holy Spirit is the fire of God.

Tradition says that in olden days, before electricity or gas-related conveniences, if someone wanted to have light or warmth or a cookstove, there was no switch to flip or button to push. Instead, in the central courtyard of most villages, a fire was kept burning. If people needed light, warmth, or fire to cook with, they took brands from the central fire to their homes for those purposes. The central fire was considered so critical to the life of the village that a fire keeper was hired to watch over the fire. If for any reason the fire keeper allowed the fire to go out—if a strong wind rose up and blew it out or rain came and drenched it or the fire keeper went to sleep and through neglect let it go out— then it cost the fire keeper his life.[1]

Throughout the Bible, fire is used to describe the Holy Spirit.[2] One of the things He does is to set our hearts on fire for God Himself, for God's Son, for God's gospel, for God's Word, for the people whom God loves, and for the purpose for which we exist, which is to bring glory to God. You and I should be fired up—all the time!

We are to be keepers of the fire. We are commanded, "Do not put out the

Spirit's fire."[3] Don't quench His fire through willful sin and disobedience. Don't neglect Him by rushing through, or skipping altogether, your daily prayer time or Bible reading. Guard your heart from the overwhelming pressure to conform to the world around you. Paul instructed Timothy, "For this reason I remind you to fan into flame the gift of God, which is in you through the laying on of my hands."[4] The gift of God was none other than the Holy Spirit, whom Timothy received when the apostle Paul led him to faith in Jesus Christ. Timothy had the "fire." It was then his responsibility not to quench Him, not to grieve Him, but to yield every part of his life to Him so that he was filled with fire . . . and deliberately maintained it.

FAN THE FLAME

Maintaining the fire requires intentionally establishing some common spiritual disciplines. They are simple choices but not always easy. They include daily prayer. Daily Bible reading. Sharing the gospel. Continuous obedience as you live out what God says in His Word. Continuous trust as you relinquish your expectations and let Him have His way. Deepening surrender to His authority—especially during times of pain and suffering.

Which discipline do you lack? Which one do you need to work to develop further? If your heart is spiritually cold or apathetic, there is a disconnect somewhere between you and the Holy Spirit. It may be directly related not only to the commission of sin and the omission of obedience but also to your lack of fellowship with other Jesus followers.

The story is told of a young man who went off to college. He came home for Christmas break, and before returning to school, he went by to see his old pastor. The pastor was delighted to see him. He invited him into his cozy study that had a warm fire crackling on the hearth. He peppered the young man with questions about school. His response was enthusiastic as he described his classes and friends. Then the pastor inquired whether he had found a church to attend. The student looked down at the floor as he replied, "No, sir. I don't feel the need to go to church anymore. My faith is strong enough without it, and with my studies and activities, I just can't find the time."

The old pastor quietly reached over and pulled a blazing log from the fire, leaving it on the hearth. Then he folded his hands and remained silent. Finally the young man thought the older gentleman had dozed off, so he cleared his throat as he rose to leave. The pastor was quickly alert, smiled, and asked, "Did you think I had fallen asleep? I was just watching that log I pulled out of the fire. Did you notice? When it was in the fire with the other logs, it burned brightly. But now that I've removed it, the fire has gone out. Son, you are like that log. If you expect your faith to stay on fire, you need to be in fellowship with other believers." So do you. And so do I.

As our world careens to an end, it will become more and more difficult to live lives that are fired up to please and glorify God, lives that maintain our focus on the goal, lives that intentionally prioritize the way we spend our time and money, where we go and what we do, who we are with and who we separate from. Such lives will be contrary to those of almost everyone around us. So for our own spiritual well-being, we are admonished, "Let us not give up meeting together, as some are in the habit of doing, but let us encourage one another—and all the more as you see the Day approaching."[5] We need one another!

Have you been trying to maintain the fire in isolation? It's hard to pursue your overall purpose of glorifying God, to set goals and achieve them through intentional priorities, all undergirded with a passionate zeal for God, if you are not in fellowship with others who are like-minded.

ABLAZE FOR HIS PURPOSE

So let me ask you. Are you on fire for the things of God? Are you still unsure what that means? While it's hard to define in words, it does not mean that you have boundless energy or that you never grow weary or that you are in Christian service 24-7 or that you always feel happy or that you bounce out of bed every morning or that you never lose concentration in prayer or that you understand everything you read in your Bible or that _____. (Fill in the blank with what you have thought it could mean.) The fire of God affects you deeper than any of those things. While it may be difficult to put it into words, I do know that if your heart is on fire, you will know it!

We see flickers of it . . .

. . . in Noah walking with and working for God when no other person in his world was.

. . . in Abraham leaving his country, his kindred, and his father's house to follow God in a life of obedient faith when he had no idea where God was leading.

. . . in Jacob, with a dislocated hip, winding his arms around God's neck and not letting go until he was blessed.

. . . in David as he went against the giant Goliath with a slingshot in the name of the living God.

. . . in Meshach, Shadrach, and Abednego being willing to be cast into the fiery furnace rather than bow down to a statue of gold.

. . . in Daniel, who prayed three times a day, knowing he would be thrown into the lions' den.

. . . in the Virgin Mary, who conceived God's Son when she knew her reputation and community standing were at stake.

. . . in Jesus of Nazareth, "who for the joy set before him endured the cross, scorning its shame, and sat down at the right hand of the throne of God."[6]

The following stanza of a poem may help us capture a glimpse of this indescribable, all-consuming passion. Use it to examine your own heart.

Has He purified you with the fire from above?
Is He first in your thoughts, does He have all your love? ·
Is His service your choice, and your sacrifice sweet?

Is your doing His will both your drink and your meat?
Do you run at His calling with glad eager feet?[7]

What is the spiritual temperature of your heart? Cold? Lukewarm? Or is it on fire? If it's not burning with love for God, His Son, His Spirit, His Word, His gospel, and people created in His image yet separated from Him, what practical steps will you take to fan into flame the fire of the Holy Spirit?

He Shapes Us

When fall rolls around each year, I enjoy going to the North Carolina State Fair with my family. We always begin at a small booth that makes the best apple dumplings imaginable. The apples are tender, the crust is crisp, and the caramelized sauce is generously slathered on top. We have learned that if we take the hot dumpling across the gravel path to another booth, where the engine of a farm tractor furnishes the power for the homemade ice cream churns, we can get a scoop of vanilla on the dumpling for only two dollars. It's the best buy at the fair. Then we make our way up the hill to the Village of Yesteryear, where artisans of every conceivable craft demonstrate their skills. From wood carving to painting to weaving to quilting to glassblowing, each booth is fascinating. I always feel so proud of North Carolina as I observe the incredible skill and giftedness of our people.

One particular craft never fails to impress me: pottery making. Shelves lined with plates, pitchers, bowls, vases, cups, and many other products all serve to display the potter's skill. But what catches everyone's attention is the potter's wheel. It's positioned in front of the display by the main aisle that circles the entire indoor village. The potter sits on a stool, with his foot on a pedal. As he pumps the pedal with his foot, the wheel begins to turn. On the wheel he has a misshapen lump of wet clay that turns quickly with the wheel. While the clay is turning, the potter places both of his hands on it. As he applies pressure with his fingers, the clay takes shape. It's amazing to see a pitcher emerging beneath the potter's hands or a beautiful vase or a goblet—all out of the same clay but shaped differently by the potter's touch.

The prophet Jeremiah in the Old Testament described the nation of Israel as a piece of clay that resisted the Potter's touch and was therefore marred and had to be reformed. The Lord instructed Jeremiah, who then recounted his experience at the potter's house:[1] "I saw him working at the wheel. But the pot he was shaping from the clay was marred in his hands; so the potter formed it into another pot, shaping it as seemed best to him. Then the word of the LORD came to me . . . 'Can I not do with you as this potter does?' declares the LORD. 'Like clay in the hand of the potter, so are you in my hand.'"[2]

While God was speaking of Israel, you and I also are described as clay in the Potter's hands.[3] The Potter is the indwelling Spirit of God. Since the overall purpose of the Holy Spirit is to bring glory to God, one of His goals is to shape us into the image of God's Son.[4] He uses everything that comes into our lives, good and bad, to apply the pressure that forms us into the shape He desires.[5] We don't have to do anything. We simply submit our lives to the Potter. Our only responsibility is to make sure we are soft to the Potter's touch. Because if we harden ourselves or resist the shape He is forming, He will have to break us in order to soften the clay of our lives and remake us into that which is pleasing to Him.

What pressure has the Potter exerted in your life? Would it help you to know that what you are experiencing is not some random problem or stressor but the Potter at work?

When my second child was a toddler, one morning I was sitting at the kitchen table. I had fixed a cup of coffee and had the newspaper in front of me, wanting just a few minutes to enjoy both in peace. Instead, my young daughter kept interrupting me. She wasn't being bad or fussy. She was just a typical toddler needing her mother's attention. Finally I'd had enough. I reached to grab her little arm and tell her to stop interrupting me. Couldn't she see I wanted to read the paper and have a cup of coffee? But I caught myself just in time. With shame I realized what I was about to do. So instead, I got up, took her into the next room, helped her find some toys to occupy her, then went back into the kitchen. I dropped to my knees on the red linoleum floor and, with tears on my face, told God how sorry I was. Right then and there, I surrendered all my time to Him. If He saw I needed some time for myself, I trusted Him to give it. But I chose in that moment to submit to the pressure of constant interruptions and allow Him to shape me into a mother who was less self-centered and more patient.

Maybe some of the other ways He has used pressure to shape me will help you recognize His touch in your own life:

- infertility that pressed me to learn to pray and fast on a regular basis
- lovelessness in my marriage that pressed me to learn to love with God's unconditional love
- caregiving that pressed me to my knees in humility and patience
- fear of an audience's upturned faces that pressed me to stay faithful to His Word
- criticism for being a woman in the pulpit that pressed me to stay focused on obeying His call on my life
- my son's cancer that pressed me to trust God when I didn't understand why
- watching helplessly as my son's marriage disintegrated so that I was pressed to accept God's will for his life that was different from my dreams
- my own cancer that pressed me to realign my priorities in order to stay focused on my life's goal
- unanswered prayers that have pressed me to want what God wants more than what I want

The types of pressure the Potter has used have been varied in size and scope. From having too much to do in one day that presses me to depend on Him for the way I use each moment; to not reaching my goals so that I'm pressed to reevaluate my priorities; to betrayal and slander that press me to live for His opinion, not that of others; to illness that brings my life to a screeching halt and presses me to look up . . . the Potter's creativity is limitless. But I am reassured by His promise that He uses "all things . . . for the good of those who love him, who have been called according to his purpose."[6] He uses all things without exception, not just some things, for my ultimate good. And my ultimate good is not health, wealth, prosperity, happiness, or sometimes the things we associate with "good." My ultimate good is to fulfill God's purpose of shaping me into the image of Jesus Christ so I bring glory to Him.[7]

Once I have grasped the ultimate purpose of the pressure, my perspective changes. Rather than indulging in self-pity or a complaining spirit or resentment or comparison or frustration, I try to see things through Heaven's eyes. But sometimes it's not easy.

The only appropriate response to pressures we don't understand is first to pray. We can ask the Holy Spirit for relief. But if the pressures persist, then we simply bow in worship before the One whose ways are not our ways. Whose touch on the clay can be soft . . . sometimes firm . . . and sometimes hard . . . as He molds us and shapes us after His will. Why? Because "we have this treasure in jars of clay to show that this all-surpassing power is from God and not from us."[8] In the end the Spirit's purpose is not just to shape the clay into a more useful vessel but to display the glory and character of God within. The more ordinary the clay, the greater the contrast with the glory so that observers are moved to praise not the clay but the God of grace who can transform the ordinary into the extraordinary.

What pressures has the Potter used to shape your life? An overextended commitment? A chaotic schedule? A career change? A health diagnosis? Has He used a person? An incompatible coworker? An unloving spouse? A critical mother-in-law? A vengeful neighbor? A neglectful parent? Has He used circumstances?

Singleness? Divorce? Job loss? Infertility? The birth of a child? The death of a loved one?

The Holy Spirit is not oblivious or uncaring about the pressures you are experiencing. He knows you. He understands you. He is intimately involved in the details of your life in a way that no one else is. And He will enable you to endure the pressures of His molding by ministering to you in a variety of ways as He shapes you into a vessel that displays the glory of God. He will guide your decisions, direct your steps, comfort your heart, teach you God's ways, enlighten your understanding, convict you of sin.

So pray now. Pour out your heart to the Potter. Ask Him to relieve the pressures, whatever the sources are. But then tell Him also that you trust Him to know exactly what He's doing. Therefore, whether the pressures are relieved or not, yield your heart, soul, mind, and life to His touch, to mold you after His will into a vessel that He can use to display God's glory. Then get ready for the ordinary to become extraordinary!

He Equips Us

Many companies and businesses require their employees to take a personality test, such as the Myers-Briggs Type Indicator, either during the job-application process or once they are hired. The purpose is to help employees identify their strengths and weaknesses, making it more likely they will be placed according to ability and therefore will be happier and more productive. Increased self-awareness and self-assurance create confidence as the employees learn what they do best and then do it.

While this approach seems pragmatic for a secular company, I wonder whether it can limit possibilities for a child of God. For instance, if we undergo a personality test and identify our strengths, will we be more likely to serve God only in the areas that utilize them and avoid serving God in areas that we've determined we "can't"?

I've never taken a personality test. I know myself well enough to recognize that in my natural self I'm shy. Timid. Self-conscious. Fearful. Prone to anxiety. With a large inferiority complex. When God called me to serve Him in a public way, my first response to Him was "I can't." And I meant it. But He responded, "I can."[1] And He meant it. I argued, "I'm weak and timid." And I am. But He responded again, *I'm strong.*[2] And He is. I tried one more excuse: "I'm inadequate." With no higher education, no formal Bible training, no resources at my disposal, no network of capable people to draw from, to say I was inadequate was an understatement. But He closed the discussion with *I'm sufficient.*[3] In other words, I felt He was saying, *Anne, never mind who you are or who you aren't. I'm all that you need. Follow Me.*

At that critical moment, I had a choice to make. Either I could shrink back into who I knew I was and into what I believed I was capable of, or I could take what seemed to be a huge risk and follow Him beyond my abilities and capabilities, my expertise and experience, my personality and preferences, my comfort and convenience. I knew that if I did shrink back from following Him, I could no longer call Him my Lord. That thought scared me enough to motivate me to follow Him. If I failed, then in my small way of thinking, He would be accountable for calling me to do something both of us knew I couldn't.

What I have discovered during the past forty years of following Him outside my comfort zone is that the Holy Spirit has always enabled me and equipped me for whatever He has called me to do. I have been on the most amazing adventure of experiencing what the Holy Spirit can do in and through me if I will simply make myself available.

The Uniqueness of the Gifts

While we have already considered the power of the Holy Spirit at work within us, it's exciting to also turn our attention to His gifting. He has supernaturally equipped every child of God who has been born again into His family, for the purpose of serving Him, building up the family of God, and bringing Him glory. No one has all the gifts. But everyone has at least one of the gifts. They are not ours to choose since their distribution is at the discretion of the Holy Spirit.[4] But they are ours to receive and exercise. In appendix D at the back of this book, I have listed and described three categories of gifts as I understand them: motivational gifts, manifestation gifts, and ministry gifts.

As we look to exercise our gifts, it's important to recognize and appreciate the unique gifting of those around us—gifting that may be radically different from our own.

Several years after Danny and I were married, we experienced increasing tension in our relationship. He was constantly finding fault with me, and I was constantly feeling resentful as a result. I remember sitting down and explaining to him that I couldn't live up to his expectations. He could not comprehend what I was saying, and I wasn't able to articulate it so that he could. The conversation actually added to the tension instead of helping relieve it.

Then one day I heard the radio broadcast of a well-known Bible teacher who was preaching on the gifts of the Spirit. Not only were his insights fascinating, but I also felt they possibly could hold the key to my relationship with Danny. I sent off for the audio recording. Because Danny also enjoyed and had been blessed by the ministry of this Bible teacher, he agreed to listen to the series of messages that I had ordered.

As the teacher described each of the gifts, the Holy Spirit opened our eyes to which gifts we had—and which gifts we did not have. It became obvious that our gifts were very different. The tension seemed to be coming from the fact that Danny expected me to express myself according to his gifting, and I, in turn, expected him to be more like someone who had my gifting. The impact of the discovery was amazing! Danny and I both ended up on our knees, thanking God for the gifts He had given each of us, while recognizing and respecting the differences between us. To say it was freeing doesn't come close to describing the release both of us felt. For the remainder of our marriage, we never again dealt with tension that stemmed from each of us expecting the other to operate according to our gifts.

Could this be the source of any tension you are experiencing with your spouse? Your coworker? Someone in your church or Bible study? While the Holy Spirit is the source of our spiritual gifting, the gifts themselves are incredibly diverse. They are also individualized specifically for us, which makes each person's unique—and uniquely crucial for bringing glory to God.

IDENTIFYING OUR SPIRITUAL GIFTS

So the sixty-million-dollar question becomes, What are your spiritual gifts? I wonder whether your response is like mine when I first heard teaching on the Spirit's gifting. I was certain I was the exception to the rule. In fact, I would have argued with someone who insisted I had a spiritual gift, because I was quite sure I did not. But I couldn't get around what the Bible says: we have each been given one or more gifts for the common good of God's people.[5]

Prompted by this knowledge, I began to explore what my gifts could possibly be. Which leads to the next obvious question: How do you and I find our spiritual gifts?

There are several ways to discover what your gifts might be:

- One way is to *try to exercise them all.* The ones you can't seem to do well and get worse at you can eliminate. Any you can do well and get better at may be one of your gifts. Keep in mind that spiritual gifts come more like seeds than full-grown plants. The gifts are developed and grow into maturity as we faithfully exercise them in obedience to God's will.

- Another way is to *ask a spiritually mature friend,* or your pastor, what that person sees in you. Then take on a small responsibility that would allow this gift to become evident if present. Try it on a small scale so if you don't have that particular gift, you won't do too much damage when you fail.

- Still another way is to *take a test* designed to help you determine your spiritual gifting, sort of like the Myers-Briggs test that people use to help identify their personality type. Some churches and ministries offer these tests for spiritual gifts.

While the messages Danny and I listened to helped us pinpoint the differences in our giftings, they didn't help me discover other gifts I had been given. (See appendix D.) The way I discovered these was simpler than the above three ways. I just obeyed the Lord. Whatever He has asked me to do, I have done my best to do. What I have discovered is that He has always . . . always . . . *always* equipped me for anything He has called me to do. If I lack a gift that I need, then He has brought someone alongside who has the gift that I lack. Not only that, but He will also never ask me to do something for which He has not equipped me. How exciting! I can be absolutely confident that whatever He calls and commands me to do, I can do—by His grace and in His power and according to His gifting.

Now that you know that you—no exceptions, *you*—have been equipped by the Holy Spirit, what's your excuse for not discovering what your gifts are? Don't just stare at your equipment. Don't just discuss or define it. Don't just analyze or argue about it. Don't envy someone else's or fight over it. Instead, try it on. Use it. Exercise whatever gifting the Holy Spirit has given you until it blossoms into a means of blessing others and glorifying God.

Part Five

LIVING BY THE PRECEPTS OF THE HOLY SPIRIT

All Scripture is God-breathed and is
useful for teaching, rebuking, correct-
ing and training in righteousness.

—2 TIMOTHY 3:16

I have always loved to read. Anything and everything. If I'm sitting at the breakfast table without a newspaper or a book in front of me, I read the yogurt label or get my laptop to read through the day's headlines. Up until I was a freshman in high school, I easily read a book a week. Once I was in high school, my studies kept me from reading as prolifically as before, but I still made time to read through all of Ayn Rand's novels. A classmate fed them to me one at a time. My father's secretary informed my mother that those novels might not be what she would want me to read, but Mother didn't say no, so I read them all.[1]

My love of reading began early in life. My grandmother taught me to read when I was five years old. She and my grandfather lived right across the street from us when I was growing up. Many times I would grab my pillow, walk through our yard, rock jump the creek, look both ways before crossing the street, then run down my grandmother's gravel driveway, across her stone bridge, through her back porch, and into her kitchen. I can still hear her voice welcoming me into her house. In fact, I can never remember not being welcomed by her.

I spent hours cuddled up to her as she sat in her customary place at the end of her blue sofa. She taught me to love books by reading them to me. And then she began to teach me to read. When I went to kindergarten, my reading was reinforced by a teacher who taught using phonics. By the time I started first grade, there wasn't much that I couldn't read.

Looking back, I believe those reading times with my grandmother were divinely inspired. While I can't remember the specific year that I confessed my sin, claimed Jesus as my Savior, and invited Him to live in my heart, I do remember, following that decision, I began to have a strong desire to read my Bible. So I did. All the way through, from Genesis to Revelation. And that began a lifelong love affair with God's Word.[2]

While my grandmother taught me how to read generally, my mother and father taught me how to read my Bible. Every day without fail, my mother led our family in devotions. She would gather everyone who was in the house into the kitchen, where she would read a portion of Scripture, then pray. I did not enjoy these times, because I always seemed to be running late for school, and it was hard to concentrate when I was trying to cram down breakfast, make sure I had my reports and schoolwork done, then get out the door to arrive at school before the bell rang. But the consistency of my mother's effort, as well as her obvious love for God's Word and belief in its relevancy for all of us as we began our day, made a deep impact.

When my father was home, he led family devotions, usually in the evening. He also would read a portion of Scripture, but he would then stop, ask questions, make comments, and lead us in a discussion of what he had read.

By her example my mother taught me to love and read my Bible every day—preferably in the morning. My father, by his example, taught me to think about what I was reading. Those two life lessons are perhaps the most valuable ones my parents handed down to me.

While I owned some child-friendly versions of the Bible, my first "real" Bible was a navy leather-bound King James Version, Scofield edition. Mother and Daddy gave it to me at my baptism. It is a treasure that I still have safely on my bookshelf. In the flyleaf, my mother wrote these words: *To Anne—(who on this January 13, 1957 publicly took her stand for Christ, her Savior), we give this Book, your one sure guide in an unsure world. Read it, study it, love it, live it. In it you will find a verse for every occasion. Hide them in your heart.* Although my mother's words were written over sixty years ago, their wisdom transcends generations, cultures, world events, time, and age. I have done my best to truly take her encouragement to heart and live it out.

My love of reading, studying, applying, and obeying my Bible has led me to the deep conviction that it is more than just great literature. There is something supernatural about it. It works! It pulsates with life! How could that be? What makes it so unique? The answer to those questions leads us straight to the Holy Spirit.

His Precepts Are True

One of the names for the Holy Spirit is "the Spirit of truth."[1]
The Bible bears witness of itself that it is inspired by the Holy Spirit. In writing about the Old Testament Scriptures, the apostle Peter made it clear: "Above all, you must understand that no prophecy of Scripture came about by the prophet's own interpretation. For prophecy never had its origin in the will of man, but men spoke from God as they were carried along by the Holy Spirit."[2]

King David, who wrote many of the psalms, testified, "The Spirit of the LORD spoke through me; his word was on my tongue."[3] When God called Jeremiah to serve Him as a prophet, Jeremiah resisted because, apparently, he felt he was too young for such a large responsibility. God rebuked him: "Do not say, 'I am only a child.' You must go to everyone I send you to and say whatever I command you. . . . Now, I have put my words in your mouth."[4] Ezekiel also bore witness, "The Spirit came into me and raised me to my feet. He spoke to me and said. . . . 'When I speak to you, I will open your mouth and you shall say to them, "This is what the Sovereign LORD says."'"[5]

As Jesus prepared His disciples for His departure, He reassured them, "The Counselor, the Holy Spirit, whom the Father will send in my name, will teach you all things and will remind you of everything I have said to you."[6] This was fulfilled when the followers of Jesus wrote down the accounts of His life and ministry that we know as the four Gospels. Jesus then promised that the same

Holy Spirit would guide them into all truth, which He did as the book of Acts and the epistles were written.[7] He went on to encourage His disciples that the Holy Spirit would "speak only what he hears, and he will tell you what is yet to come," a promise that was primarily fulfilled by the last book of the New Testament, the Revelation of Jesus Christ.[8]

While no one knows exactly how the Holy Spirit inspired the writers of both the Old and the New Testaments, we know that He did. The evidence is not only in what Scripture says of itself but also in the impact it has made on lives throughout the generations. Its truth has stood the test of time. But as followers of Jesus Christ, it's up to us to decide for ourselves the very critical issue of whether or not we believe the Bible to be true.

THE CHOICE TO DOUBT

The first temptation in human history was the temptation to doubt the truth of God's word. At the very dawn of creation, the first woman, Eve, was walking through the Garden of Eden. She seemed relaxed, enjoying what was literally paradise on earth. She was newly created with the body of a woman but the naivete of a child. As hard as it is for us to imagine a serpent being magnificent, at the dawn of history he apparently was. She was approached by this most magnificent creature, who was also the smartest of all the animals God had made.

This particular serpent was indwelt by the devil himself, who had chosen his timing with great care, catching Eve when apparently she was alone and off guard. The Bible describes him this way: The serpent was more crafty than any of the wild animals the LORD God had made. He said to the woman, "Did God really say . . ?"[9] That one seemingly innocent question plunged Eve into doubt and confusion. If I put the serpent's words into my own, he was saying, in essence, "Eve, did God really say that? Are you sure you heard it accurately from Adam? Could there have been a mistake in the translation or transmission of the text? And even if that is what God said, don't you know you can't take Him literally? We all have our own interpretations of what He really means by what He said. You might have one interpretation, Adam another, and I have still another. . . . When you've been around longer, you will know that God's Word is not quite as black and white as you want to think it is."[10]

When Eve made the choice to doubt the truth of God's word, her life began to spiral down in a whirlpool of devastating consequences—consequences that continue to devastate our world today. Because she didn't truly believe the truth of God's word, she disobeyed it. Her disobedience led her husband, Adam, into disobedience. God then held them both accountable: they were separated from Him, paradise was lost, and sin and death entered the human race.

The devil has not changed his tactics over the millennia. He is still doing his best to get people to doubt the truth of God's Word. But whenever a nation such as ancient Israel or Judah, or an individual such as you or me, or the church, doubts the integrity of God's Word, when we start picking it apart and deciding which sections to believe and which to discard, moral and spiritual decline results.

THE CHOICE TO BELIEVE

For myself, I have made the decision to take God at His Word. I believe it is all true, even though I readily admit I don't understand everything. How dangerous would it be for me to use my finite mind and human understanding to pick and choose my way through Scripture—to judge as true only the things I can understand and to discard as untrue the things I don't understand?

Jesus reaffirmed our choice to believe when He clearly and firmly stated, "I tell you the truth, until heaven and earth disappear, not the smallest letter, not the least stroke of a pen, will by any means disappear from the Law until everything is accomplished."[11] Again He declared, "Heaven and earth will pass away, but my words will never pass away."[12]

To further help us resist the temptation to disbelieve things we don't understand, Jesus specifically referred to biblical stories that critics are quick to point out as being beyond belief, such as Adam and Eve created by God, Noah saved on the ark during a worldwide flood, and Jonah swallowed by a big fish.[13] Yet Jesus cited these stories not as parables or myths or legends but as legitimate historical events. Think about it. If Jesus is the Son of God, if He is the truth incarnate, if He believed these stories to be historically and factually true, who can say they are not? I believe Jesus is exactly whom He claimed to be—the Son of God, the truth—which is why I choose to humble myself and come to God like a little child, trusting my heavenly Father, working through the Spirit of truth, to speak the truth to me.[14] And He has. He does. He always speaks the truth.

The choice is yours, to doubt or to believe. Which will it be?

———————————————

What is your opinion of the Bible? How was your opinion formed? Have you been influenced by others who are critical of what they claim it says? Have you been taught that it is a good book that contains God's word but is not God's word in its entirety? Have you been told that the Bible contains errors or myths? Think. That criticism actually slurs the integrity of the Spirit of truth.

Whatever your opinion has been up until this moment, I challenge you to decide now, once and for all, what you believe. Follow my mother's advice when it comes to the Bible. *Read it, study it, love it, live it.* For yourself. You will discover that it "works." Take God at His Word. It's backed by His character. He doesn't lie or spin the truth. He keeps His Word. Then choose to place your faith in the Bible as true. Inerrant. Inspired. Infallible. For the simple reason that it's inspired by the Spirit of truth. It's "God-breathed."[15] It's God's Word.

His Precepts Are Trustworthy

Just about every major purchase comes with a manual. Whether it's a dishwasher, oven, stovetop, washing machine, hair dryer, car, lawn mower, leaf blower—you name it—there are instructions somewhere to help the user get the most from the product and ensure it works properly.

Have you ever wished that your life also came with a manual? Amazingly, it does! But often we don't refer to it until we've made a mess, and even then, some of us think we don't have to follow the directions. It reminds me of a gift we gave our daughter Morrow one Christmas.

When Morrow was about three years old, she wanted a tricycle. Danny and I purchased one that needed to be assembled. I asked Danny to put it together in time for us to have it sitting out on Christmas morning, but he kept procrastinating. He waited until after the children had gone to bed Christmas Eve to tackle the project. When he opened the box and pulled out the pieces, his comment was "This is so simple any dummy could put it together." But by the time he finished assembling it, every wheel went in a different direction, and the handlebars were tilted. Only then did he look into the box and pull out a white sheet of paper labeled *Manufacturer's Directions for Assembly: Read carefully.* But of course, by that time it was too late. He couldn't get the nuts and bolts to loosen for readjustment, so the tricycle never did roll in a straight line as it was intended to.

In the same way as Danny had guessed how to put that tricycle together, many people seem to just guess their way through life. By the time they've made a mess and life doesn't work, they start looking around for directions. The directions are found in the Bible, the Creator's manual for life. It needs to be read and followed carefully if we want to avoid the crooked mess our guessing can get us into.

Trustworthy Practically

God is the one who designed life in the first place. He knows how it functions best and has given practical directions for us to achieve the fullest possible extent of joy and happiness. His directions are like the road markings on a highway.

When I drive down the highway, painted lines on the pavement provide helpful guidance. A dotted white line lets me know that if the lane of oncoming traffic is clear, I can pass other cars. A solid line means no passing is allowed. The highway department is not trying to take away my joy in driving. The lines on the road are intended to keep me and others safe, while I'm on my way to my destination.

You and I can push the boundaries that God has established, but we do so at our own peril. If we go outside His "road markings," the likelihood is that we will get hurt, as well as hurt other people. At the very least, we will experience life on a lower level than He intended. The alternative is to take God at His word, stay within His boundaries, and trust Him to know what's best for us.

Let's consider some of His road markings:

- When God says to have no other gods before Him, He knows that other gods—such as money, fame, sex, pleasure, power—will enslave you.
- When God says not to create and worship idols, He knows that behind them are demonic forces who will weaken you, deceive you, and suck you into evil attitudes, words, actions, and thoughts that you had no idea you were capable of having or saying or doing.

- When God says not to misuse His name, He knows that unless you reverence Him, you will not have even the beginning of wisdom with which to live and make your decisions.
- When God says to set aside one day in seven in order to focus on Him, He knows that such a lifestyle will help keep your faith anchored and remind you that the world doesn't need your effort to continue spinning.
- When God says to honor your parents, He knows it will lead to a richer, fuller, longer life.
- When God says not to murder, He knows that human life has a high value. Yours and theirs.
- When God says not to commit adultery, He knows sexual betrayal destroys a marriage bond and cracks the foundation of a nation.
- When God says not to steal, He knows that if we want others to respect us and our possessions, we need to respect them and their possessions. Without mutual trust we cannot have safe, healthy relationships.
- When God says not to lie, He knows that integrity is foundational to a successful life and a strong society.
- When God says not to covet, He knows the danger of never being content with what we have, whether it's a spouse, a home, or a job, of being dominated by greed that demands more and more until we are insatiably unfulfilled.[1]

This simple and incomplete rationale for heeding God's road markings illustrates that His practical, divine directions for living are for our own good. And while you may be questioning what the Holy Spirit has to do with what is in essence the Ten Commandments given by God to Moses, we may benefit from being reminded that the entire Bible is "God-breathed"—divinely inspired by the Holy Spirit, both Old Testament and New Testament.[2]

When you or I go outside His directions for living—His road markings—

we wind up with less than God intended us to have. This begs the question, What if you have gone outside God's road markings, hurt yourself or someone else, and now want to live according to God's directions? The first step is to just tell Him. Be honest. Whether you have been living in ignorance of His guidelines or in rebellion against them, tell Him what you have done, where you are, and that you want to start living as He directs. Then start reading your Bible. Study it, love it, and live by it. God the Holy Spirit is your helper, remember? Your strengthener. Your counselor. He is just waiting for you to turn to Him and give Him the freedom and authority to bring order out of your chaos.

TRUSTWORTHY PERSONALLY

But the Bible is more than just a manual for living a fully blessed life. It is God's living Word. He speaks through it, personally. Every day I read a few verses of Scripture, listening for His voice. While I don't hear an audible sound, there are times when a verse seems to leap off the page and speak directly into my heart. His Word comforts, encourages, rebukes, strengthens, sustains, brings peace, and gives hope. For example . . .

. . . My husband had been a great athlete and was the perfect picture of muscle-bound health. When our children were young, he never even came down with the same viruses and colds that seemed to run through the family. But when he turned fifty years of age, he was hit suddenly with adult-onset type 1 diabetes. By the time he was sixty, the diabetes began to take its toll. The year he turned seventy, my younger daughter found him incoherent and behaving strangely. I took him to the doctor, who ordered an MRA. The test confirmed that Danny had had a stroke. The next morning, God whispered to me from a devotional book that paraphrased Philippians 4:6: "Do not begin to be anxious."[3] When the nurse explained to me what I could expect, I smiled and thanked her. She looked at me more intensely and pressed the issue: "You need to understand. This will change his personality." And I looked back, thanked her again, and told her God would take care of him . . . and me. And God did.

Danny struggled with some issues for several weeks, and then his fun-loving personality returned.

. . . On August 19, 2015, my husband of forty-nine years moved to our Father's house. While I knew with sweet, blessed assurance he was safely in Heaven, my heart had a hard time letting go. I had been his caregiver 24-7 for three years. It was extremely difficult to have that role come to a screeching halt in a single moment. As ridiculous as it sounds, I was worried about him. Was he really, truly okay? The Spirit didn't let me struggle long with these emotional thoughts before He intervened. He brought Philippians 1:21 clearly to my attention: "To me, to live is Christ and to die is gain." Of course! Death for Danny was gain. Of course he was better off! I felt somewhat foolish for worrying. But then my unspoken query was *What about me?* Which is when the Spirit led me to the next verse: "If I am to go on living in the body, this will mean fruitful labor for me." Once again, a strong sense of purpose seeped into the depths of my being. I knew without question that God had taken Danny to something much better and that I still had work to do. I was filled with peace.

. . . One morning after my husband went to Heaven, I especially felt the burden of leading the family. Until then, I had taken my husband's leadership for granted. I never realized what a heavy responsibility he had carried so well on his broad shoulders. Now I was faced with guiding, counseling, comforting, encouraging, and helping my children, their spouses, and my grandchildren in a way I had never had the full responsibility of when my husband was alive. It was almost more than I felt I could handle. But one morning as I prayed about it, the Spirit lifted the burden when He seemed to whisper, *Anne, you are not alone, because the Father is with you.*[4] While I still feel weighed down at times with the responsibility, I am reassured that I am not alone and that God Himself will be a father to my children and a husband to me.

. . . Getting adjusted to living by myself after forty-nine years of marriage included putting my children at ease concerning my safety. Even though my husband could not have protected me during the last few years he was in the home because of his physical decline, somehow his presence gave my children a sense of peace. Not too long after I started living alone, the Spirit whispered a promise to me from Hosea that I could share with them: "I . . . will make them to lie down safely."[5] Even when my doorbell rang at two in the morning, I knew God would keep His promise. So while I was unsettled, I was not afraid. My dog started barking wildly, adding to the chaos and confusion. I threw on a robe, went to the door with my dog growling and lunging, and found a sheriff's deputy standing on my front porch. He had received a false alarm and was checking on me. God has kept me safe then and now in more ways than I'm sure I'm even aware.

Earlier, in chapter 5, I shared how the Counselor gave me His wisdom from Deuteronomy 29 about how to tell my family I had breast cancer. He continued to whisper to me from His Word throughout my cancer journey. I do not know how I could have possibly managed all that was involved following the diagnosis without His gentle whispers of comfort, encouragement, and guidance. Several situations stand out . . .

. . . Following my surgery and before my first chemo treatment, I met with a pharmacist who listed the side effects I would experience: hair loss, mouth sores, flu-like body aches, bone pain, metallic taste, appetite loss, fingernail loss . . . At that point it was hard to keep listening. I was overwhelmed with the thought of what lay ahead. I went straight from my meeting with her to the heart-and-vascular surgeon for the insertion of a semipermanent port in my chest. I felt as if I was being sucked into a black whirlpool over which I had no control . . . and from which there was no escape. The next morning my devotional reading was from Job 42:12: "The LORD blessed the latter end of Job more than his beginning."[6] The thought was that through Job's suffering and grief, he had come to his heritage. Peace flooded over me as the Spirit seemed to indicate that my cancer experience was not a whirlpool. It was a journey with a purpose. God would use it to lead me to my heritage—where He wanted me to be.

. . . . As I went from appointment to appointment—meeting with doctors, pharmacists, lab technicians, the heart-and-vascular surgeon . . . enduring chemo treatments, radiation, and endless waiting rooms for all the above—once again, the Spirit gave me a sense of purpose when He whispered these words from Zechariah: "'I will strengthen [Anne] in the LORD, and [she] shall walk up and down in His name,' says the LORD."[7] I seemed to walk all over the big hospital. Up and down escalators. To elevators. Between parking garages and floors and hospital wings. But the purpose came through, that as I walked, I would do so in His name. Again and again I was stopped by other patients or visitors who recognized me, people who said they were praying for me or who asked me to pray for them. I had multiple opportunities to share the gospel and to pray with nurses, technicians, doctors, and many others who treated me. His whisper changed my attitude from that of being a cancer victim to being on a mission as His ambassador.

. . . As I prayed with my two daughters following my fifth chemo treatment, God seemed to indicate He had healed me. I pondered in my heart what I believed He had said. My numbers from my blood draw before the sixth treatment were all remarkably good. After my sixth treatment, I began questioning whether or not I should continue chemo. The weakness and weariness were debilitating. The side effects were daunting. I did not want to continue treatments if they were unnecessary. So one morning I prayed specifically, asking God to confirm from His Word whether or not I was to continue chemotherapy treatments. Two hours later, Rachel-Ruth came to sit with me. She shared some of her insights from 2 Kings 5—that she was to teach her Bible class that week. She related the story of the Syrian general Naaman who had leprosy. A little Israelite slave girl told Naaman of Elisha, a man of God, who could heal him. When Naaman sought Elisha, he was told, "Go, wash yourself seven times in the Jordan . . . and you will be cleansed."[8] Naaman resisted, saying that Syria had better rivers than the Jordan. He did not want to submit himself to the "side effects" of muck and mud.[9] But at his servant's urging, Naaman did dip in the Jordan. When he came up the seventh time, he was healed![10] *The seventh time!* And I could hear the clear whisper of the Spirit answering my prayer, confirming that I was to continue chemo . . . my next and last treatment would be my *seventh time!* So as much as I resisted the "muck and mud," in obedience to God's leading, I committed to complete the seventh infusion.

There have been times when the Spirit has seemed to give me a promise that doesn't come to pass. Whenever that has happened, my faith has been challenged. I go back to reexamine the promise and pray over it. Did I misread it? Did I read into it? Was it a promise God was truly giving me or one I had just named and claimed? Recently I had a crisis of faith triggered by a promise I thought God had clearly given me but was proven over time to be unfulfilled. I was devastated. I felt empty, foolish, and, oh, so spiritually naive. Then the Spirit whispered to me, "Therefore will the LORD wait, that he may be gracious unto you."[11] And I knew His promise would be fulfilled, just not according to my time. My faith rebounded as I chose to trust His way and His time.

The previous examples are just a few of the Spirit's whispers to my heart. Would I have made the same decisions without what He had said? Would I have had the same perseverance, courage, comfort, and direction if I had not read my Bible, listening for His voice? I don't think so. Yes, I would have survived. But like many others, I would have been just guessing my way through life, afraid I would take a wrong turn and very probably doing so. Instead, the Spirit's whispers have enabled me to live with energetic confidence, making very few costly mistakes.

Once again, I'm reminded of my mother's advice and her example. Read your Bible. Every day. Study it. Learn to love it. Live by it. I urge you to take her wise counsel, then follow my father's example and think about what you are reading. Listen for the whisper of the Spirit, who speaks through the pages of the Word that He Himself has inspired and through the words on the pages, which are God-breathed.

At the conclusion of this book, in appendix A, you will find a section on how to read your Bible so you, too, can hear more discernably the Spirit's whispers. Follow the instructions; then start listening.

Part Six

REFLECTING THE PURITY OF THE HOLY SPIRIT

Set an example for the believers in speech,
in life, in love, in faith and in purity.

—1 TIMOTHY 4:12

S everal years ago I was invited to speak to a dinner gathering of the staff and faculty of a prestigious evangelical seminary. I accepted, feeling honored and humbled to have been offered the opportunity. When the evening came, I was introduced informally to those who made time to mingle at a reception before the dinner. I met professors whose names I knew from the outstanding books they had authored—books that are the textbooks for other theological seminaries. I met the dean of students, the dean of admissions, and other staff members whose leadership served as models throughout Christian academia.

I don't remember much about the dinner itself, just the fact that I felt somewhat intimidated by the accomplished and brilliant members of the audience. I was warmly introduced. After a few personal remarks to the assembled gathering, I prayed, then launched into a brief message on the Holy Spirit, the One who would lead them into all truth and empower them to pass it along to others. During the course of the message, I pointed out that the Holy Spirit is holy and that He works to make us holy. I didn't spend a lot of time on this point, because it seemed so obvious.

Following my message, when the dinner concluded, a professor came up to speak to me. "I teach here. But I learned something tonight. I had never before thought of the Holy Spirit as holy." *Really?* I hope I kept the shock I felt from being reflected on my face. How had he missed it? Is it so obvious that it was just overlooked? Afterward, I wondered whether I had misunderstood him, but I never had the opportunity to ask him.

Sometime later I was the dinner guest of the president of another well-respected theological seminary. As we conversed, he confided that the number-one problem he faced with the students at his school was pornography. Shocked again, I wanted to make sure this time that I had understood accurately what had just been said, so I asked him to repeat it. Was he talking about the men and women who were studying at his seminary in preparation for Christian ministry as pastors, youth leaders, music directors, Bible teachers, seminary professors, and other leaders within the church? Was he saying these men and women were viewing pornography? At his seminary? He answered "Yes." He then told me they had become aware of the problem because the students used the computers in the library that were tucked back behind the stacks of books. In an area they believed to be private, they were indulging their sinful habit, not realizing that what they viewed was traceable.

I'm still stunned by the seminary president's revelation. But I've seen the bitter fruit borne in the lives of pastors, some of whom have multiple academic degrees, some of whom lead megachurches, some of whom may speak in tongues or exhibit other manifestations of the Spirit, and some of whom are gifted orators, yet secretly struggle with sexual immorality or addiction. Occasionally God allows Christian leaders to be exposed for their own good so that they can get help and for the purifying of the church. But such revelations are devastating to the church congregations and do great damage to the credibility of the gospel in the public's eyes.

Years ago my husband spoke with the manager of one of the largest convention hotels in Atlanta. They had just hosted a church denomination's annual gathering of thousands of delegates. My husband remarked that the hotel must have lost a lot of revenue in the bars, assuming the delegates would not consume as much alcohol as those attending secular conventions. The manager smiled and said, "That's right. But we made up for the lost revenue with the adult movies offered on the in-room entertainment channels."

What has happened to purity? *Within the church?* Within the lives of those who call themselves by God's name? Is the lack of purity an indication that the Holy Spirit is withdrawing Himself? Because make no mistake about it, the Holy Spirit is indeed pure. He is holy.

His Purity Is Exemplified in Jesus

You and I live surrounded by a culture that has become spiritually and morally bankrupt. Right has been replaced with wrong, and wrong is the new right. Infanticide and abortion; assisted suicide and euthanasia; gay marriage; pornography; sexting; switching gender; sex trafficking; date rape; road rage; obscenity; obsession with self; greed; cruelty; the glorification of violence through video games, movies, and music—the evidence is overwhelming that there seems to be no regard for holiness or purity.

The distressing thing I've observed is that we seem to have less and less regard for purity within the church. Generally speaking, we seem to be absorbing the world around us instead of separating from it. The result is that the holiness of God is not always reflected in the way Christians think, speak, and act.

Yet as we are introduced to God in the Old Testament, one of His most striking characteristics is holiness.

From His watery destruction of the entire world in Noah's day because of its saturation in wickedness[1] . . .

. . . to the fiery destruction of Sodom and Gomorrah in Abraham's day because of their exceeding sinfulness[2]

. . . to His command to Moses to take off his shoes when approaching the place where God was because even the ground was holy[3]

. . . to His judgment on Egypt because of Pharaoh's refusal to obey His command to let His people go[4]

. . . to His terrifying presence on Mount Sinai that was accompanied with thunder, lightning, fire, and the blasts of a trumpet[5]

. . . to His design for the tabernacle, and later the temple, that specified severe restrictions regarding the place where His holy presence was said to dwell[6]

. . . to His command to Joshua to take off his shoes when he, like Moses, had an encounter with God . . . [7]

On and on and on throughout the Old Testament, we glimpse God's terrifying holiness in His dealings with people.

While love and grace seem to be the characteristics of God primarily highlighted in the New Testament, His holiness has not diminished over the millennia of human history. He is just as holy today as He was in the beginning, as He ever will be. In fact, His emphasis on holiness is unmistakably obvious in the name given to His Spirit—the Holy Spirit.

God's entire reason for the Cross is His hatred and intolerance of sin. His holy, just, righteous nature demands judgment. Equal to His holiness is His love and grace, which prompted Him to step in and take His own judgment for our sin when Jesus was crucified in our place. But we should not misunderstand. God's love, mercy, grace, goodness, kindness, and patience do not cancel out or water down His standard of perfect holiness. There is no spectrum of holiness. It is completely black and white. Just one speck of sin, corruption, or imperfection results in impurity.

So why do believers seem to be growing accustomed to, even adopting, the immorality that is all around us? We no longer seem to be shocked by what we see portrayed in movies and television, displayed in magazines, described in graphic detail in novels, dangled in front of us as pop-ups on our web pages, and glorified on the red carpet. Scantily clad women used to be in magazines sold only from behind the counter. Now we see the same type of attire on women shopping in the grocery store or traveling in airports.

While I hesitate to point a critical finger at the secular world, I can't help but be dismayed by what I see Christians tolerating, ignoring, or even emulating. We seem to have lost our vision of the holiness of God. We seem to be in desperate need of a refresher course on purity. While the standards of holiness and purity in our culture have been rendered so low as to be almost nonexistent, God's standards haven't changed. Not even a little bit. He is just as holy today as He was on Mount Sinai and as He was in the Most Holy Place of the temple. The Bible makes it clear. He still demands that you and I be holy also: "Just as he who called you is holy, so be holy in all you do; for it is written: 'Be holy, because I am holy.'"[8] But sometimes we need to be jolted out of our complacency before we get serious about being holy.

Consider how God's holiness was emphasized to the fledgling church in Jerusalem. Peter's sermon on Pentecost, the healing of the crippled beggar at the Beautiful Gate of the temple, the persecution of Peter and John by the authorities—all served to bring public attention to the gospel, and thousands placed their faith in Jesus Christ as their Messiah, Savior, and Lord. The church exploded through nothing less than the power of the Holy Spirit as God's people prayed and the gospel was preached.[9] Believers supported one another not only through their prayers and fellowship but also with their possessions so that no one was needy.

One day a man named Barnabas sold some of his property and brought the entire sales price to the church. His act of self-sacrifice impressed and influenced everyone, including a couple named Ananias and Sapphira. They wanted the same respect and recognition that Barnabas had received, so they, too, sold a piece of property. But they conspired to hold back some of the money for themselves, while telling the apostles they were giving all of it to the church. When Ananias brought the money and laid it down before the apostles, Peter saw through the ruse, demanding, "What made you think of doing such a thing? You have not lied to men but to God."[10] Immediately Ananias fell dead. Young men came and removed his body. Three hours later Sapphira came in, not knowing her husband had died. When Peter questioned her, she lied also. When he rebuked her, she also fell dead. The result? "Great fear seized the whole church and all who heard about these events."[11] It's obvious that God Himself felt the early church needed a refresher course on His holiness.

What exactly is holiness? A simple definition of *holiness* is "separation from sin." Holiness is clearly and ultimately exemplified in Jesus, because He was totally separate from sin. While He was tempted as we are, He never gave in to the temptation. He was sinless.[12] He is the spotless Lamb of God with no blemish at all in God's eyes.[13] He is holy. In Him there is no meanness, no rudeness, no selfishness, no unkindness, no bitterness, no unforgiveness, no resentfulness, no untruthfulness, no sinfulness—at all! He is absolutely pure in His methods and in His motives. In His actions and in His attitudes. In His deeds and in His decisions. In His thoughts and in His feelings. He is holy, holy, holy in His body, mind, emotions, and Spirit.

When the prophet Isaiah's life was shaken by the death of King Uzziah, he looked up and had a fresh vision of the holiness of the preincarnate Son of God. The apostle John testified that Isaiah had seen the glory of Jesus when Isaiah's eyes were opened to see Him seated on the throne at the center of the universe.[14] The fact that Jesus was seated on the throne indicated His position of absolute authority. He was and still is and forever will be supreme over all. Isaiah described Him also as being "high and exalted," which means no one in all the universe has greater authority or power than He does. At that moment, not only Isaiah's eyes but also his ears were opened to hear the angelic beings calling one to another, "Holy, holy, holy is the LORD Almighty."[15] As a result, Isaiah recognized the depth of his sinful condition so that he cried out, "Woe to me! . . . I am ruined!"[16] That acknowledgment led him to an experience of deep repentance and personal, spiritual revival. He was catapulted into a prophetic role that many believe to be among the greatest of the Old Testament.

I believe the church today is in desperate need of revival. Authentic revival. Not a tent meeting or a series of services to save the lost, but a spiritual awakening that will compel God's people to repent of our sin, return to the cross, and re-commit ourselves to living lives that reflect His purity.

But I wonder. What will it take to impart a fresh vision of the holiness of the Lord Almighty to those today who call themselves by His name? To you and me? Like King Uzziah or Ananias and Sapphira, does someone have to die be-fore we get the message that God is holy? What calamity needs to strike? What enemy needs to attack? What disaster needs to befall us before we, too, will look up? The Son of God is still seated on the throne. He is still higher and more exalted than anyone in the entire universe. He still reigns supreme. He is still just as holy today as He was when Isaiah heard the angelic beings praising Him. And He still demands that you and I be holy as He is holy!

Which is why we need the help of His Holy Spirit, who has been sent to us in His name.[17]

His Purity Is Beautified in Us

When the Holy Spirit comes into our hearts, He makes a difference. Because remember, the Holy Spirit is holy. So it stands to reason that as we are filled with Him, we will reflect His holiness and purity in who we are, in what we say, and in what we do. As a result, our lives will be in sharp contrast to those around us.

On the Sunday before Passover, Jesus entered Jerusalem riding on a donkey.[1] While it may seem strange to us that He presented Himself this way publicly, an Old Testament prophecy foretold He would enter the city in this manner, and His people understood that He was coming to them as their Messiah.[2] Jesus of Nazareth was intentionally presenting Himself to God's people as God's Son, the Messiah, the Redeemer of Israel.

When we put the four gospel accounts together, we find that after entering Jerusalem, Jesus went straight to the heart of the city—to the temple. And He just looked around. Everyone knew He was looking, and everyone must have been wondering uneasily what He saw. They didn't have to wait long to find out, because although He left the city and spent the night in Bethany, He returned to the temple the next day. This time, in righteous indignation, He took up a whip and began to drive out the merchants and money changers, overturning their tables and releasing their animals. His reason? Very likely between cracks of His whip, He explained that the temple was to be "a house of prayer"; but they had made it "a den of robbers."[3] While people needed the animals being sold for sacrifices, the merchants had moved their booths closer and closer until they had set up in the temple area itself, gouging the people with exorbitant prices. Jesus cleansed the temple area, demanding by His actions that it be holy and pure of defilement. It was one thing to have such merchants in the streets of Jerusalem, but it was another thing entirely to have them within the temple area.

Besides driving out the wicked money changers from the temple area, was Jesus also giving you and me an audiovisual aid of what the Holy Spirit does when He comes into the heart of a person? When a person's heart does not belong to Him, He may let that person get away with all sorts of things. But when a person's heart is His, He takes responsibility for cleaning it up. Have you had an uneasy awareness that the Holy Spirit is looking around in your heart? Have you begun to wonder whether it's appropriate for you to keep going to that place? Using those words? Watching those films? Reading those books? Does His presence in your heart make you a little uncomfortable? How long did you enjoy His presence before He began to drive the sin out of your life? One habit, one attitude, one relationship at a time?

The Holy Spirit Drives Out Sin

One of the responsibilities of the Holy Spirit is to make us holy as He is holy. Our responsibility is to cooperate with Him if we truly want to experience and reflect His purity. Choice by choice by choice. When He says something needs to go, get rid of it. Now. When He says a relationship needs to be severed, sever it. When He says we need to offer forgiveness to that person, offer forgiveness to that person. When He says to ask someone else for forgiveness, ask that person for forgiveness. If He says to break that habit, break that habit. Now. Don't procrastinate. Don't rationalize. Don't excuse or defend yourself. Do what He says, when He says it.

What sin in your life—in action or reaction, thought or word, attitude or habit—is tarnishing the reflection of His purity? In my experience, the first few times He convicts me of something, He is rather gentle. If I don't respond the way He wants me to, He gets firmer. If I don't let the sin go for any reason, He can get very tough. What He will not do is to let me get away with sin in my life. To be honest, I don't want to get away with it. I want Him to drive out the sin that is so repugnant to Him, which mars the reflection of His beauty and causes others to have difficulty seeing Jesus in me.

One message of the Cross itself is that God does not tolerate sin. He hates it. While we have the freedom to choose to sin if we want, we have no freedom to choose the consequences. And they can be disastrous, as we saw with the story of Ananias and Sapphira.

Sin is like spiritual cancer. It can spread, taking over areas of our hearts until its tentacles become spiritually life threatening. The Holy Spirit desires for us to be cleansed continuously of sin for our own well-being, protection, and blessing.

I've observed spouses give in to temptation and have an affair that then destroys their marriage and their family. I've seen couples coveting things they couldn't afford and piling up debt until they are buried under it. I've seen mothers buy in to the feminist movement that applauds women who have careers and belittles soccer moms who stay at home, and I've seen soccer moms who belittle those with careers and applaud those who stay at home—only to discover by hard experience neither guarantees a strong family. And the children themselves? Using obscenities in elementary school. Discussing graphic sex in middle school. Then having sex in high school—at high school. And all the above describes people old and young within "Christian" homes and churches. Why? Where is the Holy Spirit? Where is the man with the whip of conviction and correction?

The Bible says that the Holy Spirit, of course, does His job, but apparently, we are not doing ours. We are not hearing or heeding Him. Simply put, we are not reading, loving, obeying, or living by the Bible. It's as though we just wanted to add Jesus to our lives, instead of turning everything over to Him so that He is our life. When those of us who belong to Him refuse to respond to the Holy

Spirit's conviction and correction, it's possible to develop what the Bible calls a "seared" conscience.[4] It's as though a thick scab forms over our hearts and hardens them to the conviction of the Holy Spirit, while a film builds over our eyes to keep us from seeing the truth and our dulled hearing muffles the Spirit's whisper. Is it possible that the entire church today, generally speaking, is suffering from spiritual hardening?

While only God knows, I believe we desperately need an outpouring of the Holy Spirit in a spiritual awakening. Not just in every church in our nation, but in every believer's heart. We need revival. But the key to revival is repenting of sin. Starting with me. And with you. Now.

Conviction That Leads to Cleansing

Several years ago God took me through a time of repentance that was triggered by my reading a list of sins in a pamphlet on revival.[5] For seven days, it was as though He cracked a whip of deep, painful conviction and correction as He revealed to me sin that I had not been aware was in my life.

I wonder whether you, like me, have had sin in your heart and life of which you are not aware? It seems to seep in from every direction.

Because I needed help to see my sin, I have included a list of personal sins in appendix C at the back of this book that may help you. Read it prayerfully, asking God to use it to shine the light of His holiness into the darker, more remote recesses of your heart, as He used an old revivalist's list of sins to shine His light into my heart. But right now, pause and pray with me:

> *Holy Lord,*
> *We set aside these moments to look up. We see You high and exalted. You are seated on the throne of our hearts. We acknowledge Your authority and Your greatness. No one is greater than You are, and no one is higher than You are. In the stillness, we can hear the chorus of angelic praise: "Holy, holy, holy is the LORD Almighty."*[6]

You are merciful. Yes, You are!

You are loving. Yes, You are!

You are gracious. Yes, You are!

You are kind. Yes, You are!

You are faithful. Yes, You are!

How we love You for the beauty of Your character. But we would be dishonest if we did not also acknowledge that You cannot be less than Yourself. And You are also just. You are holy. You are righteous. And a just, holy, righteous Lord demands judgment for our sin. Which is the message of the Cross. If there were no accountability for sin, there would be no need for the Cross. The Cross reveals Your hatred for sin. You died so that sinners could live free from the penalty of sin. You rose from the dead so that sinners could die to the power of sin.

At the Cross we see You, the holy Lamb of glory, giving Your life for little dust people, and we stand amazed in the presence of the crucified Savior. The Cross reveals not only the heinousness of our sin but also the beauty of Your infinite love as you stepped in and took Your own judgment in our place.

I confess that my focus in life and even my focus in prayer have not been on You and You alone as the Solution to my problems and the Answer to my needs. I confess that I often have acted as though I am somebody and You are not.

I repent.

I confess that often I have been so focused on "them" that I don't see myself clearly. I turn to You now and ask that You shine the light of Your truth into my heart and what I feel, into my mind and what I think, so that I see myself as You see me and truly, deeply repent of my sin.

Strip me, most holy Lord, of any pride or self-righteousness or judgmentalism. Teach me to first take the plank out of my own eye before trying to remove the splinter in someone else's eye.[7] I long for

*You to send revival to the hearts of Your people. Let it begin right
here. Right now. With me. I want to truly experience holiness as
I reflect You from the inside out.*

To that end, right now,

*I confess _____ (fill in the blank with sins that come to
your mind).*

*I repent of _____ (write down the sins one at a time that
you are willing to repudiate and put out of your life).*

*Please cleanse me, wash me clean, for Jesus's sake. I want to be
a beautiful bride for Him.*

Amen.

The author of the pamphlet that God used to clean me up suggested that
the reader work through the list of sins three times. To humor him, I did. The
first time I read the list, I felt rather smug because I didn't see any of the sins
listed in my life. The second time I read the list, I felt spiritual because if I
stretched it, I could maybe pull out two or three things I needed to work on. The
shocking truth was revealed when I read the list for the third time. I saw every
sin on the list in my life in one form or another. Not only that, but other sins also
began coming to my mind. Every time I opened my Bible, a verse would leap off
the page and convict me of yet another sin I had not known I was harboring. To
be honest, it was a brutal experience, painful and humiliating.

I learned several things. I learned first that I wasn't as wonderful a person as
I had believed. And I learned that it takes a lot of courage to be honest enough
to see what God sees, confessing my sins by the same names He calls them, one
after another.

When the Holy Spirit led me through this experience, my heart and my life
were seared by conviction, shame, and guilt. But one afternoon He seemed to
whisper to me that He was finished. At least for that time. When I asked Him
to make sure, because I didn't want to go through this process again anytime
soon, He confirmed that He was through. And deep inside I knew. I felt as

though I'd had a bath. On the inside. An amazing afterglow settled into my heart. I was filled with joy and vitality. The air around me seemed clearer; the colors, more vibrant; the sounds, sweeter. It took me some time to process what I had gone through, but I know now it was revival. Personal revival.

Instead of reading about the Holy Spirit or talking about the Holy Spirit or studying about the Holy Spirit, has the time come for you to experience the holiness of the Spirit? If so, would you read the list in appendix C thoughtfully, sincerely, three times? The third time, pray through the list instead of reading it. Ask the Holy Spirit to point out the things in your life that are not pleasing to Him. Write down the sins that are not on the list but that He brings to your mind. Confess them. Repudiate them. Ask Him to cleanse you with the blood of Jesus. He will.

Take all the time you need in confession and repentance. Then please pray with me again:

Most holy Lord,
    With tears on our faces and shame in our hearts, we truly, sincerely, courageously rend our hearts.[8] *We repent of our sin. Not only do we name it for what it is in Your sight, but we also turn away from it.*
    We claim Your promise of forgiveness of sin through Your blood.[9]
    We claim Your promise that if we confess our sins, You will be faithful and just to forgive us and purify us.[10]
    Thank You for Your forgiveness.
    Thank You for the blood that washes us clean.[11]
    Thank You that our tears are on Your face.[12]
    Thank You that as our high priest You understand firsthand the shame and guilt of our sin.[13]

Thank You that although You were sinless, You became sin for us that we might be right with You.[14]

Thank You that when we are under Your blood and our lives are hidden in You, we become a new creation. The old has gone, and the new has come.[15]

Thank You for the Holy Spirit, who is holy and works within us to make us holy as You are holy.

Thank You for the overpowering guilt and shame and conviction of sin that are evidence of the Holy Spirit's activity in our hearts, making us pure.

Thank You for the experience of being purified, as painful as it may be.

Thank You for the blessed assurance that when we have been convicted of our sin—when we have confessed our sin, when we have been cleansed of our sin—we can look forward to a rich welcome into Your presence and into Your heavenly home because we are the bride whom the Holy Spirit is making beautiful for our Bridegroom . . . our Savior . . . the holy Lamb of glory.

We pray to You in His name—Jesus.

Amen.

Now, ask God to fill you with His Holy Spirit that you might truly be revived![16] And for the beauty of the invisible Holy Spirit to be made visible to those around you.

His Purity Is Magnified in Us

The first cataract surgery my husband underwent was disastrous. When the bandages were removed, instead of seeing more clearly as he had expected, he was blind in his right eye. For the rest of his life, he squinted, which gave him the appearance of someone who continuously winked. That expression suited his fun-loving, teasing personality. But practically, he needed magnifying glasses in order to be able to read more easily. So I bought big ones and small ones, plastic ones and glass ones, and fancy ones with silver or bone handles, and placed them all over the house. Now I find I'm using them. They help me see more clearly.

You and I are something like magnifying glasses that help the world see Jesus better. When the church was first established, it was called in the Greek language *ekklēsia*. This gathering of believers was intended to be a visible demonstration of what society would be like if it operated under the authority of Jesus Christ. In a unique way, the church is ordained by God for the purpose of revealing Jesus and sharing the gospel. But the church is the body of Christ. It is not a building down the street or an organization or a denomination or an association. The church is made up of people like you and me who have been to the cross, have confessed and repented of our sin, have received Jesus Christ by faith as our Savior, and are seeking to follow Him as our Lord. The local church is where followers of Jesus gather for encouragement and instruction and are then sent out into the world to share the gospel.

In Old Testament days and during the life of Jesus, God's people gathered at the temple in Jerusalem. It was the place where God had put His name and where He was said to dwell on earth among His people.[1] But there is no temple in Jerusalem today. The Romans utterly destroyed it in AD 70. Therefore, there is now no physical Holy or Most Holy Place where God resides among men. Yet the phenomenal truth is that, in a literal way, you and I now are each individually a living temple of the Holy Spirit. God resides within you and me! Which is why it's imperative that we keep our temples holy. "Do you not know that your body is a temple of the Holy Spirit, who is in you, whom you have received from God? You are not your own; you were bought at a price. Therefore honor God with your body."[2]

We bear the awesome responsibility of revealing God the Father, God the Son, and God the Holy Spirit to those around us by what we say and what we do, where we go and how we live, how we react and how we work, what we listen to and what we watch: "We are the temple of the living God. As God has said: 'I will live with them and walk among them, and I will be their God, and they will be my people.'"[3] Today we are the temple where others ought to be able to see Him and hear Him and get to know Him.

Even greater than the miracle that each of us is the temple of the Holy Spirit is the fact that all of us as living temples are joined together into one magnificent holy temple in which God lives by His Spirit.[4] In a similar analogy, we are described by the apostle Peter as living stones that "are being built into a spiritual house" that one day will display God's glory to the world.[5]

Think of it. Each of our lives individually is meant to reflect the glory and purity of God's character. Then together we, the living stones, are gathered with one another until a greater temple is built up of hundreds upon hundreds, thousands upon thousands, millions upon millions of individual lives who have each been to the cross, confessed and repented of sin, received Jesus Christ by faith as

Savior, and sought to follow Him as Lord. We are corporately a living temple made of living stones to display and magnify the glory, the purity, the holiness of God to the entire universe.

Our lives, our Christian witness, our faith are not just about us. We are living for a much larger purpose than just me. Or just you.

We truly are living together for the glory of God!

MAGNIFIED THROUGH OUR PENITENCE

If we are to be the magnifying glass that helps the world see Jesus better, it becomes critical that we come together and confess our corporate sins. The "glass" needs to be washed and cleaned and polished so others see through us more clearly. It stands to reason that if the light of His glory may be dimmed in us as individuals, we also are making it hard for others to see Him in the church at large. The temple is going to be only as glorious as each individual stone.

As we've seen, from time to time each of us needs a thorough "house cleaning." The following prayer is one of my own used for that purpose as I have interceded for the church. I have written it out with plural pronouns to make it easier for you to use also.

Precious Cornerstone,

We are in awe of who You are. You are the stone that the builders rejected. You are the stone that people stumble over. But You are now the cornerstone and the capstone of a magnificent temple that displays Your glory throughout eternity.[6] For every age. With all our hearts, we want our lives to reflect Your glory in such a way that the entire universe is filled with it![7] We want to live for the praise of Your glory.[8]

We come to You as sinners. We are imperfect living stones, but we have been washed clean by Your blood and indwelt by Your Spirit.

We have confessed our personal, individual sins. We believe we are now clean before You, because You promised that when we confess our sin to You, You will purify us from all unrighteousness.[9] Thank You. Again.

Now we come to You and confess our sin corporately. We confess that we, Your people, the sheep of Your pasture,[10] are constantly going astray. So many of us have turned to our own way and done what we think is right in our own eyes.[11] The noise of denominational divisions, factions, and rivalry has given an uncertain sound to the trumpet call of the gospel.[12] The wounded and the wounders, the betrayals and the bickering, the pride and the prejudices, the wealth and the wants, have tarnished the reflection of Your beauty that should rest on us as Your body, the church, the living temple of the holy, living God.

We have focused on our circumstances and have therefore been defeated.

We have focused on others and have therefore been deluded.

We have focused on ourselves and have therefore been deceived.

We have focused on political policy and have therefore been disappointed.

We compare ourselves with others rather than Your holy standard so that our perception of who we really are is distorted.

We repent.

We cry out for revival yet are too busy to turn to You in prayer and fasting, in confession and repentance of our sin.

We repent.

We dare to hold the Bible up for debate, claiming it "contains" Your word, casting doubt on its infallibility, authority, inspiration, and inerrancy. As though You make mistakes or don't tell the truth, the whole truth, and nothing but the truth. Then we substitute denominational materials for Your Word.

We repent.

We have substituted orthodoxy for obedience, church activities for the life of the Spirit, and programs for prayer.

We have substituted _____ (fill in the blank with what comes to mind).

We repent.

We have rationalized, denied, or covered up sin for the sake of numerical membership growth. We don't give the whole counsel of Scripture for fear of offending the hearers.

We have rationalized _____.

We repent.

We switch labels to make sin seem less sinful. We call lying, exaggeration. We call fornication, safe sex. We call murder, a right to choose. We call drunkenness, illness. We call jealousy, ambition.[13] *We call pride, self-esteem.*

We call _____, _____.

We repent.

We have expected pastors to be CEOs. We have made spiritual leaders into celebrities. We have turned ministries into businesses. We have given You glory while claiming for ourselves a 10 percent commission of the credit.[14]

We have _____.

We repent.

With deep shame, we confess that there are people in the world whom You love and for whom You died . . .

who don't want to know You because they know us.

who reject You because they reject us.

who don't believe You because of what we say and the way we say it.

who don't know You love them because we don't love them.

who don't know You can give them victory over sin because we live in defeat.

who are hopeless because we wring our hands in despair.

who don't come to You for freedom from the power of sin because we agree they were "born that way."

who don't look to You as the solution for what's wrong because we are looking to politics and power.

who are terrified of the future because we are afraid.

With shame, we confess _____.

Why do we wonder that people are leaving the church? Leaving the faith of their fathers? Doubting Your love? Questioning Your very existence? Making up gods to suit themselves? Our sins have tarnished Your glory, hidden Your face, bound Your hands, and diminished the perception of Your love. But now we bring to You words of specific confession. We humbly, sincerely say to You, "Forgive all our sins and receive us graciously."[15]

You have promised that You will heal our waywardness and love us freely.[16] We hold You to Your Word. Clean us up, living, holy Lord. Make us a temple that clearly reflects the eternal strength of the Chief Cornerstone and the glory of the Capstone so that one day the entire universe will rock and reverberate with rejoicing: "Great and marvelous are your deeds, Lord God Almighty. Just and true are your ways, King of the ages. Who will not fear you, O Lord, and bring glory to your name? For you alone are holy. All nations will come and worship before you, for your righteous acts have been revealed"[17] through us, Your people, the living stones.

For the glory of Your great name,

Amen.

Magnified Through Our Praise

As I shared with you, one of the effects of the purifying of my heart, mind, and body through the convicting, cleansing work of the Holy Spirit is that I have been released from guilt and shame. I am free! I am confident that I am right with God and that He sees me under the blood of His dear Son. I am acceptable to Him.[18] And while I am filled with humility and gratitude for what He has done, my heart overflows with praise!

King David had the same experience. When he committed adultery with Bathsheba, arranged for her husband to be murdered, then sometime later was confronted by Nathan the prophet, he was convicted to the core of his being. He stopped trying to cover up, ignore, defend, and excuse what he had done. Instead, he confessed his sin.[19] When he did, the joy of his salvation returned and he exclaimed, "Rejoice in the LORD and be glad, you righteous; sing, all you who are upright in heart!"[20]

Genuine praise that bubbles up out of a repentant heart overflowing with gratitude is evidence of the Holy Spirit at work within us to cleanse us and then fill us with Himself.

Perhaps no song of praise in the universe is quite as thrilling as the song of the redeemed that will one day be sung around the throne in Heaven. It's not about Creation or deliverance from bondage in Egypt or the destruction of Pharaoh's army in the Red Sea or the giving of the law on Mount Sinai. It's a new song that will be sung in Heaven prior to the return of the Son of God to rule and reign on earth. What are the words? "You are worthy to take the scroll and to open its seals, because you were slain, and with your blood you purchased men for God from every tribe and language and people and nation. You have made them to be a kingdom and priests to serve our God, and they will reign on the earth."[21]

The song of redemption will become contagious as the voices of thousands upon thousands and ten thousand times ten thousand angels encircle the throne and join in with loud voices: "Worthy is the Lamb, who was slain, to receive power and wealth and wisdom and strength and honor and glory and praise!"[22] The entire universe will explode in a crescendo of praise that will penetrate its farthest reaches! The entire universe will rock in praise of the One who alone is worthy![23]

As it was in the very beginning of time, when the Spirit of God hovered over planet Earth, pulsating, energizing, preparing it to be transformed through the power of God's Word, will it also be at the very end of time? Will the ricocheting praise that rocks the entire universe be evidence of the pulsating power of the Holy Spirit infusing every living thing that has breath with praise of our Lord Jesus Christ?

Witnessing a time still to come, the apostle John said he "heard what sounded like a great multitude, like the roar of rushing waters and like loud peals of thunder, shouting: 'Hallelujah! For our Lord God Almighty reigns. Let us rejoice and be glad and give him glory! For the wedding of the Lamb has come, and his bride has made herself ready.'"[24]

What you and I have just been through, as we have confessed our sin and repudiated it, is preparation for that day. Because not only are we living stones built into a magnificent temple in which the triune God will showcase His glory, but we are also the bride of Christ! With the essential, indispensable, purifying help of the Holy Spirit, we are getting ready to greet our Bridegroom! We are getting ready to see the King!

Why wait until that day to begin to raise your voice in praise of the One who alone is worthy of all praise? Remember, the Holy Spirit inhabits your praise![25] While I can't explain the unexplainable, I do know that praise cleanses the invisible spiritual atmosphere. Unloving spirits have to flee. Going room to room in your home praising the names of Jesus out loud, filling your home or your car with Christian music, making a habit of beginning your prayers—and your day—with praise of the One from whom all blessings flow, will make a difference. Try it and see.

As my two daughters and I made the first thirty-minute trip to the breast cancer center to meet with the medical team, we used the time to praise the names of Jesus. Starting with the first letter of the alphabet, we each gave one of

His names that begin with *A*—He is the Alpha, the Almighty, the Anointed One. We continued through the alphabet, filling the car with praise for who He is.[26] By the time we arrived at the hospital, our hearts overflowed with joy because our focus was on Him, not on our circumstances.

Ask the Holy Spirit to fill you to overflowing with joy and gladness for what His purifying work has done in your life; then take a moment and express in words of praise what God has done for you. If it helps, use the words of a favorite praise chorus or hymn, such as

> My sin—oh the bliss of this glorious thought—
> My sin, not in part, but the whole,
> Is nailed to His cross, and I bear it no more;
> Praise the Lord, praise the Lord, O my soul![27]

Part Seven

TRUSTING IN THE PROVIDENCE OF THE HOLY SPIRIT

The Spirit helps us in our weakness. We do not know what we ought to pray for, but the Spirit himself intercedes for us with groans that words cannot express. And he who searches our hearts knows the mind of the Spirit, because the Spirit intercedes for the saints in accordance with God's will. And we know that in all things God works for the good of those who love him, who have been called according to his purpose.

—ROMANS 8:26–28

When I received Jesus as my Savior, my assumption had been that the Holy Spirit was "assigned" to me. I thought He had come into my life because He had no option. I was now His "job"—His responsibility. My view of Him was that He was strictly professional, a perfectionistic stickler for details and Someone who would keep me in line until one day He would present me to the Father and say something like "Here she is. I've done My best to work with what I had." This harmful attitude could have led me to living a lie, as I would have tried hard to impress Him. I could have burned myself out trying hard to earn His love.

Then one day while reading my Bible, I was gripped by the following: "Do not grieve the Holy Spirit of God, with whom you were sealed for the day of redemption."[1] While I understand that Scripture is warning us not to intentionally, willfully sin, the word *grieve* caught and held my attention. I reflected on grief in my own life and knew I had experienced that emotion only when I deeply cared about someone or something. I grieved when my mother went to Heaven. I grieved when my husband followed her there about eight years later. I grieved when my father joined them both. And I realized that *grief* is a love word. I grieve because I loved my mother and my husband and my father.

This realization turned the light on in my thinking as I realized that if I can grieve the Holy Spirit, it's because He loves me. The Holy Spirit loves me! That was a profound, revolutionary thought. He's not just a professional partner. He's not just assigned to me. He doesn't live within me because He has to—He lives within me because He wants to live within me. He deeply cares about what I do and who I become. When I do the right thing, He rejoices. When I do the wrong thing, He grieves. Not only is He spiritually and practically involved in my life, but He is also emotionally caught up in who I am and who I am to become. What a difference that simple truth has made in my perspective. I can be myself with the Holy Spirit. I don't have to be "on." I can relax and be transparent with Him. I can trust Him completely because He truly loves me!

And the Holy Spirit loves you too! He cares deeply about what you care about because He cares about you.[2] It doesn't matter how small or how large your concern is. He cares. He understands. He wants what's best for you. He desires for you to fulfill your God-given potential. He wants to ease your burden, solve your problem, comfort your broken heart, bind up your wounds, bring you through the valley of the shadow, shower you with blessing upon blessing. And yes, He wants to make you holy—because He loves you! He will work all things—*all things*—for your good.[3] So relax. Stop trying to impress Him. Stop working so hard to earn His love. Be open and honest and transparent. Live with the confidence that you are deeply, unconditionally, permanently loved by Him.

Trust in His Pledge

When I traveled through the city of Hyderabad, India, in order to speak at their National Day of Prayer as I shared earlier, I couldn't help but notice jewelry store after jewelry store after jewelry store. It was amazing! Signs along the city streets and large billboards along the highway featured photographs of beautiful Indian women displaying spectacular gold jewelry. The women in the photographs wore necklaces so large that they looked like solid gold Puritan collars, bracelets that stretched from the wrist to the elbow, wide gold armbands or cuffs that gripped the upper arm, and earrings that hung like chandeliers from the earlobes to below the shoulders.

It was so over the top that I inquired whether the city was a jewelry center for the entire country. My hostess replied that when a woman is pledged to marry a man, the man pays a dowry to her, not in money or cows or land but in jewelry. One purpose is that if anything happened to the man, through either death or divorce, the woman could then sell her jewelry and have something to live on. As it turns out, Hyderabad is indeed one of the national centers for this very special type of jewelry.

The spectacular pieces of Indian jewelry I saw displayed on billboards, in magazines, and in stores reminded me of the piece of jewelry Danny gave me for essentially the same purpose—as his pledge of marriage. Except that Danny Lotz proposed marriage to me without a ring! I agreed to marry him, and practical male that he was, he asked what kind of ring I would like. I told him I wanted one like my mother's. Just a single diamond in a Tiffany setting.

About two weeks after his marriage proposal, Danny presented the ring to me. We were sitting in the same place where he had proposed marriage—the couch beside the fireplace in my parents' living room. Inside a little black velvet box was the most beautiful engagement ring I had ever seen. It was exactly what I would have selected had I done so myself. Just a single diamond in a Tiffany setting. I was thrilled!

That night when I went to bed, I couldn't sleep. I kept gazing at the ring on my finger. It seemed to glow in the dark. Early the next morning, I slipped down the stairs to my mother's room so I could show it to her. She agreed with me that it was as beautiful as any engagement ring she had ever seen.

But the ring was more than just a beautiful piece of jewelry because I knew it carried with it Danny Lotz's pledge of marriage. Every time I saw it, I was reminded that the day would come when his promise would be fulfilled. I would become his wife, and we would live together until death separated us. The ring remained on my finger until the moment during my wedding ceremony when I slipped it off so Danny could place a wedding band on the same finger. Then I placed the engagement ring next to the wedding band, where it remains to this day. It is a constant reminder of my husband's love and commitment to me, and mine to him, even beyond his death.[1]

The Holy Spirit within us is our "engagement ring." He Himself is the promise . . . the guarantee . . . the pledge . . . that Jesus loves us. That He is committed and faithful to us. And that one day He will return to take us to live with Him forever in the home that He is preparing.[2]

A GIFT FOR THE FUTURE BRIDE

In *The Book of Mysteries,* Rabbi Jonathan Cahn has given an enriched understanding of this divine pledge based on Jewish betrothal.[3] With his permission, I have used his thoughts in the following allegory.

The woman was as beautiful as any fairy-tale princess. The man was as dashing and strikingly handsome as any Disney Prince Charming. The man had been in love with her from the beginning of their relationship, but he patiently had made time for her to get to know him. She then fell in love with him too. When he finally professed to her his all-consuming love and proposed marriage, she agreed with joy! They both were ecstatic with happiness. Then with a sorrowful yet resolute expression, the man explained there would be a necessary time of separation before they could be married. He would be going away to prepare a home in which they would live together. She was understandably distraught. In response to her protests, he reassured her that although he had to leave, he would send her a gift to confirm his love for her. It would also guarantee his faithfulness to her while they were separated and that he would return for her. And the gift would beautify her in his absence.

She was almost inconsolable when he left. But several days later, as promised, she received an exquisite gift from him—a gorgeous ring with a fifteen-carat diamond surrounded by other, smaller diamonds. It was her engagement ring, his pledge that one day she would be his bride. He would not forget her, because he truly loved her. He would be faithful to her while they were separated, and he would return for her when preparations for their home were completed. In the meantime there was no doubt that the ring would beautify her in his absence.

A PLEDGE FROM THE FAITHFUL GROOM

Rabbi Cahn pointed out that the bridegroom's gift of love—the piece of jewelry or other gift that he gave to his bride—is called the *mattan*.

Even more fascinating is the following: The day God gave the law, or Torah, to Moses on Mount Sinai is remembered in the Jewish calendar as Mattan Torah—"the giving of the Torah." The law was considered God's gift of love to His people. It is commemorated by the Feast of Shavuot,[4] which is the same day on which Pentecost took place two thousand years ago. On the Feast of

Shavuot, the Holy Spirit was given as a gift of love to the betrothed bride of the Son. The Holy Spirit is our "mattan," our "engagement ring." He works to beautify us in the Son's absence, while He also guarantees the Son's faithfulness to us, His bride. The Holy Spirit is His pledge of commitment to us now and His pledge that one day He will return to take us to live with Him forever in the home that He is preparing.

Gaze at your "engagement ring," the Holy Spirit. How would you describe Him? What does it mean to you that He is the guarantee of your relationship with the Son? If He truly loves you fully, unconditionally—if He truly desires what's best for you, if He truly cares about everything you care about because He cares for you—what reason do you have for not trusting in His providence and pledge? So would you choose to trust Him? Relax. Rest in Him. You are precious to the Son and therefore precious to the Father and precious to the Spirit. The Holy Spirit is absolutely committed to fulfilling His responsibility to take good care of you until the day you are presented as a glorious bride to your Bridegroom.

25

Trust in His Seal

In olden days, a seal was a picture or a symbol or writing of some type that was carved into a hard surface of metal or stone. When pressed into clay or wax, the seal left an impression that carried with it the authority of the person to whom it belonged. It was commonly attached to documents in order to convey their authenticity, authority, or ownership.

The apostle Paul stated, "You also were included in Christ when you heard the word of truth, the gospel of your salvation. Having believed, you were marked in him with a seal, the promised Holy Spirit."[1] The indwelling of the Holy Spirit—the seal—guarantees that we belong to God. It serves as the divine "proof of purchase." While you and I can't see the seal, God sees it. "The Lord knows those who are his."[2] The seal apparently is also visible in the unseen world because it identifies us throughout the universe as authentic children of God.

The Christians to whom Paul wrote, explaining that the promised Holy Spirit sealed them in God's eyes, lived in the port city of Ephesus. Merchants from all over that part of the world came to buy timber, which arrived on the ships that docked there. When the merchant selected and purchased the timber he wanted, he stamped it with his signet, indicating his ownership. He then sent a trusted representative to claim and collect all the timbers that carried his seal.

The thrilling application for you and me is that the Holy Spirit is God's proof of ownership! Have you ever doubted your salvation? Questioned whether you are an authentic child of God? Lacked the blessed assurance that you are His and He is yours? Well, God doesn't doubt or question or lack assurance of His ownership, because He has sealed you with His stamp of proof, the Holy Spirit. When the Enemy hisses his insidious accusations against you, God dismisses him. *God knows* you are His. One day, if we are alive on earth at the end of the age, God will send His special agents to gather all those who are sealed with His seal, and "we will be caught up . . . to meet the Lord in the air" to live with Him forever![3]

You and I can rest in the security of knowing that nothing can ever separate us from our Owner—not "trouble or hardship or persecution or famine or nakedness or danger or sword"[4]—because we are sealed with His seal, the Holy Spirit! Jesus Himself reaffirmed that no one can snatch us from His hand or His Father's hand.[5] Not any sin, not any person, not any circumstance, not any disease, not any demon, not ourselves, not even death.

As my mother lay dying, I knew she in no way lacked assurance of her salvation and eternal life. Nor was she afraid of death. But I wanted to read to her a passage of Scripture that I knew she loved and had been memorizing. The words were written by the apostle Paul to reaffirm and refocus the faith of those who were seeking to follow Jesus while living in the wicked Roman world. This is what he was inspired by the Holy Spirit to write, and this is what I read to my mother on her deathbed: "I am convinced that neither death nor life, neither angels nor demons, neither the present nor the future, nor any powers, neither height nor depth, nor anything else in all creation, will be able to separate us from the love of God that is in Christ Jesus our Lord."[6]

Praise God! My mother and you and I are secure for all time because we are sealed!

Do you ever feel spiritually insecure? Do you lack assurance of your salvation? Of God's love for you? Of your heavenly home? Then take another moment to gaze on your "engagement ring" . . . the Holy Spirit. He guarantees God's ownership of your life. As God's own child and the beloved bride of God's only Son, you can be certain He also guarantees the fulfillment of all of God's promises to you. The Holy Spirit is your pledge and your proof that God is committed to you. He will be faithful to you. And—glorious hope—He will one day return for you to live with Him. Because you are His and He is yours. Forever!

26

Trust in His Understanding

One of the things I miss most about my mother is her understanding. She knew me so well that I didn't have to explain or defend myself to her. She drew on the depth of her knowledge and discernment to give me wise counsel, comfort, and encouragement. As I entered adulthood, on rare occasions she would gently correct or rebuke me. Often when I asked her a question or shared with her a concern, she would come out with a very pithy statement that spoke to the heart of what I had just brought up. My mother had the ability to quickly wrap her mind and her heart around whatever the issue was. She just "got it." How I miss the sparkle in her eyes, the warmth of her smile, the way she would throw her arms out wide to embrace me when I walked into her room, and the conversations we would have beside her "laughing fire."

I also never tired of hearing Mother's voice in prayer. Even toward the end of her life, when physical weakness affected her voice, I would still ask her to pray. Her voice wavered. Sometimes it was tentative and raspy. But there was no doubt she knew the One to whom she was speaking. In my mind's eye I can visualize her now, with head bent over her folded hands, praying for me, my husband, my children, and whatever situation we had just been discussing. The tone of her prayer was as though she was speaking to a powerful and well-connected friend whom she had known for a long time and had grown to trust and love completely. Her relationship with the Lord was contagious. I wanted to know Him as intimately as she did. But that's another subject for another time.[1]

What I miss most are Mother's prayers of understanding for my family and me. When she moved to Heaven, I felt a great vacuum in the spiritual realm. Now who would intercede for us? Who would be covering us in prayer, doing battle in the heavenly realms on our behalf? The answer, of course, is the One who had prayed for us through my mother—the One who was still praying and is still praying: the Holy Spirit.

He Knows Us Inside and Out

The Holy Spirit is utterly trustworthy. He has no needs of His own to be concerned about. He is consumed with yours. He has said He prays for you, and He does. He is praying. He will pray. He is eternally committed to your well-being. And He is devoted to you.

Because He lives within us, He is intimately familiar with all our ways: our desires and our doubts, our decisions and our dreams, our feelings and our fears, our problems and our pressures, our sickness and our suffering, our wounds and our worries, our secrets and our selfishness. Actually, there is nothing that the Holy Spirit does not know or understand about us. There is nothing that we can hide from Him. He knows. The psalmist described it this way: "O Lord, you have searched me and you know me. You know when I sit and when I rise; you perceive my thoughts from afar. . . . Before a word is on my tongue you know it completely, O Lord. . . . Where can I go from your Spirit? Where can I flee from your presence?"[2] The answer to those rhetorical questions is "Nowhere." The Spirit of God is within us. We can never be separated from Him. He is with us everywhere and He knows everything.

Unlike some companies that apparently mine every shred of information with which online users can be manipulated, the Holy Spirit works with our best interests as His goal. He uses what He knows about us in order to intercede effectively in life-altering, circumstance-changing, people-molding, problem-solving, obstacle-moving, powerful ways.

He Prays for Us

The Holy Spirit knows how to pray and how to get answers to His prayers. He understands us because He is God, who lives within us and therefore knows us inside and out, backward and forward. He has 24-7 access to the inner sanctum of the throne room in Heaven, and He knows precisely what the will of God the Father is. He applies all this to His prayers to articulate accurately our issues and sync them up perfectly with God's will. The Bible explains, "The Spirit helps us in our weakness. We do not know what we ought to pray for, but the Spirit himself intercedes for us with groans that words cannot express. And he who searches our hearts knows the mind of the Spirit, because the Spirit intercedes for the saints in accordance with God's will."[3]

Have you ever had a burden so great, a wound so deep, a longing so profound, a grief so heart wrenching, a problem so all-consuming, that you didn't know how to pray? You didn't even know where to begin in prayer, much less what to ask for or how to ask? At such a time, what a relief and comfort to know that the Holy Spirit intercedes for you.

Years ago my husband invited me to go with him to Williamsburg, Virginia, for a Fellowship of Christian Athletes special event. I was excited to get away from the responsibilities of home and small children. But I was more excited to get away with Danny and explore an old town that I had read about but had never visited. I visualized the two of us walking hand in hand through the village streets, then stopping to get something to eat in a quaint café.

Instead, when we arrived in Williamsburg, my husband deposited me in the hotel room, then took off with his friends. All day. Later I realized we had not talked through the schedule at all and had communicated very poorly with each other about our expectations for the weekend. But at the moment, I was truly devastated. I lay down on the bed and cried until I went to sleep. When I woke up, I experienced a strange phenomenon. While I was no longer crying on the outside, deep inside I was still weeping. And I knew it was the Spirit of God who was weeping within me. In a strange way, I felt comforted that He understood.

When my husband came back to the room right before supper, he was on a high, so excited to tell me about the pickup basketball games and the tennis matches he had played that I didn't have the heart to tell him about my day. I knew we needed to work on our communication, but I left that for after we returned home.

Communication is what the Holy Spirit excels in. When we don't know what to say, He does. When we don't know what to ask for, He does. When we don't know how to express the depths of our feelings, He does.

Recently a young wife poured out her heart to me in desperation. She was carrying pain from wounds so deep she could barely speak between sobs. Her words came out in shards. She would never know how I related to her pain, yet I still had no words in response. No answers. No "fix." Not knowing what else to do, I asked whether I could pray with her. She agreed. At a loss as to what to pray, I just bowed my head, closed my eyes, opened my mouth, and trusted that the same Holy Spirit who had wept with me when I was wounded would give me His words. He did. When I finished praying for her, I could hear the change in her voice as she thanked me. The nightmare had eased, and the burden was lighter.

HE SPEAKS TO US

Our prayers are not always answered by a specific action. Sometimes our prayers are answered with a shift in our attitude or in our emotions. After prayer, we may find that confidence has replaced our fear, contentment has replaced our desire, hope has replaced our despair, comfort has replaced our grief, patience has replaced our frustration, joy has replaced our spirit of heaviness, and love has replaced our anger.

Years ago a person who had authority over me made a decision that I felt was not only wrong but also unjust. I knew it would hurt many people. I wrote a letter, respectfully protesting the decision, then explaining what I felt was a wise, workable alternative. Not only was my suggestion forcefully rejected, but the response was also accompanied by a stern tongue-lashing.

Generally I find anger takes more energy than I care to invest, but on this occasion, I was white-hot angry. I experienced the unfamiliar emotion of deep-down rage that seemed almost uncontrollable. For three days I fumed as I conducted imaginary conversations with the person in my head, brilliantly winning every argument.

I became so irate and distracted that I knew I couldn't continue to live for the Lord and serve Him with the inner turmoil I was experiencing. Finally, I had the courage to get down on my knees and talk honestly to the Lord about it. I reiterated to Him the decision that was being forced on me, the havoc and hurt it would create, and my anger at the unreasonable injustice of it. When I finished unloading my burden in prayer, I was quiet. The Lord was quiet. I continued to kneel, waiting. To my mind came a whisper: *Anne, your anger in God's eyes is as wrong as this person's decision.* That rocked me back on my heels to a sitting position on the floor! *Really?* As I began to think about it, I knew the thought came from the Holy Spirit. And He was right. As always.

Now I had a problem that was different from the injustice of the other person. I had a problem with me. Instead of a problem with the decision, I now had a problem with my reaction to the decision. So I began to confess my anger to the Lord. In the end I told Him I would rather live with the injustice than offend Him with my anger. I told Him He would have to remove my anger, as I didn't have the ability to release it in my own strength. I was willing to give it up, but I couldn't. I continued to pray and talk to Him about it.

When I got up off my knees, the anger was gone. *Gone!* The dramatic difference on the inside of me was actually stunning. I knew it was the supernatural work of the Holy Spirit within my heart. I could never have rid myself of such a strong, overwhelming emotion, especially when the circumstances remained the same. I knew it was an answer not only to my prayer but also to His prayer. Through an invisible yet powerful miracle, He replaced my anger with a quiet, gentle peace. The result? I sent a bouquet of flowers to the person who had made the decision. Three days after the flowers were delivered, I called, and God helped me work out a compromise that I know would not have been possible if I had continued to harbor anger in my heart.

What anger resides in your heart? What fears are rooted in your memory? What desires seem to consume your thoughts? What despair has plunged you into hopelessness? What grief has turned on the faucet of your tears? What frustration has triggered your temper? What joy robber has left your spirit heavy?

Would you get down on your knees, as I did, and talk to the Holy Spirit about whatever it is? He already knows, but He is waiting for you to come tell Him about it. Honestly. Without any *buts* or excuses. Give the burden to Him. He will take it as He releases you from it. Because He understands. And He is praying for you.

Trust in His Prayers

I am so grateful that the Holy Spirit prays for us with total understanding. As we saw in the last chapter, this means we don't have to pretend or excuse or defend or hide or rationalize anything. We can be brutally honest with Him since He knows it all anyway.

It's out of His heart of love that the Holy Spirit prays for you and me. Since the Bible says He prays without words,[1] it's impossible to find one of His prayers in Scripture on which we can base our thoughts. But the Holy Spirit is Jesus in us. So in the prayers of Jesus we find the closest verbal prayers to what the prayers of the Holy Spirit must be like. When Jesus prayed, in a very real way, the Holy Spirit was praying through Him.

HE PRAYS FOR OUR FAITH TO BE STEADFAST

The night He was betrayed, and less than twelve hours before He would be crucified, we get two glimpses of how Jesus prayed for His disciples. In the first instance we don't actually hear Him pray, but during the final meal He enjoyed with His disciples, Jesus described His prayer for one of them. He had led them through communion when He shared the drinking of the cup that represented His blood that would be shed for them, then the eating of the bread that represented His body that would be broken for them. At this holy moment, instead of worshipful, humble attitudes regarding what had just been taught, His disciples had broken out in an argument as to who among them was the greatest![2] It would be almost humorous if it wasn't so ludicrous. And serious.

Just before He predicted Simon Peter's denial, Jesus revealed, "Simon, Simon, Satan has asked to sift you as wheat. But I have prayed for you . . . that your faith may not fail."[3] I can almost see the tears in His eyes and hear the pain in His voice. He knew all hell was about to break loose in just a few hours when He would be betrayed by one of them, arrested, tried, tortured, then crucified. In anticipation of that horror—and Simon's failure—He prayed for Simon to be strengthened in faith.

What situation has suddenly challenged your faith? The death of a loved one? The diagnosis of a chronic or deadly disease? The termination of a job? The fiery destruction of your home? The rebellion of a child? The split in your church? The infidelity of your spouse? Life is not easy. But God is great. He loves you. And He is praying that your faith will not fail.

Several years ago the entire Christian world witnessed the dramatic answer to His prayers in the life of Greg Laurie. Greg was, and still is, the pastor of a megachurch in Southern California. He is also a gifted evangelist who packs stadiums in order to present the gospel clearly and powerfully, inviting anyone and everyone to come to Jesus for forgiveness of sin, salvation from judgment, and eternal life. On July 24, 2008, word spread quickly through the family of God that Greg Laurie's thirty-three-year-old son, Christopher, had been suddenly killed in a car accident on a California freeway. Christopher was a husband to Brittany and a father to two-year-old Stella, with another baby on the way. How could this have happened? How could a loving God have allowed such a devastating horror? How would Greg react?

Greg has shared that, at the time, the question seared on his heart was "Do you trust Christ, really, or don't you?" He testified that he didn't want to coast in his life's journey. In Greg's words, the time of Christopher's death "wasn't the time to let down his guard against the enemy and have an affair, or turn to a little or a lot of social drinking, or to fall into bitterness. This was the time to gamble it all." It was a time for radical faith. Greg reacted by grabbing hold of God and what he knew to be true, branching out, and planting another church, which effectively more than doubled his church ministry in Southern California.[4]

It has been my privilege to be a friend to both Greg and his wife, Cathe. I serve with him on the board of directors for the Billy Graham Evangelistic Association. I have preached for him in his church and led women's meetings for Cathe. What I have witnessed is authentic faith. Faith that I'm convinced is an answer to the Holy Spirit's prayers. If God can bring Greg through such a horrific nightmare with a faith that is even stronger than before, He can do the same for you and for me.

Do you trust Jesus, *really*, or don't you? The choice is yours, but the strength to trust at such a time comes in answer to the prayers of the Holy Spirit.

HE PRAYS FOR OUR RELATIONSHIP WITH THE FATHER

Returning again to Jesus in the upper room with His disciples, we see a second glimpse of how the Holy Spirit prays for us. Jesus was talking to His Father, and they overheard His very private, personal conversation. Because John wrote it down for us in John 17, we, too, can listen in.

He began the prayer by addressing God as Father. Right there, you may want to stop listening. If your father was abusive, angry, an alcoholic, an adulterer, or an absentee parent, you may struggle with the concept of God as a father. My own father was an absentee parent. It's been estimated he was gone 60 percent of my growing-up years. When he was home, he never tucked me in bed at night, never told me a bedtime story, never helped me with homework—all the things I saw my husband do with our children. In fact, it wasn't until I saw the way Danny fathered our children that I realized what I had missed. To be honest, I don't want to think of God as a father in that sense, either. I will insert that my father modeled our heavenly Father in many ways other than in the everyday types of activities, and I would rather have had Billy Graham as an absentee father than anyone else full time.

However, Jesus was not implying that God is like your father or like my father. One of the most personal relationships available to humanity is that between a parent and a child. So the Spirit of Jesus was underscoring that the relationship between the members of the Trinity is a personal love relationship. As Jesus continued pouring out His heart, He prayed, "I pray . . . that all of them may be one, Father, just as you are in me and I am in you. May they also be in us so that the world may believe that you have sent me. . . . I have made you known to them, and will continue to make you known in order that the love you have for me may be in them and that I myself may be in them."[5] This request was answered at Pentecost when Jesus came into the disciples through the person of the Holy Spirit.

And lest there be any misunderstanding, the indwelling of the Holy Spirit ushers you and me into a personal love relationship with God the Father, God the Son, and God the Holy Spirit. Let that sink in for a moment. God loves you! *God loves you!* God really does *love you!* There is nothing you can do to make Him love you less. Or make Him love you more. He loves you completely. Fully. Unconditionally.

After focusing on a personal love relationship with God by addressing Him as His Father, Jesus acknowledged that God had given Him the authority to give us eternal life,[6] a relationship with God that is not only personal but also permanent. It's forever. For all time. It is not even interrupted by death. Death is just the transition from faith to sight. Death is closing your eyes to this life and opening them to the face of Jesus. And the relationship you established with the Father at the cross when you were first saved continues on . . . and on . . . and on . . . *forever!*

Are you one of those dear people who live with the fear that you can lose your salvation? You can't. Eternal life is given to you when you are saved, and if you could lose it, then it wouldn't be eternal, would it? It would be temporary. And if you did nothing to earn or deserve salvation, which you didn't because it's a free gift that you received by faith, then you can do nothing to lose or undeserve your salvation. So instead of living in fear . . . apprehension . . . uncertainty . . . never really sure you belong . . . never really sure you are going to Heaven . . . live in the light of the Father's love for you and His relationship with you. His love will never die or grow dim or wear out. God the Father, Son, and Holy Spirit will never get tired of you. You are loved. Forever. How do you know? Because you are sealed, remember? And because He says so![7]

Jesus then defined eternal life not just as living forever but as knowing God the Father and God the Son.[8] The word He used for "know" is one used for the intimate relationship between a husband and a wife.[9] So the word *know* does not describe intellectual, academic, or theological knowledge of God only. It implies something much more.

The phenomenal truth is not only that He *allows* us to know Him intimately but also that He *invites* us to do so when He gives us eternal life. This increasing, intimate knowledge of the living God is evidence of the Holy Spirit at work, because He is the one who takes the things of God and makes them known to us.[10]

As we exercise the privilege of pursuing a personal, intimate relationship with the living God, the Holy Spirit is praying for us. How else does He pray? What more besides our faith and our relationship with the Father does He pray for? Let's turn back to the scene in the upper room as Jesus prayed for His disciples.

HE PRAYS FOR OUR NEEDS

As we pick back up in John 17, the specific requests Jesus made give us further insight into how the Holy Spirit prays for you and me even now. What are the requests that He made? He seems to cover a wide range of our needs.

For Our Protection

Jesus prayed for His followers to be protected from the world.[11] While Jesus was with the disciples, He protected them from the intense questioning, scrutiny, hatred, rejection, and danger that swirled around them. Like a mother hen with her chicks under her wings, He had taken on Himself the full storm of people's hostility. His desire for the disciples' protection was clearly evident at the scene of His arrest when He commanded the soldiers to let His disciples go.[12] But Jesus knew that when His visible presence and His audible voice were removed, His disciples would be vulnerable. Hatred and persecution would be aimed at them because of their association with Him.

I remember when my children were in high school and wanted to go to the beach with their friends for spring break. My concern for their protection from things they would be exposed to and the temptations they would face led me to say no. But when they went off to Baylor University and I was half a continent away from them, I knew they would be vulnerable and exposed to all sorts of things I would have protected them from had I been physically present. So I prayed. In much the same way, in the absence of our Lord's visible presence, the Holy Spirit prays for our protection from the distractions, diversions, temptations, and downward pull of the world around us.

What are you afraid of? Who are you afraid for? Take your fears to the One who understands and is praying even now for your protection.

For Our Joy

Jesus also prayed for His followers to have the full measure of His joy.[13] Unlike some people's perception that Christians live miserable lives filled with a checklist of dos and don'ts . . . that it's spiritual to have a serious, even sour demeanor . . . that it's unspiritual to laugh and enjoy life . . . the Holy Spirit actually prays for us to be filled with joy! Joy that comes from having genuine peace with God. Joy that comes from being confident our sins are forgiven. Joy that comes from knowing we are wrapped in God's love. Joy that comes from living for something bigger than ourselves so our lives have purpose and meaning. Joy that comes from the privilege of increasingly knowing God in a relationship that is personal and permanent. Joy that comes from knowing our lives are not careening out of control but orchestrated for a divine purpose. Joy that comes from the hope of a heavenly home to come. Joy that comes from experiencing one blessing after another.

The Holy Spirit knows that if you and I have the fullness of God's joy, then the world will lose its charm. Sin won't seem so attractive. Worldly positions, possessions, popularity, and prestige will seem tawdry, cheap, and superficial in comparison with knowing Jesus. So the Holy Spirit prays for our joy to be in Jesus, not in our circumstances or in anything else. Just Jesus.

Who or what has robbed you of your joy? Try counting your blessings.

Years ago our house was broken into in broad daylight. The thieves took just about everything of measurable value. That night when I went to bed, I was aware they had also robbed me of my joy, peace, and ability to sleep. As I lay staring into the darkness, terrified they would return, the Spirit seemed to whisper, *Anne, count your blessings.* So I began to do so. There were so many I couldn't keep them straight, so I began to alphabetize them. As I went through two alphabetical lists, then started on the third one, I went to sleep. The next morning, the joy was back.

For Our Deliverance from the Devil

Jesus also prayed for our protection from the Evil One—the devil or Satan—who is our archenemy.[14] While the devil cannot interfere with our salvation, since we already are sealed with God's unbreakable seal of ownership, he will do his best to keep us from being effective. He will make it his priority to get you and me to waste our Christian lives so that we make no eternal impact on our world for Jesus. He will work through others to slander you, accuse you, distract you, tempt you, and ultimately defeat you. Watch out! The enemy is not your neighbor or your spouse or your boss or your coworker or your child's teacher. Your enemy is the devil, which is why Jesus prayed for your protection from him and why the Holy Spirit surely continues in this line of prayer. He knows the devil is much stronger, smarter, and slyer than we are. But the devil is no match for the Spirit of God.

So when the devil attacks, don't run and hide. Don't even turn your back. Paul challenged the Ephesian followers of Jesus to stand against the devil's schemes.[15] And keep standing firm. Don't give in or give up, back down or back up. The Spirit's prayers assure us of ultimate victory.

For Our Undivided Devotion

Jesus also prayed for us to be sanctified, set apart from the world around us for God's exclusive use.[16] As we have already seen, the Holy Spirit works in our lives to separate us from sin so that increasingly we are holy as He is holy. But this particular request in the prayer of John 17 carries with it the thought of being separated from secondary things so that we can be devoted to our primary goal, which is to fulfill our God-given potential and complete the work He has given us to do.

When Jesus said that for our sakes He sanctified Himself, He wasn't saying He had separated Himself from sin, since He was always separate from sin. He was saying He had separated Himself from many good things in order to give His undivided devotion, attention, time, and energy to do the best thing, which was to finish His Father's work. In doing so, He set an example for His disciples, including you and me.[17]

What have you separated from in order to have time to serve Jesus? What else have you separated from in order to set an example for your children and grandchildren of a holy, sanctified life? I have felt the Holy Spirit's prayers as I have separated from my warm, cozy bed in the morning in order to get up early and spend time in prayer and Bible reading. At times I have separated from lunch or shopping with friends, yardwork and housework, even from watching some of my granddaughters' basketball and soccer games, in order to write this book. For the sake of setting an example for my children and grandchildren, I have separated from certain television programs that I will not watch, movies that I will not attend, books that I will not read, magazines that I will not look at, and places that I will not go.

What do you need to separate from in order to set a godly example for someone else? Think about it. What right have you denied yourself to avoid causing another person to stumble and instead to draw that person to Jesus? "For them I sanctify myself,"[18] Jesus prayed. I am quite sure the Holy Spirit prays that you and I will do likewise.

For Our Unity

As Jesus continued to pray, we can hear the Holy Spirit asking for us to be one with the Father and the Son.[19] His prayer was answered initially when you and I received Jesus Christ as our Lord and Savior, then were sealed with the Holy Spirit. At that moment, we were given an organic unity with the triune God, similar to a branch that is organically attached to the vine. Unity is our position in Jesus Christ. But Jesus prayed, and the Holy Spirit continues to pray, for our unity to be experienced in everyday practice.

As I've shared with you, I was married to Danny for forty-nine years. As much as I loved him and as secure as I was in our relationship as husband and wife, at times we disagreed and argued. It's humorous now because I can't think of one example to give. But I do know we had plenty of arguments, and when we did, tension set in, silence reigned, and a barrier went up between us. I was still his wife, and he was still my husband, but I no longer felt in unity with him.

It's the same in my relationship with the Lord. Any argument, disagreement, or disobedience—if sin and rebellion can be called that—immediately throws up a barrier. Tension settles in as I wrestle with conviction and that guilty feeling. Silence reigns as I no longer can pray freely, without restraint. Although I am still sealed with the Holy Spirit, my sin robs me of the awareness of oneness and sweet fellowship with God. The remedy? I must apologize. Confess my sin for what it is. Say I'm sorry. Then surrender to His will and obey whatever direction I had resisted. When I'm brutally honest about my sin, naming it for what it is in His sight and asking Him to cleanse me, He does![20] Our relationship is then restored to the sweet intimacy that is the very core of my being. And that's an answer to the Holy Spirit's prayer.

But Jesus also prayed for us to be unified with other believers.[21] In many ways this is His most challenging request. My mother quipped that this was evidence that even our Lord had unanswered prayers. And she may have been right, because the answer to this prayer is based on our choice to be more concerned with the well-being of others and our unity with them than we are with our own opinion. Or our own church or denomination. Or our own leadership position. Or our own race or economic status or political affiliation. Or our own right to be heard or deferred to or respected or honored or obeyed. Or our own right to be right.

What is dividing you from another follower of Jesus? What has broken the unity that the Holy Spirit is even now praying for? Would you ask Him to show you what you can do to restore it? It may mean you have to give up or give in. You may have to leave something or someone behind or let something or someone go. You may have to place a phone call, write an email, or be the first to say you are sorry. If you don't know why the relationship is broken, ask the other person, "Are we all right? Have I done something to offend you? How can I make it right?" Then follow through and do whatever it is.

Remember, the Holy Spirit is praying for you.

For Our Eternal Perspective

The last specific request Jesus prayed in John 17 is truly life defining and priority setting. He prayed for us to one day be where He is and see Him in His glory.[22] As the world around us becomes more anti-Christ, more blasphemous, more dangerous for followers of Jesus, we need to keep eternity in view. While others are living for themselves, working hard to be popular, to accumulate more possessions, to build up their portfolios, to achieve prominent positions, to wield power, to enjoy a variety of pleasures, or just to live a good life and get along without causing too much of a stir or controversy, you and I are to live for the glory of God. You and I need to know that this life is not all there is and live accordingly.

What has caught your eye? Your neighbor's late-model car? Your friend's designer clothes? Your sibling's larger home? Shoppers in the mall carrying bulging shopping bags emblazoned with the logos of store brands you can't afford? Do you ever find yourself looking twice and wishing . . . ?

While we all have been there, my mother urged me not to be envious of the wealth or pleasures or prestige or possessions or position or power of the ungodly in this life. Because—think about it—that's all they will ever have. On the other hand, " 'no eye has seen, no ear has heard, no mind has conceived what God has prepared for those who love him' . . . but God has revealed it to us by his Spirit."[23] You and I are to live in anticipation that the best is yet to come.

Have you ever experienced the blessing of having someone pray with you? For you? Over you? Have you ever had one or more prayer partners that you confide in? Friends who pray specifically because they know, love, and understand you? Prayer partners are one of the sweetest blessings in my life. From my mother to my husband to my children to my prayer team to my executive assistant to a few beloved friends, I have experienced the ministry of the invisible Holy Spirit praying specifically for me through visible people.

If you don't have a prayer partner, ask God now to give you one. Just be still. Let Him bring a name to your mind. Then reach out and invite that person to pray with you and for you. You can exchange email addresses, phone numbers, or postal addresses. You can pray together once a day, once a week, once a month. The time, place, and manner of meeting is up to you. Who knows? You may be the answer to that person's prayers.

And if no one comes to mind or no one will make that commitment, remember that the Holy Spirit is praying for you. Specifically. Personally. With full understanding and a heart of love.

Conclusion

The Unwavering Focus
of the Holy Spirit: Jesus

If the purpose of the Holy Spirit is to glorify Jesus . . .

if the goal of the Holy Spirit is to make Jesus known to you and to me . . .

if the priority of the Holy Spirit is to guide us into all truth—truth revealed in the written Word of God so that we might know and reflect with our lives the living Word of God, who is Jesus, the truth incarnate . . .

. . . then the purpose, the goal, and the priority of the Holy Spirit can be summed up in one word: *Jesus*. When we wrap our minds around the laser-like focus of the Holy Spirit, a lot of things become clearer, including the Bible itself.

The Bible is more understandable when we grasp what the entire book is about. In some ways, it reminds me of the jigsaw puzzles I learned to put together as a child.

Whenever I became ill, my mother would send me to my grandmother's house. My grandmother was a medical nurse who had directed a large women's clinic in China for twenty-five years before she and my grandfather were run out during the Japanese invasion. She was the best nurse ever for a sick little girl. One of the ways she invariably distracted me from my aches and pains was to involve me in putting together one of her jigsaw puzzles. She almost always had one going that contained five hundred to one thousand pieces.

If you've worked one of these puzzles, you know that it consists of a picture pasted on cardboard that is cut up into lots of little shapes. The picture is also on the front of the puzzle box. My grandmother taught me to turn the puzzle pieces face up, see the little bits of the picture, and connect them to other puzzle pieces that showed similar pieces of the picture. The puzzle was completed when all the pieces were connected and the picture on the box was replicated.

The Bible can seem like a jigsaw puzzle, with lots of disconnected pieces, which is why we need to turn the pieces over. The Holy Spirit shows us how to put the pieces together so that we discover the full picture. It's the picture of Jesus! The entire Bible, which is "God-breathed" by the Holy Spirit,[1] reveals Jesus, and Jesus reveals God.

This unwavering focus of the Holy Spirit on Jesus can be seen throughout all of Scripture. In the following paragraphs I will try to describe some of the major puzzle pieces that come readily to my mind as thrilling evidence of His focus.

Focused in Creation

Beginning with Genesis 1, the Bible reveals that God created the heavens and the earth and that the Spirit of God hovered over the face of the deep. Then in verse 3 we are given the words *God said*. Beginning with calling forth light, when those words are repeated all the way through Genesis 1, whatever God said was so.

We would think that God was speaking in some sort of language with nouns and verbs until the Holy Spirit takes that puzzle piece and connects it to the first verse of John's gospel, which plainly says, "In the beginning was the Word [God said], and the Word was with God [a distinct person because He was with God], and the Word was God." Farther down in that same chapter, the Holy Spirit connects these two puzzle pieces with another one that makes the astounding assertion when John testified, "The Word became flesh and dwelt among us, and we beheld His glory, the glory as of the only begotten of the Father, full of grace and truth."[2] What an amazing revelation! The Holy Spirit connects the puzzle pieces to show us that right there in the beginning is the picture of Jesus, by whom and for whom everything was created. Jesus—the Creator—became flesh at Bethlehem, but that was not His beginning. He always has been!

Since no one has ever seen God at any time, when God does reveal Himself to us in physical form, He reveals Himself to us through Jesus.[3] From time to time throughout the Old Testament, before God became flesh in Bethlehem, He appeared in the physical form of the preincarnate Jesus so He could be seen.

In Genesis 2:8 we are told, "The LORD God had planted a garden in the east, in Eden." It's logical to assume that in order to plant a garden in Eden, God would be in a physical form. And the Holy Spirit turns over the puzzle piece and shows us the picture of the man on the other side, digging in the dirt, planting flowers and grass, arranging the trees and shrubs as He prepared a home for our first parents, Adam and Eve. Think about it! Look at the other side of the puzzle piece! The preincarnate Word of God, who was in the beginning, who was with God, who was God, was the first homemaker. Jesus! And He is still in the homemaking business today.[4] He said so. He promised He has gone to prepare a place for you and me to live with Him forever.[5] When it's finished, one day He will come for us.

Returning to our puzzle, we find another foundational piece in Genesis 2. It reveals that "the LORD God formed the man from the dust of the ground and breathed into his nostrils the breath of life, and the man became a living being."[6] Acknowledging that it wasn't good for the man to be alone, the Lord God fashioned a suitable companion—a woman—and gave her to the man.[7] Turning over the puzzle pieces, once again we glimpse the preincarnate Son of God personally creating and forming man and woman, then breathing His own life into them. Jesus is our creator![8]

Our bodies, how they look and how they function, are His idea and the work of His hands. Our very breath comes from Him. Do you know people who say they don't need Jesus? Don't believe in Him? Those people should turn over the puzzle pieces. Because all human life and breath, including theirs, come from Him!

In Genesis 3, when Adam and Eve disobeyed the Lord God, they were filled with shame and tried to hide from Him. But He sought them out. The Bible describes the Lord God walking in the garden, calling for them, clearly indicating He was in a physical form.[9] He found them cowering in the bushes. He didn't want to leave them forever in their sin, so He led them in confession before explaining to them the consequences of their sin and the curse that would fall on them and all their descendants because of it.[10] But before He separated them from Himself, "the LORD God made garments of skin . . . and clothed them."[11] In order to make garments of skin, it stands to reason that some animal had to be sacrificed. I sense this puzzle piece turning over slowly as I can't help but wonder whether the Lord God had tears in His eyes as He clothed His children. Surely the preincarnate Son of God was keenly aware that one day their sin and ours would require another sacrifice so we could be cleansed of our sin, shame, and guilt, then clothed in a restored right standing with God. And that the sacrifice would be that of a lamb, Jesus Himself.

In Genesis 4 we glimpse Adam and Eve's dysfunctional family. Their first-born son, Cain, became insanely jealous of their second-born son, Abel. The Holy Spirit turns over the shadowy puzzle piece and shows us the preincarnate Son of God seeking out the rebellious and belligerent son of Adam and Eve, challenging him to master his strong bent toward sin. But instead, Cain rose up and murdered his brother, then Cain refused to repent, whining instead that God's judgment was too great to bear. He lived the rest of his life wandering from place to place, with no peace in his heart or in his life.[12] The encouragement the Holy Spirit gives us from this piece of the puzzle is that Jesus will seek out our prodigals and make every effort to reconcile them to Himself. But the choice to repent, return, and reconcile is theirs to make.

In Genesis 6 we discover that the world had become saturated in evil. As a result God's heart was filled with pain.[13] As He surveyed the wickedness of humanity, His eye fell on one man, Noah, who lived in such a way that he found favor with God. In the entire world, Noah was the only one who was right with God and blameless among the people of his generation. The primary reason for his godliness in the midst of godlessness had to have been that Noah walked with God.[14] This puzzle piece is intriguing because the Bible lets us overhear a rather one-sided conversation. As Noah and the preincarnate Son of God, Jesus, walked together, Noah discovered what was on the heart and mind of God: judgment. "God said to Noah, 'I am going to put an end to all people, for the earth is filled with violence because of them.'"[15] That surely was as terrifying a revelation to Noah as it would be today if we were told we were going to be hit by nuclear weapons that would destroy us and the entire world! While I'm sure Noah was still gasping to catch his breath and collect his thoughts, God directed, "Make yourself an ark."[16] Judgment was on God's mind but so was salvation! The Holy Spirit turns over this puzzle piece and reveals that judgment for sin, and salvation from judgment, have been on the heart and mind of God's Son from the very beginning of human history. And still are today. And will be until the end of human history.

When we make the time to walk and talk with God, we, too, will become aware of what's on His mind and in His heart. His burden for people will become our own, and our hearts will burn to "build an ark"—to present the gospel, the good news of God's salvation from judgment, to our generation. Lest there be any misunderstanding, the Holy Spirit connects this puzzle piece to another one found in the New Testament: "Salvation is found in no one else, for there is no other name under heaven given to men by which we must be saved."[17] Only Jesus. He is the ark. Don't get caught up in the popular opinions, philosophies, and perspectives as the people did in Noah's day. They denied the truth. They thought a loving God would never send judgment and destroy His own creation. They must have been convinced that there was safety in numbers. They were wrong. Dead wrong. The flood came and, along with it, the destruction of every living thing that was outside the ark.[18]

God used Noah and his family to repopulate the earth. After several generations went by, the Bible focuses on one man, Abraham, and his family.

FOCUSED THROUGH THE CENTURIES

Abraham had been living in Ur of the Chaldeans, which was in modern-day Iraq. God leaned out of Heaven and told Abraham that if he would follow Him in a life of obedient faith, He would bless him. One of the primary blessings God promised to give Abraham in his lifetime was a son.[19]

But after years of being unable to bear children, Abraham's wife, Sarah, urged him to use Hagar, her Egyptian servant, as a surrogate mother. He did. Hagar became pregnant with Abraham's child, then arrogantly treated the barren Sarah with contempt. Sarah reacted by abusing Hagar, and she fled. Somewhere out on a forsaken desert road, the angel of the Lord—whom scholars refer to as a "theophany," a unique revelation of the preincarnate Son of God—sought her and found her. He talked her through her actions and revealed that she was carrying a son and that God had heard of her misery. He then sent her back to Sarah.[20] We can almost hear the emotion choking her voice when she realized that Abraham and Sarah's God was hers, too, when she responded, "You are the God who sees me . . . I have now seen the One who sees me."[21]

The astounding revelation is that the very first time in Scripture that the angel of the Lord appears, it's not to Abraham or one of his descendants. It's not to a man, not to a free person, not to a wealthy person, but to an Egyptian, a pregnant woman, a poor slave, with no rights of her own. And the Holy Spirit turns over the puzzle piece and shows us the One who sees us, who loves us whoever we are, who hears our cries of misery, who seeks us out in our wilderness wandering, who answers our prayers, and who is with us when we return to our circumstances and have to remain there.[22]

Thirteen years after Hagar's son was born, Abraham was sitting in the doorway of his tent, in the heat of the day, when three men suddenly appeared. We are given an incredible scene when Abraham not only offered his three visitors hospitality but also then served them a meal of fresh-baked bread and grilled steaks! While eating, one of the men revealed that he, Abraham, at ninety-nine years of age, and his barren wife, Sarah, at eighty-nine years of age, would have their own son within the year. Abraham knew only the Lord would have such knowledge! The man was the preincarnate Son of God, Jesus Himself, coming to tell Abraham that his long-awaited answer to prayer, the desire of his heart, was soon to come![23] Abraham learned firsthand that God can do the impossible.

Abraham and Sarah did have a son, Isaac, who eventually had two sons, Esau and Jacob. Jacob desperately wanted the birthright that belonged to his brother, Esau, as the firstborn. That birthright included the covenant blessings that God had given to his grandfather Abraham, which had then passed to his father, Isaac. So Jacob conspired to steal the birthright from Esau. With his mother's help, he succeeded. Esau was enraged, forcing Jacob into exile for over twenty years.[24] When Jacob returned to claim the birthright, he proceeded in his own strength and by his own wits. But as he crossed the river that served as a border to the land God had promised Abraham, he was met by a man who would not let him pass. Jacob wrestled with the man. All night. I'm not sure when Jacob realized he was in God's grip, but it may have been when, finally, the man reached down and dislocated Jacob's hip with a touch. Instead of collapsing in a heap of self-pity, Jacob wound his arms around the man's neck and said he would not let Him go until He blessed him. The man did.[25] The Holy Spirit turns over that puzzle piece, and we see the incarnate Son of God refusing to allow us to seize the fullness of God's blessing through our own strength, manipulation, knowledge, effort, or willpower. He breaks us first. Breaks us of our pride, self-reliance, cockiness so we are totally, sincerely, humbly yielded to Him. Jacob was radically changed as a result. Even his name was changed to Israel. His twelve sons became the founding fathers of the nation that bears his name.

Years later Jacob's sons and their families relocated to Egypt during a time of famine. The family remained in Egypt for generations until they grew in such numbers that Pharaoh felt threatened and enslaved them all. As with Hagar,

God heard the Israelites' cries of misery and sent Moses to liberate them. Moses led them out of bondage and into the wilderness where they wandered for forty years.[26] This sets us up for the next puzzle piece that comes to mind.

Joshua had been an aide to the great liberator and lawgiver, Moses. When Moses died, Joshua was called by God to lead the Israelites out of the wilderness and into the land God had promised to give them.[27] But there was one major obstacle to their advance: Jericho. The great enemy fortress was the most impenetrable of all the Canaanite strongholds. Joshua sent in spies to assess the situation.[28] As Joshua set out to walk near the walled city in a reconnaissance mission, he came upon a man with a drawn sword. The man identified Himself as the commander of the Lord's army. He commanded Joshua to take off his sandals because he was standing on holy ground. The man then gave Joshua instructions on how to overcome the enemy stronghold.[29] And the Holy Spirit turns over the puzzle piece to reveal the Commander of God's army, the incarnate Son of God, who still gives His people victory over the enemy today. The victory has nothing to do with military strategy, financial resources, educational degrees, plotting, or planning, and everything to do with obedience to the Word of God, then wrapping the stronghold in prayer and praise.

Years later, when Israel was settled in the land of promise, they seemed to forget the Lord their God, and all the people did what was right in their own eyes. Again and again God used an enemy to turn the people back to Himself. As a result of danger, threats, and oppression, His people would cry to Him for help and He would answer by raising up someone to deliver them. Things would be good for a while; then His people would go right back to their idolatrous, rebellious ways. The next puzzle piece took place during one of those times.

"The Israelites did evil in the eyes of the LORD," and God sent the Midianites to oppress them.[30] For seven long years, the Midianites swarmed over the land at harvesttime, seizing crops and livestock so that nothing was left. Once again, the Israelites cried out to the Lord. In answer to their cry, the angel of the Lord intervened. He sat down under an oak tree and observed a man named Gideon, who was hiding from the enemy in a winepress as he threshed wheat.[31]

The angel of the Lord remarked to Gideon, "The LORD is with you, mighty warrior."[32] Gideon must have looked around, wondering whom the man was talking to. Mighty warrior? He was a terrified farmer. But the Lord was addressing him. Although Gideon's obedience got off to a somewhat shaky start, he followed the clear instructions God gave him. The Midianites were supernaturally defeated and God's people were set free.[33] The Holy Spirit turns over the puzzle piece, and we discover that the incarnate Son of God raises us up to serve Him and to help liberate others based not on who we are but on who we can become when the Lord is with us.

"In the year that King Uzziah died," Isaiah saw the Lord, seated on the throne of Heaven, "high and exalted."[34] The Holy Spirit connects this piece to another one in the New Testament that confirms Isaiah saw the glory of the Lord Jesus Christ.[35] When the puzzle piece is turned over, we, too, see the preincarnate Son of God giving Isaiah a fresh vision of His glory when his world was rocked and his life was shaken. And we are encouraged to look up when our lives are shattered by death, disease, divorce, disappointment, or some other disaster. The Lord God is seated on the throne, in absolute control of everything taking place in the world at large, as well as in our own world.

Ezekiel knew all about disappointment and disaster. He had been studying for the priesthood in Jerusalem when he was captured and enslaved by the Babylonians. Whereas Daniel, who had been captured around the same time, wound up in the king's palace, Ezekiel was discarded. He was a human piece of trash, thrown away to live in a refugee camp located on a garbage dump beside a dirty irrigation canal.[36] Just when he surely thought things couldn't get any worse, a windstorm swept in from the north. As he gazed at the threatening approach of an immense cloud reverberating with thunder and lit by strobes of lightning, he looked closer. He saw in the center of the storm four living creatures with wings outstretched. Above their heads was a throne of sapphire, and high above the throne was "a figure like that of a man."[37] The Holy Spirit turns over another puzzle piece, and we see the incarnate Son of God, who reveals His glory to "throwaways." Because their lives matter to Him. And sometimes

God uses disaster to redirect our course. Ezekiel never did become a priest. Instead, he became one of the major prophets in the Old Testament.

Also during the Babylonian exile, Shadrach, Meshach, and Abednego had a confrontation with the king of Babylon, Nebuchadnezzar, on the plain of Dura. The king had erected a ninety-foot-tall statue of himself made out of gold and demanded that everyone bow down in worship. Of him! When Shadrach, Meshach, and Abednego refused to bow down, they were threatened with execution in a fiery furnace.[38] Their reply to the king demonstrated stunningly courageous faith: "O Nebuchadnezzar, we do not need to defend ourselves before you in this matter. If we are thrown into the blazing furnace, the God we serve is able to save us from it, and he will rescue us from your hand, O king. But even if he does not, we want you to know, O king, that we will not serve your gods or worship the image of gold you have set up."[39] What an amazing, in-your-face answer! They didn't need to discuss the decision among themselves. They knew God could save them. But even if He didn't, they were not going to worship a golden idol.

God did not save Shadrach, Meshach, and Abednego from the fire. The king heated the furnace seven times hotter, then had them thrown into it. But our eyes grow wide with astonishment as we, too, look with the king into the flames and see not three men but four, walking unscathed in the midst of the furnace. And the fourth, the king said, looked like "a son of the gods."[40] The Holy Spirit turns over the puzzle piece, and we see the incarnate Son of "the only God" in the fire with His children. He has promised to be with us when we walk through "the valley of the shadow of death" or when we "walk through the fire." In fact, He has promised never to leave or forsake us.[41]

FOCUSED ON THE CRADLE AND THE CROSS

Perhaps the most astounding puzzle piece of all focuses on a little Judean village. It was a starry night outside Bethlehem. Shepherds were out in the fields, keeping watch over their sheep and sacrificial lambs. Suddenly the inky black sky was split with what must have looked in contrast like a laser beam of light. An angel appeared surrounded by God's glory and, in a voice that has been heard around the world and through the centuries, announced, "Today in the town of David a Savior has been born to you; he is Christ the Lord."[42] They would find Him wrapped in cloths, lying in a manger! In a stable in the nearby town! Before the shepherds could react, the sky was filled with angels, all praising God: "Glory to God in the highest, and on earth peace to men on whom his favor rests."[43]

How long was it before the shepherds took the first step? When they did, they must have raced through the fields, stumbling over rocks, dodging the olive trees, jerking free of brambles, entering Bethlehem, looking into every stable, until they found one that, sure enough, had a newborn baby lying in a manger bed.[44] As we join the shepherds, who must have approached quietly, respectfully, and expectantly to peer at the tiny form, the Holy Spirit turns over the puzzle piece and we find ourselves looking into the face of God! The Messiah. The Lord God. The Son of God, who was no longer preincarnate. The Word that was in the beginning had become flesh! His name? Jesus!

We see Him through the pages of Scripture, growing "in wisdom and stature, and in favor with God and men."[45] We see Him enter the public arena and preach, teach, heal, comfort, and forgive until He became such a threat to the jealous and fiercely territorial religious leaders that they plotted to take His life. We see Him betrayed by one of His own disciples, set up for arrest and trial by the religious leaders, who should have been the first to recognize Him since they knew the Scriptures. In shock we see Him crucified by the Romans in a mockery of justice. And as we stare in horror, we see Him hanging on a cross. But the Holy Spirit turns over the puzzle piece, and we no longer see evil triumphing over good, or hate triumphing over love, or the guilty triumphing over the innocent. We see the Lamb of God intentionally being sacrificed on the altar of the cross to make atonement for the sin of the world.

Take a moment now to just kneel at the cross. Ask the Holy Spirit to turn over this particular puzzle piece for you in a fresh way. Ask Him to reveal to you the enormity of your sin and guilt that must be infinite in its evil in order to demand such a price. The price of the blood of God incarnate.

We see the Lord of life dead, buried in a borrowed tomb. But the puzzle is not yet completed, because three days later we see that same tomb empty! And the Holy Spirit turns over the puzzle piece and reveals to us the risen Lord Jesus Christ. He's alive! Our hearts are thrilled! The disciples . . . the followers of Jesus . . . we . . . the world . . . will never be the same! The sting of death and the victory of the grave have been defeated. We are no longer slaves to fear or guilt or shame or self or the devil. Our sins have been forgiven. Our guilt has been atoned for. We have been reconciled to the Father and have peace with God. We have the sure hope of a heavenly home.

After the Resurrection, we hear the risen Lord Jesus Christ commanding His followers to go into all the world and make more followers by sharing the glorious good news that He saves, He lives, He reigns, and He's coming again![46] We see Him raise His hands in blessing as He ascends back into Heaven.[47] And the Holy Spirit turns over the puzzle piece and shows us that Jesus is *still alive*!

Through His Spirit, He is invisibly present in our world today. Our lives are not about us. Our lives are to be lived for a greater purpose, with greater goals and greater priorities than just the everyday variety. It's all about Jesus! Loving Him and living for Him and obeying Him and serving Him and in the process multiplying ourselves so that the number of His followers is increased.

If we are tempted to disbelieve or doubt the presence of the living, risen Christ enthroned in the glory of Heaven, then the Holy Spirit starts flipping the puzzle pieces, giving us evidence when Stephen, one of the deacons of the early church, was stoned to death. Just before Stephen closed his eyes in death, he saw Heaven open, and Jesus was standing at the right hand of the Father in Heaven.[48] And the Holy Spirit shows us that when we are absent from the body, we are present with the Lord. Immediately.

When Saul of Tarsus, a religious fanatic, was doing all he could to eliminate the followers of Jesus, whom he thought were blasphemous, he saw a brilliant, blinding light while traveling on the Damascus Road. He then heard a voice from Heaven ask why he was persecuting Him. When Saul asked who He was, the response was stunning: "I am Jesus, whom you are persecuting."[49] And Saul of Tarsus, persecutor of Christians, was transformed by his encounter with the ·risen Lord Jesus Christ into the apostle Paul, who proclaimed the gospel all over the known world of his day.[50] And the Holy Spirit shows us that if Saul of Tarsus could be transformed into Paul the apostle, no one is so hostile to Jesus that he or she is beyond God's power to change.

When the disciple whom Jesus loved, John, was exiled to Patmos, a small rocky island in the middle of the Aegean Sea, because of his testimony of faith and the Word of God, he heard a loud voice like a trumpet. When he turned to see who was speaking to him, he saw with his own eyes the risen Lord Jesus Christ in all His glory.[51] And the dark night of John's soul turned to day in the light of the presence of the living, risen Lord Jesus Christ.[52] And the Holy Spirit shows us that when we are in exile . . . cut off . . . isolated . . . confined to a hospital bed, or to a small home with small children, or in an undesirable job, or in a loveless marriage, or to a military barracks . . . Jesus draws near and can turn our night into day.

FOCUSED ON THE CROWN

Perhaps the ultimate puzzle piece is found at the end of the Bible. God's Word clearly states that the armies of the world will gather in Israel on the plain of Armageddon to engage in a final, apocalyptic war.[53] If they were to unleash the ferocity of their firepower, the entire world would be annihilated. But just at the pinnacle of their confrontation,[54] the sky unfolds and a rider on a white horse appears.[55] "His eyes are like blazing fire, and on his head are many crowns. . . . He is dressed in a robe dipped in blood, and his name is the Word of God."[56]

The Holy Spirit turns over the puzzle piece and shows us that the same Word that was in the beginning, who was with God, who is God, and who became flesh and dwelt among us,[57] is the rider on the white horse. Jesus, returning to judge and rule the world with justice and righteousness. Forever and ever and ever! "Hallelujah! For our Lord God Almighty reigns. Let us rejoice and be glad and give him glory!"[58]

How would we know the thrilling end of the story without the Holy Spirit turning over the puzzle pieces and revealing it to us? Praise God that He does! And the Bible no longer seems quite like the puzzle we thought it was, does it?

FOCUSED ON JESUS CHRIST

You and I will not know what the world is coming to unless we read our Bibles. Because the Holy Spirit reveals the living Word of God through the written Word of God. From Genesis to Revelation, He reveals that . . .

underneath everything that's going on in our world . . .

over everything in the universe . . .

and around everything on this planet . . .

through everything as empires rise and fall . . .

at the beginning of everything in human history . . .

and at the end of everything in human history . . .

Jesus Christ reigns supreme!

He is King of kings and Lord of lords.[59] One day every knee will bow to Him, and every tongue will confess that He is Lord, whether willingly or not.[60] He will be absolutely victorious! Triumphant! Undisputed in His power, unequaled in His position, and unsurpassed in praise and adoration.

Jesus is the reason for everything that exists, including you and me. He is our ultimate purpose, our ultimate goal, and our ultimate priority. If your life's purpose, goal, and priorities are about anything less than Jesus only, anything other than Jesus only, anything more than Jesus only, then there is a disconnect between you and the Holy Spirit. Because, remember, the Holy Spirit's ultimate purpose is to glorify Jesus, His ultimate goal is to make Jesus known to you and to me, and His priority is to guide us into all truth as He transforms us into the image of Jesus.

So stay focused. Stop looking all around and comparing yourself with others. Stop looking back at what might have, could have, should have been. Stop rolling your eyes in cynical doubt or confusion. Ask the Holy Spirit to guide you into all truth. Get to know Jesus so you will love Jesus and trust Jesus and obey Jesus and serve Jesus and bring glory to Jesus.

If, at the end of this book, that is your commitment, live it out by opening your Bible *and reading it,* listening for the Spirit's gentle whispers! Let Him turn over the puzzle pieces for you. He will. I know. Because He has turned over the puzzle pieces for me, revealing He is my constant companion—Jesus in me.

APPENDIXES

Learning How to Hear the Holy Spirit's Whispers When You Read Your Bible

As I have grown older, I'm embarrassed to confess that I seem to be getting harder of hearing. I have had the awkward experience of conversing with people, seeing their mouths move, yet not really being able to hear what they were saying. This is especially true if someone speaks softly.

I used to have a similar experience when I read my Bible. I have always loved reading it, but I didn't always "hear" God speaking to me. It's as though I knew His mouth was moving—He was saying something because the words were on the page—but I couldn't really hear what He was saying. That changed when I started applying a simple form of meditation to my Bible reading. It has transformed not only my daily time with the Lord but even my life, as I am now able to hear when He speaks softly in His gentle whispers.

Each morning, I set aside time to read my Bible. I do so in a designated chair beside a table on which I keep a pair of glasses, pen, pencil, notebook, and tissues so I don't have to waste valuable time running around looking for any of those items. The passage of Scripture that I read is not a randomly selected portion of God's Word; instead, it's a book of the Bible that I have felt God leading me to work through from beginning to end.[1] But my aim is not to get through the book. My aim is to hear the Spirit's whispers as I read. So I don't tackle an entire chapter each morning, as that would become a time-consuming burden. I focus on just one paragraph of verses. The next morning, I pick up where I left off and meditate on the paragraph that follows the one I worked through the previous morning. As I write this, I'm reading the gospel of John, from beginning to end, paragraph by paragraph, chapter by chapter.

As I read the paragraph of verses, I ask four questions of the text.

The first is, *What does God's Word say?* To answer this question, I reread the verses, then list in my notebook the outstanding facts that I find in them. I do not paraphrase, which would be to put words in God's mouth. I just omit some of the "extra" words or descriptions, like adjectives and prepositional phrases, then focus especially on nouns and verbs as I pinpoint exactly what the facts are.

The second question is, *What does God's Word mean?* To answer this I go back to my list of facts and try to learn something from each one. I look for a command to obey, a promise to claim, or a warning to heed. I also look to see what the people are doing or saying that I should also do or say . . . or that I shouldn't do or say. Then I write down the lessons in my notebook verse by verse.

The third question is, *What does God's Word mean in my life?* This is where so often I begin to hear the Spirit's whisper. Because the answer to this question is found when I go back to the lessons I've written down and rewrite them in the form of questions I would ask myself or someone else. It's amazing to me that as I'm writing out the questions, I often hear the Spirit whispering His comfort, instruction, warning, encouragement, or answers to my private prayers. This doesn't happen every morning, but it does happen more mornings than not.

The fourth question is, *What is my takeaway?* I write down whatever God seems to have said to me to make sure that I am applying what He has said, then live it out. I date it to hold myself accountable to follow through in obedience. Then I conclude in prayer as I talk to the Lord about what I've just read.

In my private devotions, I am in the gospel of John. I have drawn from it for the following example in order to lead you through this exercise.

Step 1: Read God's Word Look at the passage	Step 2: What Does God's Word Say? List the facts
Read John 1:35–39	*Since facts are facts, and if we are using the same translation of the Bible, then our lists will be similar. You may have more facts, and I may have fewer facts, or vice versa. The important thing is that we do not paraphrase but use the actual words of the passage itself. Having reread John 1:35–39 the following are the facts I pulled out:*
v. 35 The next day John was there again with two of his disciples.	v. 35 The next day John was again with his disciples.
v. 36 When he saw Jesus passing by, he said, "Look, the Lamb of God!"	v. 36 When he saw Jesus, he said, "Look, the Lamb of God!"
v. 37 When the two disciples heard him say this, they followed Jesus.	v. 37 When the disciples heard, they followed Jesus.
v. 38 Turning around, Jesus saw them following and asked, "What do you want?" They said, "Rabbi" (which means Teacher), "where are you staying?"	v. 38 Turning, Jesus saw them following. Jesus asked, "What do you want?" They said, "Where are You staying?"
v. 39 "Come," he replied, "and you will see." So, they went and saw where he was staying, and spent that day with him. It was about the tenth hour.	v. 39 "Come," He replied, "and see." They went and spent that day with Him.

Step 3: What Does God's Word Mean? Learn the lessons	Step 4: What Does God's Word Mean in My Life? Listen to His whispers
The following lessons are ones I have extracted from each of the facts on the previous page in answer to the above question:	*As I rewrite the lessons in the form of questions that I ask myself, I listen carefully for the Spirit's whisper:*
v. 35 Discipleship is a longer commitment than just one day.	v. 35 Having read this book, am I willing to choose be a disciple?
v. 36 A true man or woman of God points others to Jesus.	v. 36 At the end of this book, have I heard the whisper of the Spirit pointing me to Jesus?
v.37 We may need to separate from someone we love and respect in order to choose to follow Jesus for ourselves.	v. 37 Am I willing now to follow Jesus for myself, even if it means separation from others?
v. 38 When we choose to follow Jesus, we discover we have His undivided attention. Jesus challenges us to tell Him what we want. Those who want to follow Jesus desire to be where He is that they might know Him better.	v. 38 If I have chosen to follow Jesus, am I aware He is giving me His full attention? Why do I want to follow Him? Do I really want to be where Jesus is—to spend time daily in His presence so that I might know Him better?
v. 39 Jesus invites us to get to know Him. It's our choice to spend time with Jesus. *There can be multiple lessons from one fact depending on your perspective. The above is just a sampling. The same is true when we rewrite the lessons into questions. There is no limit to what you can come up with.*	v. 39 Will I accept Jesus's invitation to "come"—to get to know Him better? If so, what part of this day…and every day…will I carve out in order to spend time with Jesus, asking the Spirit of Truth to guide me?

```
┌─────────────────────────────────────────────────────────────┐
│                  Step 5: What Is My Takeaway?                 │
│                      Live out God's Word                      │
├─────────────────────────────────────────────────────────────┤
│  The last step in this exercise is to write down what I'm     │
│  going to do about what the Spirit seems to have whispered    │
│  from John 1:35–39 in order to hold myself accountable.       │
│                                                               │
│  Example:                                                     │
│  I want to be a Jesus follower, so I choose to spend time     │
│  with Him each day through prayer and meditating on His       │
│  Word, asking the Holy Spirit to take from what is His and    │
│  make it known to me in order to get to know Jesus for        │
│  myself...then make Him known to others.                      │
├─────────────────────────────────────────────────────────────┤
│  Date:                                                        │
│                                                               │
└─────────────────────────────────────────────────────────────┘
```

This exercise is simple but challenging in that it requires you and me to think for ourselves. It effectively removes the "middleman" and allows us to hear directly from the Spirit through God's Word. Don't be intimidated. Some days I have a hard time getting the lessons from the facts, and some days it seems easier. And the Spirit doesn't seem to whisper to me every day. But meditating on His Word as I listen for His voice has transformed the time I spend with Him.

If you need further help, please visit my website: www.annegrahamlotz.org. We have free worksheets, Bible studies, and videos, all for the purpose of helping you read your Bible so that you, too, can hear the Spirit's whispers. But remember, Jesus said, "The Holy Spirit . . . will teach you all things and will remind you of everything I have said to you."[2] So before you read your Bible, pray and ask Him to teach you through it. He's eager to get started.

Appendix B

Learning How to Be Filled—and Stay Filled—with the Holy Spirit

The family home of my childhood is located in a cove that is accessed by a narrow drive that winds around the mountainside. Almost three-quarters of the way to the house, the drive takes a sharp right-angled turn. A mountain spring is located at this bend in the road. When I was young, the spring flowed across the drive, and in the winter when the temperature dropped, the water would freeze and form a serious hazard to anyone trying to drive up or down. So my mother took an old wooden bucket and placed it at the base of the spring. She then drove one end of a pipe into the spring itself, with the other end of the pipe protruding over the bucket. Sure enough! The water from the spring flowed through the pipe and into the bucket. When the bucket filled with water, instead of flowing across the drive, it overflowed into a ditch beside the road, and the hazard was removed.

From time to time we would find the pipe dry as water once again seeped through the ground and flowed across the drive. When that happened, Mother would take a straight stick and run it through the pipe to remove whatever was clogging it. Sometimes it was a rotten leaf, sometimes it was a slippery salamander, and sometimes it was a small, hard pebble. As soon as she dislodged and removed whatever it was, the water once again began to flow through the pipe, into the bucket, then into the roadside ditch.

If we use Mother's creative solution to the ice hazard as a spiritual illustration, the water is like the power and presence of the Holy Spirit, the pipe is His access to us, and the bucket represents our lives that should be overflowing with Him as a blessing to others. But sometimes His access is hindered. We seem to dry up and fall into our old ways. When that happens, we need to take the "stick" of the cross and apply it to the Spirit's access. Maybe His flow is clogged by a rotten leaf—something from the past like a failure or a disappointment. Or maybe the Spirit's access is blocked by a slippery salamander—a sinful habit that seems to elude our effort to change or a memory that pops up in the middle of the night. Maybe the obstruction is a hardened pebble of unforgiveness, bitterness, resentment, or anger.

Whatever it is, bring it to the cross. Ask the Holy Spirit, "Search me, O God, and know my heart; test me and know my anxious thoughts. See if there is any offensive way in me, and lead me in the way everlasting"[1]—the way that leads to the foot of the cross. He will show you what the blockage is. Then you need to choose to remove it.

To be filled with the Holy Spirit is not mystical or emotional. It's not reserved for an exclusive group of people. It is actually a command that we are to obey: "Be filled with the Spirit."[2] And because commands are obeyable, they involve decisions we intentionally make with our wills. Think about it. If obedience depended on our emotions or feelings, we could never consistently be obedient since we can't control our emotions. So obedience rests strictly on the intentional choice we make to follow through on whatever God has said. Being filled with the Spirit is not an option or an exception.

To obey the command to be filled with the Spirit, choose to bring your sin to the Cross, then take whatever action is necessary to remove it. The Holy Spirit will empower you to make this decision and follow through.

My prayer for you is that, as a result of reading this book, you will make the choice to be filled with the Holy Spirit, if you have not already done so. The necessary actions involve simple disciplines in the Christian life. While much of the following has been covered in this book, it bears repeating here to give you the opportunity to apply what you have read. Follow me as together we walk through these simple steps. Please consider each question, carefully look up each scripture, and sincerely ask God to fill you with His Spirit, who, as you now know, is Jesus . . . in you.

1. A Heart Where He Dwells

Since the Holy Spirit is Jesus living inside you, take a moment to examine your heart. Does the Holy Spirit truly live within you? At what point in time can you remember inviting Jesus, with your conscious mind, to come into your heart? If you cannot remember a time when you deliberately issued that invitation, how can you be sure He lives within you? Let's make sure together.

NOTE: If you are certain without any doubt that your heart is one in which Jesus dwells, then skip the following steps and begin the exercise with section 2, "A Heart That He Fills." But before you do, take a moment to thank God for the priceless provision of His Spirit.

Because you cannot be filled with the Holy Spirit until He dwells in your heart, it's very important to make sure that He lives within you. I know you won't misunderstand. To invite Jesus into your heart is the *same thing* as inviting the Holy Spirit into your heart.

If you have any doubt whatsoever that Jesus, in the person of the Holy Spirit, lives within you, then take a few minutes right now to make sure that He does by humbly coming to God in prayer:

- Acknowledge that you are a sinner (Romans 3:23).
- Confess specific sins that come to your mind (1 John 1:9). Make sure that you don't rationalize the sin by the label you give it. Name it for what it is in God's eyes.

- Repent of your sin, which means to stop sinning in your actions and to change your mind about it in your attitude as you turn away from it (Luke 13:5; Acts 3:19).
- Ask God to cleanse and forgive you (Ephesians 1:7; 1 John 1:7).
- Invite Jesus, in the person of the Holy Spirit, to come into your life (Luke 11:13; John 1:12; Revelation 3:20).
- Surrender the control of your life to Him as your Lord (Acts 2:36).
- To help you with the deep, blessed assurance that Jesus now lives within you in the person of the Holy Spirit, tell someone of the decision you have made, then publicly declare your decision through baptism (Acts 2:37–39; Romans 10:9–10).

Once you have prayerfully, sincerely gone through these steps, take a few moments to rejoice! Praise God! Based on what He has said in His Word, your sins—all of them—are now forgiven! You have established a personal, right relationship with Him. You have received eternal life, which means you have entered into a personal relationship with God the Father, God the Son, and God the Holy Spirit, as you are now a member of His family. A heavenly home is your birthright. And Jesus now lives inside you in the person of the Holy Spirit.

If you doubt any part of this, go back and reread the Scripture references once again—and again if necessary—until you claim by faith what God has said. Jesus accepts your invitation when you issue it by faith in what God has said, holding God to His own Word, claiming His promises for yourself. It's critical that your faith is based not on what I or anyone else has said or written but on what God Himself has said. He keeps His Word. You can count on His Word because it is backed by the integrity of His own character. What's more, once you belong to Him, He will never leave you and never forsake you regardless of what you do or someone else does or says! (Romans 8:35, 37–39; Hebrews 13:5–6).

The Holy Spirit—Jesus inside you—is also God's pledge or guarantee that He will keep all His promises because He is permanently, personally, passionately committed to you! You now bear His seal of ownership (Ephesians 1:13).

2. A HEART THAT HE FILLS

If you are indwelt by the Holy Spirit because you have been born again into the family of God by faith in Jesus, then are you filled with His Holy Spirit? As we have discovered in this book, the Holy Spirit living inside you is not the same thing as the Holy Spirit filling your life. I shared with you the analogy that while I may invite you to come into my home, I may allow you only restricted access. You may come into my living room or kitchen or some other more public room but not into my messy laundry room or my private bedroom and bath or the neglected upstairs. In other words, it's possible for you to be invited into my home without having access to every room.

Likewise, it's possible to invite the Holy Spirit into your life, fully intending to give Him access to everything, but then when He enters areas you want to keep hidden or keep under your own control, you bar the door. You refuse to surrender that habit, relationship, pleasure, memory, goal, or method for fear that if you do, the change He will bring about will be less than what you want for yourself. The trade-off is that when you restrict His access in your life, you give up being filled with the Spirit and you deny yourself access to all His spiritual blessings, including His power and eternal purpose for your life.

I'm going to assume that because you are still reading this, you want to be filled with the Holy Spirit. You want to give Him unrestricted access to every nook and cranny, every dark recess, every relationship, every attitude, every dream, every action in your life. You deeply desire to place everything under His authority, then live out that surrender moment by moment in a life that overflows with Jesus. I do too!

The following steps to being filled with the Holy Spirit are simple but not necessarily easy.

Confess all known sin to God.

- Ask God to bring to your conscious mind those sins you need to confess to Him (1 John 1:9).

- Don't worry about the sins you are not aware of. It may help you to list your sins as they come to mind (1 Corinthians 6:9–11, 18–20; Galatians 5:19–21; Ephesians 4:29–32; James 2:10; 4:17).
- Read the list of sins in appendix C of this book in order to sharpen your focus and clear away any remaining cobwebs of denial, rationalization, excuses, defensiveness, or pride that may lurk in your heart.

Repent of your sin.

Repentance means to repudiate sin, stop it, and turn away from it. Is there a sinful attitude or action you need to stop? Or a habit you need to break? Or a relationship you need to forsake? Name it, reject it, and turn away from it (2 Corinthians 6:14–18; Ephesians 4:17–28; Colossians 3:5–10).

Get right with others.

Choose right now to name the person with whom you have a severed relationship, confess honestly anything you contributed to the wounding, and set it right to the best of your ability—now. Place a phone call or write an email or text. Just reach out and offer the person forgiveness or ask that person to forgive you (Matthew 5:23–24; Hebrews 12:15).

Destroy any idols in your life.

An idol is anything that you put before God. It can be your child or your desire for a child, your spouse or your desire for a spouse, your career, your goals, your friends, your image, your reputation, your money, your entertainment, your pleasures, your eating or dieting, your health or your healing, your exercise or your laziness, your church or your ministry, your position, your home, your material possessions, sex, technology, web surfing, texting, social media. An idol is anything that preoccupies your thoughts to the extent God is shut out or relegated to the leftovers of your mind or your time or your money or your affection. Whatever the idol is, destroy it! (Exodus 20:3–4; 1 John 5:21).

Intentionally, humbly, and sincerely surrender all that you are and have to God.

Open every door, every room, every closet, every dark recess of your heart and life to the Holy Spirit. If there is anything you are still clinging to and refusing to surrender, let it go now. Think carefully.

- Give God first place in your priorities (Matthew 6:33).
- Give God first place in your time (Psalm 63:6).
- Give God first place in your thoughts (Joshua 1:8).
- Give God first place in your heart (Deuteronomy 6:5–6).

The following words of an old hymn penned by J. Edwin Orr may help you articulate your prayer:

Search me, O God, and know my heart today;
　Try me, O Savior, know my thoughts, I pray;
See if there be some wicked way in me;
　Cleanse me from every sin, and set me free.

I praise Thee, Lord, for cleansing me from sin;
　Fulfill Thy Word, and make me pure within;
Fill me with fire, where once I burned with shame;
　Grant my desire to magnify Thy name.

O Holy Ghost, revival comes from Thee;
　Send a revival—start the work in me;
Thy Word declares Thou wilt supply our need;
　For blessings now, O Lord, I humbly plead.[3]

Ask God to fill you with His Spirit.

When you have surrendered everything to God as far as you know and understand, ask Him now to fill you with His Spirit (Galatians 2:20).

Believe by faith that you are now filled with His Spirit and thank Him.
When you finish your prayer, having completed the previous steps, you can assume, by faith that you are now filled with the Holy Spirit! Take a moment to thank Him!

For some, the filling of the Holy Spirit is a crisis-type experience that can be triggered by great pressure or problems. For others, it is more of a growth process, without crisis.

For some, the filling of the Holy Spirit is accompanied by emotion, while for others it is simply a series of deep, daily, earnest choices without emotion.

For some, the filling of the Holy Spirit can be more overwhelming than their conversion. For others, it is simply the quiet awareness that God is in complete control.

I've already noted that people in Scripture were described by others as being filled with the Holy Spirit, but people didn't make this claim about themselves (Luke 1:15, 41, 67; Acts 4:8, 31). Don't get caught up in feelings or comparisons with others.

Walk in the Spirit.
You are now ready to begin the process of walking in the Spirit as you live, surrendered moment by moment to His moment-by-moment control (Romans 8:1–16; Galatians 5:25; 1 John 1:7; 2:6).

Don't be discouraged.
As you live out your Christian life, you will still continue to sin, although a Spirit-filled person does not sin willfully or consciously (1 John 3:6).

But Spirit-filled people do sin! Our sin may be disobedience or neglect or an attitude or a habit we struggle to overcome. But any and all sin grieves or quenches the Holy Spirit, who lives within us (Ephesians 4:30). As soon as you sin, you are no longer filled with Him.

When this happens, as it will . . .

Return to the Cross.
When you become aware that you have sinned and therefore grieved the Holy Spirit, repeat the previous steps. Do not feel embarrassed or ashamed to return to the Cross and ask God for cleansing and refilling.

The Bible records not just one but many fillings of the Holy Spirit in the lives of the apostles.[4] Remember, the Christian life is a journey, step by step, day by day. Growth into maturity takes time. There are no shortcuts. Increasingly, as you follow these steps, they will become a habit. You will more quickly recognize your sin, return to the Cross, and receive cleansing and refilling.

Pray with me now:

Dear Spirit of Jesus,
When You first hovered over chaos, order came to birth, beauty robed the world, fruitfulness sprang forth.
I have learned so much about You that I long to be filled with You until I overflow. You who proceed from the Father and the Son, look on me and have mercy.
Please, move, I pray, upon my disordered heart;
Take away the infirmities of unruly desires and hateful lusts;
Lift the mists and darkness of unbelief;
Brighten my soul with the pure light of truth;
Fulfill in me the glory of Your divine offices;
Be my helper, comforter, advocate, intercessor, counselor, strengthener, and standby.
Take the things of Jesus and show them to my soul;
Through You may I daily learn more of His love, grace, compassion, faithfulness, beauty;
Lead me to the cross and show me His wounds, the hateful nature of evil, the power of Satan;
May I there see my sins as . . .

the nails that transfixed Him,
the cords that bound Him,
the thorns that tore Him,
the sword that pierced Him.
Help me find in His death the reality and immensity of His love.

Increase my faith in the clear knowledge of atonement achieved,
guilt done away, my debt paid, my sins forgiven, my person redeemed,
my soul saved, hell vanquished, Heaven opened, and eternity made
mine.

Make me a pure vessel. A clean temple. A polished living stone
that reflects His purity and glory.

O Holy Spirit, deepen in me these saving lessons.

Write them upon my heart that my walk would be sin loathing,
sin fleeing, Christ exalting, glory giving,[5] until all see Jesus overflow-
ing in me. And until You rejoice as the universe erupts in applause for
the One who alone is worthy of all praise and honor and glory and
power forever and ever!

For the glory of His great name—Jesus.

Amen.

Appendix C

A Self-Examination
of Personal Sin

Below is the list of sins that triggered my own repentance and experience of personal revival several years ago. The booklet from which it is taken included more explanation for most of these sins.[1] I have simply listed them. The author did say to read the list through prayerfully three times.

- ingratitude
- lack of love for God
- neglect of Bible reading
- instances of unbelief
- neglect of prayer
- neglect of spiritual disciplines
- a poor attitude when performing spiritual duties
- lack of love for the souls of others
- lack of concern for unreached people
- neglect of family duties
- neglect of watchfulness over my own life
- neglect of watching over my brothers and sisters in Christ
- neglect of self-denial
- worldly mindedness

- pride
- envy
- a critical spirit
- slander
- lack of seriousness
- lying
- cheating
- hypocrisy
- robbing God
- bad temper
- hindering others from being useful

For a similar list with more explanation, please see my own list as published in *Expecting to See Jesus*.[2] And remember, "If we claim to be without sin, we deceive ourselves and the truth is not in us. If we confess our sins, he is faithful and just and will forgive us our sins and purify us from all unrighteousness. If we claim we have not sinned, we make him out to be a liar and his word has no place in our lives."[3]

Appendix D

Gifts of the Spirit

In chapter 18 we considered the Holy Spirit's equipping of the believer, which includes spiritual gifts. The gifts are supernatural and given to us by the sovereign choice of the Holy Spirit. They are not natural talents.

There are three categories: motivational gifts, manifestation gifts, and ministry gifts.

MOTIVATIONAL GIFTS

The following is the list Paul gave to the Roman believers, along with my understanding of each gift's description and the characteristics of the person who possesses it.[1] They have been described as motivational gifts because they tend to dominate our perspective on life, decision-making, friendships, and our relationship with God.

Prophecy is the ability to give out God's Word in a relevant way to the hearers. In the Old Testament God's prophets were responsible for receiving a message from God and then relaying it to God's people. The message they were given often involved foretelling the future. To be deemed authentic divine messengers, they were required to be 100 percent accurate 100 percent of the time. Anything less was an offense that carried with it the death penalty.[2]

Today a person who has the gift of prophecy is still responsible for receiving a message from God and relaying it to God's people. But the message is based on the revelation God has given in the Bible. A person who has this gift is not satisfied to just present the truth of God's Word in an academic fashion but seeks to apply the truth to the lives of others and persuade them to receive and live by it. This person feels compelled to express thoughts about what is right and wrong and is willing to suffer for faithfully speaking the truth. People with this gift have a keen ability to discern the motives of others. They can be painfully direct, make quick judgments, and are open and honest about their own weaknesses. A biblical example of someone who possessed this gift is the apostle Peter.[3]

Ministry is what we sometimes call a gift of service or helps. A person with this gift is content to work behind the scenes doing practical things and is delighted to apply this gifting to free others to exercise their own giftings. A biblical example is Timothy, the apostle Paul's "son in the faith,"[4] pastor of the Ephesian church, and superintendent of some of the churches in Asia.[5]

Teaching is a gift that thrives on searching out and validating truth. A teacher is more academically minded than the prophet and is satisfied to present truth, not necessarily to get it across to others. This person loves to study, dissect Scripture, and present truth in a systematic order. A person with this gift emphasizes facts and details and may challenge the credentials of a pastor or Bible teacher. Luke would be a good example of a biblical teacher.[6]

Exhortation is a gift of encouragement. A person who possesses this gift stimulates others to walk more closely with Jesus. This person is good at one-on-one ministry and can visualize another person's potential. And rather than be discouraged by personal tribulation, this person sees it as a means of spiritual growth. The apostle Paul would be the best biblical example of someone with this gift.[7]

Giving is an unusual gift that has nothing to do with financial status. This person lives to give, not accumulate. People with this gift provide for the needs of others with joy but do so privately, not publicly. While they are usually thrifty and frugal in their personal lives, they give generously, even sacrificially, to meet the needs of others. The Macedonian believers had this gift.[8]

Administration or ruling is a gift of organization. People who have this gift are leaders, delegators, coordinators, or facilitators who can keep an entire operation on track. They are self-starters with the ability to take a large task and break it into smaller pieces that others can carry out. They never seem to be overwhelmed by the size of the challenge before them. They are thick skinned, know what should and should not be delegated, and demand loyalty from those under them. In the Old Testament Nehemiah was a gifted administrator.[9]

Mercy is the ability to empathize with the need, pain, or heartache of others. People with this gift are great at healing relationships and bringing restoration. They are attracted to the distressed. They tend to lack firmness because they don't want to cause more hurt. They desire physical closeness and quality time, sensitive to the emotional needs of others. The apostle John would seem to exemplify someone who has this gift.[10]

What difference does knowing and operating according to your gifting make? Let's consider this question in the context of the local church. What if the person with a gift of mercy were put in charge of the budget? It would soon be in the red because few who asked for help would be refused. Or what if the prophet were put in charge of visitation? We can almost hear the angry shouts as people would slam the doors of their homes to the visiting team, offended by the bluntness of the prophet. Or if the person with the gift of encouragement or exhortation were put in charge of evangelism? I doubt many would be told they needed to renounce their sin.

Instead, it stands to reason that a person with the gift of prophecy would serve as the pastor; a person with the gift of ministry would serve as the office manager or be placed in charge of community outreach; teachers would be at the lecterns of the Sunday school classrooms; exhorters would be small-group leaders; givers would handle the treasury; an administrator would be the executive pastor or director of education; and those with the gift of mercy would be placed on hospital visitation. Paul wrote specifically that these gifts are given for the common good.[11] They are not toys to be played with but tools to be used for blessing and building up others in their faith.

Manifestation Gifts

Manifestation gifts of the Spirit are given for the edification of others to the glory of God.[12] While each believer has one dominant motivational gift, a person can have multiple manifestation gifts. These work with the motivational gift to create an infinite variety of combinations that make each person's gifting unique. We are told to seek these gifts,[13] yet that does not necessarily mean we will receive them. Once again, "all these are the work of one and the same Spirit, and he gives them to each one, just as he determines."[14]

Word of Wisdom

This is a gift of understanding God's revealed truth. I have observed this gift most clearly in third-world countries where God's people have not had access to Bible schools and theological seminaries. One of my first commitments when I left teaching my weekly Bible class was to a pastors' conference in Suva, Fiji. I had been asked to give several messages to about six hundred pastors who had come in from the hundreds of surrounding islands. While I was humbled and honored to do so, I asked the organizers whether I could also be given a women's meeting. I was told that, in that culture, women did not gather for separate meetings. When I asked them to try to arrange one anyway, they agreed. The result was a small women's meeting in the back storeroom of the facility where the men's meetings were taking place.

There were no chairs, so the women sat on boxes arranged in a semicircle. They were barefoot, and most had walked for miles to attend the meeting. To this day I can see their beautiful round faces, sparkling dark eyes, heads crowned with brown hair as they looked at me expectantly. They clutched tattered Bibles on their laps. As I opened my Bible and taught them, then threw open the meeting for back-and-forth discussion, their insights were mind blowing! I could hardly take in the depth of their knowledge and understanding. I knew what I was witnessing was a manifestation of the Holy Spirit's equipping of these women to understand spiritual things at a level even some of my friends back home would have difficulty grasping. It was the Holy Spirit's supernatural equipping of God's children.

Word of Knowledge

This gift involves ordinary truth that is supernaturally revealed. Its most effective use seems to be for insight in how to pray. My daughter Rachel-Ruth has this gift.

Several years ago I was in a cabin at the Billy Graham Training Center at The Cove, preparing to lead my fall seminar. I stepped outside the cabin to take a walk, realized I did not have my cell phone in my pocket, so I stepped back into the cabin to get it. When I stepped back outside, I saw movement in the woods below the cabin. As I focused on the disturbance, I saw a black bear walking through the trees. Fascinated, I continued to watch until I realized he was coming straight for the cabin! I quickly turned around, went back inside, then watched in consternation as the bear, who seemed somewhat sickly, staggered up onto the cabin porch, tore up the pillow I had just been sitting on, turned over my glass of ice tea, reared up on his hind legs to stare at me through the window, then circled the cabin two more times before ambling off into the woods!

When Rachel-Ruth called that night to check on me, I told her what had happened. She asked me what time the bear had been there, so I told her it was late morning—the very time she had been on her knees in prayer with eight other ladies. She said she had felt led to pray out loud for my protection from bears. When she finished praying, the other ladies chuckled at her strange request. But no one was laughing the next time they met when she related to them what had happened. I know if I had not gone back into the cabin to retrieve my cell phone, I would have quickly walked away from the cabin—and right into that bear.

The insight Rachel-Ruth received was a manifestation of the Spirit's word of knowledge. I've also experienced, from time to time, random people coming up to me after I have spoken or catching me while I'm out in public, who say they have a word of knowledge for me. They seem to be sincere, well meaning, and I usually make the time to let them share what's on their hearts. Following the encounter, I take to the Lord in prayer what the person said, and leave it there. I know if the word of knowledge is from Him, it will come to pass. I have never acted on what someone has told me. I simply tuck it away for the encouragement, warning, preparation, or confirmation that it may be.

Faith

This refers not to saving faith but to trusting God against enormous odds. This gift is most obvious when it is exercised by church planters and missionaries, although laypeople can possess it also. One of my favorite examples is that of Matt and Misty Hedspeth. Matt came from a fine family in our city, gave his heart to Jesus while in college before he began a real-estate development business. Soon after, he married Misty, who began practicing family law, and they seemed headed for a typical southern, good-life type of future.

Matt loved to surf, scuba dive, and engage in other water sports, so he and Misty decided to vacation in Panama. But that's where their lives were invaded by God. Instead of kicking back and enjoying leisure activities, they were gripped by the thousands of orphans and homeless children that seemed to be everywhere, children with no hope and no future.

As a result, Matt and Misty felt called to Panama. Misty went to work to change the adoption laws in the nation—and succeeded! Matt used his real-estate development background to build orphanages and most recently completed Panama's first temporary home and therapy center for special-needs orphans, Casa Providencia.[15] Their ministry also provides adoption and foster-care services, legal counsel, psychological assessments, and education—at no charge! They are surely exhibit A of the gift of faith.

Another example is Wes and Vicky Bentley. In 1999 they had a vision to train chaplains for the South Sudanese army. So far Wes has trained over four hundred chaplains. The former deputy governor of South Kordofan, Abdel Aziz, has stated that the chaplains are the best men in his army. The Islamic enemy forces know them to be fearless. The jihadists call them "the army of God that is not afraid to die for their faith."

While Wes has trained chaplains, Vicky has founded a missionary-aviation ministry as well as ministries that provide discipleship and literacy training for women and basic needs for children. Their organization, Far Reaching Ministries, has a Bible college in Kenya as well as outreaches in South Sudan, Uganda, the Congo, Mauritius, South Africa, France, Ireland, Russia, Asia, and the United States.[16]

How I praise God for Wes and Vicki Bentley, and Matt and Misty Hedspeth. They have been and are faithful to exercise the gift of faith to the glory of God. And I praise God for the thousands of other missionaries and ministry leaders who are exercising their gift of faith as they take the gospel to the four corners of the globe, caring for the least of these in the name of the Lord Jesus Christ.

Healing

Praise God! He still heals today physically, emotionally, mentally, and spiritually. Joe's story, which I shared earlier, is evidence of multiple facets of healing. But another example I will never forget involved my youngest granddaughter, Anne Riggin. I had invited a counselor into our family to help us talk through multiple issues. He was kind, wise, gifted, and amazingly helpful. He was also a healer. After a couple of days, he had accomplished all he felt he could at that time. Promising to return several months later, he gathered his things to leave. Anne Riggin, about age six at the time, ran over to me and tugged at my hand. "But, Mimi. He hasn't prayed for my warts." She had patches of warts on her legs, torso, and hands. I looked at the intensity of her little expression and her eagerness to be helped. I caught him as he was literally walking out the door and asked whether he would pray for her to be healed of her warts. He stopped right where he was, put his things down, and called her to him. She walked over to him and he took both of her hands in his. Looking her right in the eye, he asked whether she believed Jesus could heal her. She nodded with a child's simplicity. "Yes." So he prayed. Then he left. The next day, every single wart was gone! And they have never returned!

While Anne Riggin's healing may seem small in comparison with other experiences, it was nonetheless a manifestation of the Spirit's gift.

Sometimes God heals as He did for Riggin, in answer to believing prayer. Sometimes He uses doctors and nurses to bring it about as He did when my husband's dialysis port became infected with MRSA. The looks on the faces of the medical personnel as they put my severely diabetic husband in quarantine had me in tears. I knew they were giving him a very small chance to recover. I sent an email to one of his men's Bible studies, described what we were facing, and asked for prayer. The email went viral. Messages began pouring in from all over the world as people began praying. And my husband miraculously recovered! While I know God used doctors, nurses, a wound VAC, intravenous antibiotics, and meticulous cleansing and care, I also know God healed my husband.

Miracles

A miracle is something that takes place in the physical world that has no natural or human explanation. God is a God of miracles, because He is not bound by conventional means or ordinary methods.

While I was writing this appendix, a friend called to tell me about something that had happened recently in a Bible study she leads. The group was watching a video on the topic of prayer when an elderly lady sitting at the same table with my friend collapsed. The woman's eyes had rolled back, the color had drained from her face, and she was perfectly still. My friend immediately laid hands on the woman and prayed, boldly defying death by commanding, "Not today." The request went out for any doctors or nurses in the Bible study to help, while a 911 call was made. A nurse came forward who said she worked in the hospital ICU. When the nurse checked the woman, she could not find a pulse. As women in the Bible class gathered around and continued to pray, the paramedics arrived. The woman opened her eyes and asked, "What happened? Did I faint?" She was then taken to the hospital, where she was given a clean bill of health. She followed up with her own doctor who said he could find nothing that could have triggered such a collapse. Two weeks later she was back in the Bible study to give testimony to the power of prayer! That was undoubtedly a miracle!

In my own life I've witnessed miracles, most often in answer to prayer rather than as a result of an individual's gifting. A very personal miracle that I will never forget involved the beautiful Tiffany diamond that Danny had given me as an engagement ring. I was traveling at the time, and although I never took off my wedding band, I took off my diamond ring before I went to bed in an airport hotel. The next morning when I went to put it on, I couldn't find it. I searched everywhere, even calling in the head of housekeeping to help me look. But the ring was nowhere to be found.

I knew if I didn't catch the shuttle, I would miss my flight, so with a truly broken heart, I left the hotel. When the shuttle deposited me at the airport check-in curb, I tripped. My pocketbook fell over upside down, spilling the entire contents on the sidewalk. I almost wept while I picked everything up with shaking hands and deposited the contents back in my bag, then carefully zipped it all the way shut. As I stood in line at the airline check-in counter, I silently prayed, *"Father, You know how precious that ring is and all that it represents. If You could put a coin in a fish's mouth for Peter to pay taxes with,"*[17] *You can bring me my ring. Please return it to me.*

When it was my turn to check in, I reached for my ticket while placing my pocketbook on the counter. To my stunned amazement, my engagement ring was sitting on top of my pocketbook! That was a miracle![18]

Prophecy

As with the motivational gift, this gift is the ability to give out God's Word in a relevant way to the hearers. I experienced its manifestation during my father's funeral service.

I had been advised to prepare well in advance for any remarks I might be asked to give at my father's memorial service, but for the life of me, I could not come up with anything. I trusted that God would give me what He wanted me to say, if and when the time came.

That time did come, when my father went to Heaven on February 21, 2018. His death set in motion an entire series of events that ran almost 24-7 until his funeral service on March 2.

Each of my four siblings and I had agreed to briefly share personal remarks at the noontime service, and God had used a friend to plant a seed of thought in my mind the day after Daddy went to Heaven. But in the days that followed, I literally had had no time at all to prepare. While I was waiting to ride in the first of several motorcades the day of the service, the Spirit seemed to speak to me in a gentle whisper, letting me know how I could flesh out the thought that had already been given to me. But with the busy schedule before the funeral, I had no set-aside time to craft a message.

One hour before the service began, I was so overcome by the fear of standing up to speak at my father's funeral when I had nothing prepared to say that I put my head down on a table, closed my eyes, and thought I would pass out. I couldn't even pray.

About thirty minutes before the service was to begin, I was called to stand by Daddy's casket and wait with my siblings to greet the president and first lady, and the vice president and his wife. When they entered the main lobby of the library, greetings were given, and then the four of them walked to the tent. My siblings and I followed with Daddy leading the way. After special music, my aunt, my two sisters, and my youngest brother and I were escorted to the platform to await our turn to speak. I had not one moment to even collect my thoughts.

We went in birth order, which meant I would be the third to speak, following my aunt and my older sister. And this is when the miracle occurred. When I stood at the podium, all the fear, dizziness, and grief fell away. What was left was a clarity of thought and a prophetic message that I knew, even as I heard my own words pouring forth, was a manifestation of a gift of the Spirit. To this day, I'm not sure whether it was the gift of miracles or healing or prophecy. I know only that it was the Spirit's supernatural equipping of God's feeble child for that moment. I believe my father was honored, Jesus was exalted, and God was glorified as His Word went forth to the entire world through television, livestream, and social media.

Distinguishing Between Good and Evil Spirits

Several years ago I was invited to speak to pastors and ministry leaders in Uganda. The first commitment took me to Gulu, an area that had been dominated for years by satanic rituals, human sacrifice, and witch doctors. About forty minutes into the first session, I felt myself getting dizzy, then collapsed. The organizers gathered around, put their hands on me, and prayed against the spiritual forces that had come against me. I went back to the platform and finished out the day with great victory. But I will never forget the sound of the military jets that buzzed the roof of the pavilion we were in as I spoke, attempting to scare all of us. Or the huge vultures that circled in the sky, swooping over the courtyard where hundreds of people had gathered for lunch—birds that I was told could eat and digest a car engine. While I didn't see the evil spirits, I knew they were all around.

At times I have entered a store and felt my spirit clash with the atmosphere—and I've walked out. I have talked with spiritual leaders, looked into their eyes, and known I was seeing unloving spirits. How I pray for greater discernment for myself, my children, and my grandchildren during these wicked days when truth is exchanged for a lie, light is marginalized by the darkness, and sin is applauded while purity is vilified. Demons seem to be unleashed, as they know their time is short to wreak as much havoc and destruction as they possibly can.

Tongues

This unknown prayer language seems to be a source of division within the Christian community. Rather than build up and edify the body of Christ, it seems to set us against one another. Those who have this gift are so blessed by it, they sometimes think everyone should have it. Those who don't have it sometimes are made to feel less spiritual than those who do. As a result, the Holy Spirit Himself has been considered a dangerous, dividing force within some Christian circles. God must weep.

I do not have the gift of tongues. But I have seen it used in powerful ways to bring healing and restoration to broken people. Years ago our city was blessed to have Nicky and Gloria Cruz move to town. Nicky had been a notorious gang leader from the streets of Brooklyn. He was deemed hopeless by the authorities. One day he was in the audience when a country preacher, David Wilkerson, shared the gospel. Not long after, he was gloriously converted.

When Nicky moved to our city, I was invited to a coffee hosted in his honor, along with several prominent women from our city, including the governor's wife. Nicky shared that his dream was to open a halfway home for girls—a place where they could receive counseling, love, and a second chance at life when leaving prison. The meeting resulted in separate teams of women taking on the responsibility to fix up various portions of the house so that no one bore the burden of the entire project. As a result, the Nicky Cruz Girls' Home on Hillsborough Street became a reality.

And this was where I witnessed a valid use of the gift of tongues. The young women who came into the home desperately needed a manifestation of the Spirit to set them free from drugs, alcohol, sex, and so many of the addictions that had landed them in their helpless state. Most of them, as soon as they repented of their sin and received Jesus as Savior and Lord, began to pray in tongues. For some reason, being able to pray in this way seemed to be a higher high than any drug they had been on, and God used it to help set them free! The prayer language seemed to jump-start their faith. One after another, the home graduated girls who went on to lead productive lives.

Interpretation

When exercised, the gift of interpreting the unknown prayer language of tongues becomes more like prophecy. The Bible gives strict instruction that if the gift of tongues is exercised in public, as in a church setting, then it is to be followed immediately by someone who can clearly state what was just prayed.[19] While I don't have personal experience with this gift, I have been in meetings where people prayed in tongues with no interpretation, and the result was chaotic. Not only was it *not* a blessing; it was also not edifying to the general congregation and was very unsettling to others. On the other hand, I was recently in a meeting where an elderly woman prayed in tongues, then interpreted herself phrase by phrase. It was very dramatic and very meaningful.

I also know of a dear young friend who was visiting with a person who began to speak to him in Hebrew. When the person asked my friend what he had said, my friend interpreted it verbatim. He had never studied Hebrew. He had never been around anyone who spoke Hebrew. Yet he knew exactly what had been said. This gift is most likely the one that was exercised at Pentecost when "a crowd came together in bewilderment, because each one heard them speaking in his own language."[20]

I share these stories because you and I can't put God in a box. His ways are not our ways. He operates in the here and now, but He also operates outside time and space.

Ministry Gifts

The third category of spiritual gifts is more of a list of ministry positions within the church. They are introduced by the apostle Paul to the Ephesian church,[21] as having been given "to prepare God's people for works of service, so that the body of Christ may be built up until we all reach unity in the faith and in the knowledge of the Son of God and become mature, attaining to the whole measure of the fullness of Christ."[22]

The first one listed is that of *apostles*. In the primary sense of the word, this position is no longer active since one of the requirements for an apostle is that he had to have met the risen Lord Jesus Christ in person.[23] But in a secondary sense, one could use the word *apostle* to describe those whom God uses to break ground for fresh ministry, such as church planters and missionaries.

Second, *prophets* are listed. These are not necessarily people who foretell the future but those who are Bible expositors and who give out God's Word in a relevant way.

Third, *evangelists* are gifted at sharing the gospel in such a way that people are stirred in their hearts, are convicted of their sin, and respond by receiving Jesus Christ as Savior and Lord.

Fourth, *pastors* are shepherds of God's people who lead local congregations, making sure the people are fed God's Word, protected from heresies, and brought back if they wander away from the faith. They warn, guide, and counsel.

Last, there are *teachers* or instructors, men and women who present and preserve the truth of God's Word that has been handed down generation after generation.

EMBRACE AND EXERCISE YOUR GIFTS

Discovering your spiritual gifts is not optional. Each of us will be held accountable by God for exercising the ones we've been given as we build up our Christian family. The solemn thought shared with me by one of my mentors is this: When I stand before Jesus face to face and see the scars on His brow where the thorns were and the wounds in His hands and feet where the nails were—when for the first time I fully comprehend what it cost Him to open Heaven for me—I know I will want to give Him something in return. And while nothing I could ever give Him would be sufficient to repay what He has done for me, a crown that has been given me in reward for a life lived for Him on earth would be something. On that day, will I have a crown to lay at His nail-pierced feet?

The choices you and I make today will determine how our lives are viewed when we meet Jesus face to face. Please. Embrace fully the Holy Spirit's gifting, then exercise your gifts in service to Him so that on that day you will not be empty handed but will have something to lay at the feet of Jesus in return for all He has given you.

With Gratitude to My Families

The first person I would like to acknowledge with a heart overflowing with gratitude is the Holy Spirit. I could never have written this book, much less met on time all the deadlines associated with it, if I had not had His help. He has comforted, strengthened, encouraged, and inspired me—especially when during the process of writing, my adored father went to Heaven and I began my cancer journey.

One way the Holy Spirit helped me practically was to place me in families . . .

My Publishing Family

Since this is the first book I have written in partnership with my new publishing house, Multnomah, I would like to acknowledge the team that has believed in me, come alongside to guide me, supported and encouraged me during this difficult year.

I met my new publisher, **Tina Constable,** at an ECPA Awards banquet. The buzz around the room was not who would win Book of the Year but the considerable honor of having Tina Constable in attendance. I was a little intimidated to meet her, but from our first meeting, I found her to be a kindred spirit. She loves God's Word and has thrown her impressive publishing muscle behind *Jesus in Me.*

Laura Barker has been my editor, exercising her exceptional skills with patience, gentleness, and excellence. This book is much better because of her touch.

Donald Fairbairn gave a detailed, thorough theological review of the first draft. His insights and perspective were invaluable. As a result of his effort, the reader can trust the factual and biblical accuracy in this book.

Ginia Hairston Croker laid out for our publishing team an incredibly detailed, thorough marketing plan that was not only uplifting in its scope and vision but gave evidence that she shared my heart to help people experience the Holy Spirit as a constant companion.

Bev Rykerd fleshed out Ginia's marketing plan with an extensive, intense publicity campaign that was thrilling! She thought of every opportunity, from every angle, to help promote the message that we have not been abandoned by Jesus. To the contrary, He will never leave us nor forsake us because He has come to live within us in the person of the Holy Spirit.

Helen Macdonald took the edited manuscript and shepherded it through the production process. She was attentive to deadlines while being respectful, kind, and understanding.

Kristopher Orr graciously inquired whether or not I had any ideas for the cover design of this book. I had no ideas. How do you picture the Holy Spirit . . . *Jesus in Me*? When Kristopher first submitted his idea, I knew he had visually captured something that is actually invisible . . . the glory of God on the inside of ordinary people. The cover is a bold, striking, elegant interpretation of the title.

And lastly, **Bryan Norman** expertly guided me during the transition from Zondervan Publishing to Multnomah and continues to oversee my publishing efforts with creative, prayerful energy.

My Ministry Family

My nonprofit ministry, AnGeL Ministries, is like a special-ops team. We are small but laser focused on getting people into God's Word that they might know Him in a personal relationship through faith in Jesus. While I could not function effectively in ministry without the 24-7 help of **Helen George**, my executive assistant for over forty years, the director of operations, **Ross Rhudy**, shouldered much of my organizational ministry responsibilities. He oversees my ministry staff of fourteen people, two prayer teams, and dozens of volunteers. While writing this book I was sidelined from active ministry not only by hours spent at the computer but also by grief and cancer, yet under Ross's servant leadership, AnGeL Ministries continued to function smoothly and with excellence.

My Church Family

When I was first diagnosed with cancer, God seemed to promise me through James 5:16 that I would be healed through the prayers of others. I took Him at His Word, publicized my condition, then was totally unprepared for the continuous tsunami of prayer on my behalf! My church family includes thousands of people worldwide who have been faithful to track with me on this journey, bearing me up on the wings of their prayers. I have no doubt that my increasing restoration to health, as well as this book, give evidence to a prayer-hearing, prayer-answering God.

My Personal Family

I have three children: **Jonathan** and his wife, Jenny; **Morrow** and her husband, Traynor; **Rachel-Ruth** and her husband, Steven. Jonathan came frequently to take care of the "honey-do" list—everything from changing light bulbs to cleaning out the garage. Morrow did the grocery shopping, cooking, and upkeep of my medical appointments and tests. Rachel-Ruth led my weekly prayer team of seven spiritually powerful women, inspiring them with insights into Scripture, while keeping everyone laughing with her zany sense of humor. And the prayers of all three of them brought Heaven down and raised me up during the most difficult days. I could not have endured as triumphantly as I have, nor met the deadlines for this book, without their practical, physical, emotional, and spiritual help.

My three granddaughters, **Bell**, **Sophia**, and **Riggin**, kept a smile on my face and joy in my heart with their presence and their prayers.

> For this reason I kneel before the Father, from whom his whole
> family . . . derives its name. I pray that out of his glorious riches he
> may strengthen you with power through his Spirit in your inner
> being, so that Christ may dwell in your hearts through faith . . .
> that you may be filled to the measure of all the fullness of God.
>
> EPHESIANS 3:14–17, 19

Notes

*Introduction: Experiencing
the Holy Spirit as a Constant
Companion*
1. John 14:16.

*Part 1: Loving the Person
of the Holy Spirit*
1. John 16:7–14. The number of
   pronouns used for the Holy Spirit
   occurs in the 1978 version of the
   New International Version of the
   Bible. This number may vary
   according to different
   translations.
2. The dramatic story of Jacob's
   name change is found in Genesis
   32.
3. Matthew 1:21.

Chapter 1: Our Helper
1. Hebrews 13:6.

Chapter 2: Our Comforter
1. Numbers 6:24–26.
2. 2 Corinthians 1:4.
3. John 20:11–14.

Chapter 3: Our Advocate
1. In the years that followed,
   Danny helped establish a growing church, where once again he
   chaired the board of elders and
   taught the largest adult Sunday
   school class. In time, he helped
   plant two other churches that are
   thriving today.
2. Genesis 39:1–23; 41:1–44.
3. Nehemiah 1:1–2:12; 6:15–16.
4. Esther 5:1–9:16.
5. Acts 13:13.
6. Acts 15:39.
7. 2 Timothy 4:11.
8. John 14:16, NLT.

Chapter 4: Our Intercessor
1. The story is true, but the names
   have been changed to protect the
   privacy of those involved.
2. Psalm 139:23–24.
3. I have written more about
   lessons I have learned on my
   healing journey in *Wounded by
   God's People: Discovering How
   God's Love Heals Our Hearts*
   (Grand Rapids, MI: Zondervan,
   2013).

Chapter 5: Our Counselor
1. 2 Chronicles 1:10.
2. 2 Chronicles 1:1–12.
3. Psalm 23:4.
4. Psalm 31:15; Job 14:5.
5. Proverbs 3:5–6.
6. James 1:5.

Chapter 6: Our Strengthener
1. 2 Corinthians 12:10.
2. Genesis 37.
3. Genesis 39.
4. Psalm 105:18, YLT.
5. Genesis 41.
6. Jeremiah 1:18–19.
7. Isaiah 41:10–12.
8. Revelation 3:7–13.
9. Daniel 9:4–19.

Chapter 7: Our Standby
1. Each one of these examples comes from my own extended family.
2. Mark 6:45–48.
3. Mark 6:48.

Part 2: Enjoying the Presence of the Holy Spirit
1. John 14:16–17.
2. John 14:26.

Chapter 8: His Presence in Eternity
1. "Apollo 8: Christmas at the Moon," NASA, December 19, 2014, www.nasa.gov/topics /history/features/apollo_8.html.
2. Psalm 139:7.
3. Matthew 28:19.
4. 1 Peter 1:2.
5. The symbol of the dove at the baptism of Jesus has often led to the misconception that the Holy Spirit is a dove. In the same way, the flames that rested on the

heads of disciples at Pentecost cause some people to mistakenly believe that the Holy Spirit is a fire. But the Holy Spirit is a spirit. He does not have a visible form. So in Scripture symbols are often used to indicate His presence. See Genesis 15:17; Zechariah 4:1–6; Acts 2:3–4; Revelation 4:5.
6. Matthew 3:16–17.
7. You can explore further the topic of the Trinity in the book *Life in the Trinity* by Dr. Donald Fairbairn, the theological reviewer of this book. He also recommends *Delighting in the Trinity* by Michael Reeves and *The Deep Things of God* by Fred Sanders.
8. "Apollo 8's Christmas Eve 1968 Message," December 24, 1968, video, 2:01, May 19, 2013, www .youtube.com/watch?v=ToH hQUhdyBY.

Chapter 9: His Presence in History
1. In chapter 18 we will explore ways the indwelling Holy Spirit equips believers today.
2. Exodus 31:3; 35:31.
3. Numbers 11:16–17.
4. Judges 6:33–35.
5. Judges 14:5–6.
6. 1 Chronicles 28:11–12.
7. Isaiah 61:1.
8. Ezekiel 3:10–15.

9. 1 Samuel 10:10.
10. 1 Samuel 15:1–9.
11. 1 Samuel 16:13–14.
12. 1 Samuel 16:14; 17:4–53; 18:6–7; 31:1–4.
13. 1 Samuel 16:13.
14. 2 Samuel 23.
15. 1 Samuel 13:14.
16. Psalm 19:1; 23:1; 27:1; 34:18; 31:1–2.
17. Matthew 1:1; Luke 1:32–33.
18. 2 Samuel 11.
19. Psalm 32:3–4.
20. 2 Samuel 12:1–12.
21. 2 Samuel 12:13.
22. Psalm 51:3–4.
23. 1 John 1:9.
24. Psalm 51:17.
25. John 13:3–30; 14:2–6; 15:1–25.
26. John 14:18; 16:7.
27. John 20:22; Acts 1:4, 8.
28. Acts 1:14.
29. Acts 2:1–4.
30. Acts 2:7–8, 12.
31. Acts 2:14–33.
32. Acts 2:33.
33. Matthew 27:22–23.
34. Luke 23:34; Acts 2:23, 36
35. Acts 2:36.
36. Acts 2:38.
37. Psalm 51:17.
38. Matthew 1:21.

Chapter 10: His Presence in Humanity

1. Genesis 3:21.
2. Leviticus 17:11; Hebrews 9:22.
3. "The Precious Blood," in *The Valley of Vision*, ed. Arthur Bennett (Edinburgh: Banner of Truth, 1975), 74.
4. Leviticus 4:4, 14, 22–23, 27–28, 32–35; 5:7, 11. The sin offering varied from a bull to a goat to a lamb or to a dove for the very poor. But the principle was the same for each: the sinner was required to place his hands on the offering, confess his sin, and kill the animal and, then the priest would sprinkle the blood on the altar to make atonement for the person's sin.
5. Hebrews 10:4.
6. John 1:29.
7. Ephesians 1:7; 1 John 3:1; 5:11.
8. John 1:46.
9. Luke 1:28–29.
10. Luke 1:30–33.
11. Luke 1:34.
12. Luke 1:35, 37.
13. Luke 1:38.
14. Romans 3:23; 6:23; John 3:16; Ephesians 1:7; 1 John 1:9; John 17:1–3; 1:12; Ephesians 1:13–14; John 3:3–6.
15. Titus 3:4–7.
16. 2 Corinthians 5:17.
17. Romans 10:9–10.
18. Ephesians 1:13–14.
19. John 14:16–17; Hebrews 13:5.
20. The doorbell rang at two in the morning, during a major thunderstorm when I was by myself.

While it was very unsettling, I was not afraid because I knew I was not really alone. I threw on my robe and found a police officer standing at the front door who said that his dispatcher had received a 911 call from my house and that he had been sent to check on me. I reassured him I was fine, then reported the error to the telephone company. Apparently in the storm, wires had been crossed and my phone was repeatedly dialing 911 in error.

Chapter 11: His Power to Transform

1. Genesis 1:3.
2. Genesis 1:26–27.
3. Genesis 1:31.
4. John 1:41.
5. John 1:42.
6. Luke 5:5.
7. Luke 5:1–11.
8. Matthew 16:15.
9. Matthew 16:16.
10. Matthew 16:17.
11. Matthew 16:22.
12. Matthew 16:23; see also Revelation 2:18.
13. Matthew 26:31–35.
14. Matthew 26:69–75.
15. Matthew 14:25–30.
16. Matthew 17:1–5.
17. Mark 14:38.
18. Acts 2:14–41.

19. Acts 3:6.
20. Acts 3:12.
21. Acts 4:8–10, 12.
22. Acts 4:19–20.
23. Acts 4:31.

Chapter 12: His Power to Transform You and Me

1. Alan Redpath, *The Making of a Man of God: Lessons from the Life of David* (Grand Rapids, MI: Revell, 2007), 9.
2. Acts 2:4; 4:8, 31.
3. Ephesians 5:18.
4. We will discuss in more detail what it means to grieve the Holy Spirit in part 7 of this book.
5. Acts 2:4; 4:8, 31; 13:9, 52.
6. 2 Corinthians 3:18.
7. Judson W. Van DeVenter, "I Surrender All," 1896, public domain.
8. At the end of this book, you will find an exercise designed to lead you through the biblical steps to being filled with the Holy Spirit.
9. John 1:16; Romans 8:28–29.

Chapter 13: His Power to Transform Others

1. Deuteronomy 6:4.
2. John 3:16.
3. John 16:8, 13.
4. John 3:3.
5. Zechariah 4:6.
6. Ephesians 3:16–19.

Part 4: Embracing the Purpose of the Holy Spirit

1. To those who disagree because you know people who are unbelievers who seem very happy and satisfied, all I can say is that the happiness and satisfaction they experience is a smaller, limited version of what they would have if they were in a personal, right relationship with the One for whom they were created.
2. 2 Corinthians 3:18.

Chapter 14: He Quickens Us

1. There is a time yet to come when the Holy Spirit also will quicken our dead bodies and raise us up into physical life (Romans 8:11).
2. Ephesians 2:1–10, kjv.
3. John 6:63, kjv.
4. 2 Chronicles 20:7; Isaiah 41:8; James 2:23.
5. Hebrews 13:8.
6. For more details about my journey and Abraham's life, see *The Magnificent Obsession: Embracing the God-Filled Life* (Grand Rapids, MI: Zondervan, 2009).
7. Matthew 5:16.
8. Ephesians 2:10.
9. Luke 7:36–50.
10. Romans 5:5.
11. Philippians 2:13.
12. Matthew 13:52.

Chapter 15: He Guides Us

1. *The Shorter Catechism of the Westminster Assembly of Divines* (London: 1647), 1.
2. John 17:4.
3. John 4:4.
4. John 4:28–29.
5. John 4:32.
6. John 4:34.
7. Isaiah 50:7.
8. Romans 5:10.
9. John 19:30.
10. Hebrews 12:2.
11. John 16:13.

Chapter 16: He Ignites Us

1. While I can't find a source for this "tradition," the point the story makes is valid.
2. Genesis 15:17–18; Exodus 3:1–2; Deuteronomy 5:1–5; Acts 2:1–4; Revelation 4:5.
3. 1 Thessalonians 5:19.
4. 2 Timothy 1:6.
5. Hebrews 10:25.
6. Hebrews 12:2.
7. L. B. Cowman, August 7, in *Streams in the Desert,* ed. James Reimann, rev. ed. (Grand Rapids, MI: Zondervan, 1997), 303.

Chapter 17: He Shapes Us

1. Jeremiah 18:2.
2. Jeremiah 18:3–6.
3. Romans 9:19–21; 2 Corinthians 4:7; 2 Timothy 2:20–21.

4. Romans 8:29; 2 Corinthians 3:17–18.
5. Romans 8:28.
6. Romans 8:28.
7. Romans 8:29.
8. 2 Corinthians 4:7.

Chapter 18: He Equips Us
1. Philippians 4:13.
2. Colossians 1:11.
3. 2 Corinthians 12:9.
4. 1 Corinthians 12:11.
5. 1 Corinthians 12:7.

Part 5: Living by the Precepts of the Holy Spirit
1. I did not recommend Ayn Rand's books to my children. Or to anyone else. But they were interesting reading at the time.
2. God's Word is different from every other book I've ever read. It's different from any other book ever written. The Bible includes sixty-six books written by approximately forty authors over a span of about fifteen hundred years. It continues to be the bestselling book of all time, with sales estimated to be over five billion copies. At last count, the complete Bible is available in over 680 languages. See Brian H. Edwards, "Why 66?," in *The New Answers Book 2: Over 30 Questions on Creation/Evolution and the Bible,* ed. Ken Ham

(Green Forest, AR: Master Books, 2008), 169; "Best-Selling Book of Non-Fiction," Guinness World Records, www.guinness worldrecords.com/world-records /best-selling-book-of-non-fiction; "Scripture and Language Statistics 2018," Wycliffe Global Alliance, www.wycliffe.net /statistics.

Chapter 19: His Precepts Are True
1. John 14:17.
2. 2 Peter 1:20–21.
3. 2 Samuel 23:2.
4. Jeremiah 1:7, 9.
5. Ezekiel 3:24, 27.
6. John 14:26.
7. John 16:13.
8. John 16:13.
9. Genesis 3:1.
10. This imaginary conversation is in Anne Graham Lotz, *God's Story* (Nashville: Thomas Nelson, 2009), 63.
11. Matthew 5:18.
12. Matthew 24:35.
13. Matthew 12:40; 19:4; 24:37–39.
14. Matthew 18:1–4; Mark 10:13–16; Luke 18:15–17.
15. 2 Timothy 3:16.

Chapter 20: His Precepts Are Trustworthy
1. Exodus 20:3–17.
2. 2 Timothy 3:16.

3. L. B. Cowman, "October 8," in *Streams in the Desert* (Grand Rapids, MI: Zondervan, 1996), 298.
4. John 16:32.
5. Hosea 2:18, KJV.
6. Job 42:12, KJV.
7. Zechariah 10:12, NKJV.
8. 2 Kings 5:10.
9. 2 Kings 5:11–12.
10. 2 Kings 5:13–14.
11. Isaiah 30:18, KJV.

Chapter 21: His Purity Is Exemplified in Jesus
1. Genesis 6–7.
2. Genesis 19:1–28.
3. Exodus 3:1–6.
4. Exodus 7:14–12:30.
5. Exodus 19:1–24.
6. Exodus 26:30–35; 28:31–38.
7. Joshua 5:13–15.
8. 1 Peter 1:15–16.
9. Acts 4:31.
10. Acts 5:4.
11. Acts 5:11.
12. Hebrews 4:15.
13. 1 Peter 1:18–19.
14. John 12:41.
15. Isaiah 6:1–3.
16. Isaiah 6:5.
17. John 14:26.

Chapter 22: His Purity Is Beautified in Us
1. Matthew 21:1–11.
2. Zechariah 9:9.

3. Luke 19:46; see also Matthew 21:1–17; Mark 11:1–17; Luke 19:28–46; John 12:12–15.
4. 1 Timothy 4:1–2.
5. Charles G. Finney, *How to Experience Revival* (New Kensington, PA: Whitaker, 1984), 19–27.
6. Isaiah 6:3.
7. Matthew 7:1–5.
8. Joel 2:13.
9. Ephesians 1:7.
10. 1 John 1:9.
11. 1 John 1:7.
12. Psalm 56:8; John 11:35.
13. Hebrews 4:15.
14. 2 Corinthians 5:21.
15. 2 Corinthians 5:17.
16. Acts 3:19.

Chapter 23: His Purity Is Magnified in Us
1. 1 Kings 8:27–30; 9:3.
2. 1 Corinthians 6:19–20.
3. 2 Corinthians 6:16.
4. Ephesians 2:19–22.
5. 1 Peter 2:5.
6. 1 Peter 2:4–8.
7. Isaiah 6:3; Revelation 5:11–13.
8. Ephesians 1:11–12.
9. 1 John 1:9.
10. Ezekiel 34:31.
11. Isaiah 53:6.
12. 1 Corinthians 14:8.
13. Galatians 5:16–21.
14. Isaiah 42:8.
15. Hosea 14:2.

16. Hosea 14:4.
17. Revelation 15:3–4.
18. Ephesians 1:6, KJV.
19. 2 Samuel 11:1–12:13; Psalm 32:3–5.
20. Psalm 32:11.
21. Revelation 5:9–10.
22. Revelation 5:12.
23. Revelation 5:11–13.
24. Revelation 19:6–7.
25. Psalm 22:3, KJV.
26. We couldn't give names for some of the letters, like X, Y, and Z, so we shifted to adjectives.
27. Horatio G. Spafford, "It Is Well with My Soul," 1873, public domain.

Part 7: Trusting in the Providence of the Holy Spirit
1. Ephesians 4:30.
2. 1 Peter 5:7.
3. Romans 8:28.

Chapter 24: Trust in His Pledge
1. My wedding band remained on my finger for fifty-two years . . . until my breast cancer surgery when the surgeon demanded I take it off. So, with tears streaming down my cheeks, I removed it for the first time since Danny had placed it on my finger. As soon as surgery was over, I put my rings back on. But about two months later, chemotherapy made my hands swell so badly I had to take all my rings off once again.
2. John 14:2–3.
3. Jonathan Cahn, *The Book of Mysteries* (Lake Mary, FL: FrontLine, 2016), 220.
4. *Encyclopaedia Britannica,* s.v. "Shavuot," www.britannica.com /topic/Shavuot.

Chapter 25: Trust in His Seal
1. Ephesians 1:13.
2. 2 Timothy 2:19.
3. Matthew 24:30–31; 1 Thessalonians 4:16–17.
4. Romans 8:35.
5. John 10:28–29.
6. Romans 8:38–39.

Chapter 26: Trust in His Understanding
1. My desire to know God in the kind of relationship I had witnessed in my mother's life is described in my book *The Magnificent Obsession: Embracing the God-Filled Life* (Grand Rapids, MI: Zondervan, 2009).
2. Psalm 139:1–2, 4, 7.
3. Romans 8:26–27.

Chapter 27: Trust in His Prayers
1. Romans 8:26.
2. Luke 22:17–24.
3. Luke 22:31–32.

4. Greg's story can be found in his book *Jesus Revolution: How God Transformed an Unlikely Generation and How He Can Do It Again Today* (Grand Rapids, MI: Baker Books, 2018).
5. John 17:20–21, 26.
6. John 17:2.
7. John 6:51; 14:16; Romans 8:37–39; 1 Thessalonians 4:17; 1 John 2:17.
8. John 17:3.
9. Genesis 4:1, NKJV.
10. John 16:14.
11. John 17:11.
12. John 18:8.
13. John 17:13.
14. John 17:15.
15. Ephesians 6:11, 13–14.
16. John 17:17.
17. John 17:17–19.
18. John 17:19.
19. John 17:21.
20. 1 John 1:9.
21. John 17:23.
22. John 17:24.
23. 1 Corinthians 2:9–10.

Conclusion: Jesus: The Unwavering Focus of the Holy Spirit
1. 2 Timothy 3:16.
2. John 1:14, NKJV.
3. John 1:18.
4. Do you remember where Jesus performed His first miracle when He began His public ministry on earth? It was at the wedding feast in Cana. It was to benefit and bless a young couple's marriage. Jesus prepared our first home in Eden, He is preparing our last home in Heaven, and He will also help make your home today into a place of blessing, love, and joy. He can still turn water into wine. Make Him Lord of your marriage, do whatever He says, and watch Him perform a miracle.
5. John 14:2.
6. Genesis 2:7.
7. Genesis 2:18, 21–22.
8. Colossians 1:15–17.
9. Genesis 3:8–9.
10. Genesis 3:10–19.
11. Genesis 3:21.
12. Genesis 4:1–16.
13. Genesis 6:6.
14. Genesis 6:8–9.
15. Genesis 6:13.
16. Genesis 6:14.
17. Acts 4:12.
18. Genesis 7:6–23.
19. Genesis 12:1–3; 15:4.
20. Genesis 16:1–12.
21. Genesis 16:13.
22. For more on Hagar's moving story, read Anne Graham Lotz, *Wounded by God's People: Discovering How God's Love Heals Our Hearts* (Grand Rapids, MI: Zondervan, 2013).
23. Genesis 18:1–14.

24. Genesis 27:1–31:55.
25. Genesis 32:22–32.
26. Genesis 46:5–6; 47:4; Exodus 1:7–11; 3:7–10; 12:31–41; Numbers 14:33–34.
27. Joshua 1:1–2.
28. Joshua 2.
29. Joshua 5:13–6:5.
30. Judges 6:1.
31. Judges 6:3–11.
32. Judges 6:12.
33. Judges 7:1–8:12.
34. Isaiah 6:1.
35. John 12:41.
36. Ezekiel 1:1–3.
37. Ezekiel 1:4–26.
38. Daniel 3:1–15.
39. Daniel 3:16–18.
40. Daniel 3:25.
41. Psalm 23:4; Isaiah 43:2; Hebrews 13:5.
42. Luke 2:11.
43. Luke 2:14.
44. Luke 2:8–16.
45. Luke 2:52.
46. Matthew 28:18–20.
47. Luke 24:50–51.
48. Acts 6:5; 7:55–60.
49. Acts 9:5.
50. Acts 9:1–19.
51. Revelation 1:9–16.
52. For more on John's incredible vision, read Anne Graham Lotz, *The Vision of His Glory: Finding Hope Through the Revelation of Jesus Christ* (Dallas: Word, 1996).
53. Revelation 16:16.
54. Zechariah 14:1–11.
55. Revelation 19:11.
56. Revelation 19:12–13.
57. John 1:1, 14.
58. Revelation 19:6–7.
59. Revelation 19:16.
60. Philippians 2:9–11.

Appendix A: Learning How to Hear the Holy Spirit's Whispers When You Read Your Bible

1. From time to time I feel led to make an exception and turn to a psalm. If so, after meditating on the psalm for as many days as it takes to work through it paragraph by paragraph, I return to where I left off in the book and then I continue meditating paragraph by paragraph and chapter by chapter.
2. John 14:26.

Appendix B: Learning How to Be Filled—and Stay Filled—with the Holy Spirit

1. Psalm 139:23–24.
2. Ephesians 5:18.
3. J. Edwin Orr, "Cleanse Me," 1936, public domain.
4. Acts 2:4; 4:8, 31; 13:9, 52.
5. Adapted from "The Spirit's Work," in *The Valley of Vision,* ed. Arthur Bennett (Edinburgh: Banner of Truth, 1975), 56–57.

Appendix C: A Self-Examination of Personal Sin

1. Charles G. Finney, *How to Experience Revival* (New Kensington, PA: Whitaker, 1984), 19–27.
2. Anne Graham Lotz, *Expecting to See Jesus: A Wake-Up Call for God's People* (Grand Rapids, MI: Zondervan, 2011), 146–48.
3. 1 John 1:8–10.

Appendix D: Gifts of the Spirit

1. Romans 12:6–8.
2. Deuteronomy 18:14–22.
3. For an example of Peter exercising his gift of prophecy, see Acts 2:14–40.
4. 1 Timothy 1:2.
5. For an example of Timothy exercising his gift of ministry, see 1 Corinthians 4:17; Philippians 2:19–23.
6. For an example of Luke exercising his gift of teaching, see Acts 1:1–2.
7. For an example of Paul exercising his gift of exhortation, see Philippians 4:4–9.
8. For an example of the Macedonian church exercising this gift of giving, see 2 Corinthians 8:1–5.
9. For an example of Nehemiah exercising his gift of administration, see Nehemiah 2:1–9.
10. For an example of John exercising his gift of mercy, see 1 John 2:1–2.
11. 1 Corinthians 12:7.
12. 1 Corinthians 12:7–10.
13. 1 Corinthians 14:1.
14. 1 Corinthians 12:11.
15. Please visit Matt and Misty Hedspeth's ministry website to learn more: www.heartscrychildren.com.
16. Please visit Wes and Vicky Bentley's ministry website to learn more: https://frmusa.org.
17. Matthew 17:24–27.
18. When I arrived home, I went straight to the jeweler and had my ring sized so tight I can get it off only with a lot of soap and effort. The only times I have removed it since have been for surgeries. Otherwise I never take it off, even to this day, three years after Danny has gone to Heaven.
19. 1 Corinthians 14:27–28.
20. Acts 2:6.
21. Ephesians 4:11.
22. Ephesians 4:12–13.
23. 1 Corinthians 9:1.

About the Author

Called "the best preacher in the family" by her late father, Billy Graham, Anne Graham Lotz speaks around the globe with the wisdom and authority of years spent studying God's Word.

The *New York Times* named Anne one of the five most influential evangelists of her generation. Her Just Give Me Jesus revivals have been held in more than thirty cities in twelve countries, with hundreds of thousands of attendees.

Anne is a bestselling and award-winning author of eighteen books. She is the president of AnGeL Ministries in Raleigh, North Carolina, and served as chairman of the National Day of Prayer Task Force from 2016 to 2017.

Whether a delegate to the World Economic Forum's annual meeting, a commentator in the *Washington Post*, or a groundbreaking speaker on platforms throughout the world, Anne's aim is clear: to bring revival to the hearts of God's people. And her message is consistent: calling people into a personal relationship with God through His Word.

ANNE GRAHAM LOTZ

AnGeL MINISTRIES

5115 Hollyridge Drive
Raleigh, NC 27612-3111
(919) 787-6606
info@AnneGrahamLotz.org

STEPS TO PEACE WITH GOD

1. RECOGNIZE GOD'S PLAN—PEACE AND LIFE

The message in this book stresses that God loves you and wants you to experience His peace and life.

The BIBLE says, "For God so loved the world that He gave His only begotten Son, that whoever believes in Him should not perish but have everlasting life." *John 3:16, NKJV*

2. REALIZE OUR PROBLEM—SEPARATION FROM GOD

People choose to disobey God and go their own way. This results in separation from God.

The BIBLE says, "For all have sinned and fall short of the glory of God." *Romans 3:23, NKJV*

3. RESPOND TO GOD'S REMEDY—THE CROSS OF CHRIST

God sent His Son to bridge the gap. Christ did this by paying the penalty of our sins when He died on the cross and rose from the grave.

The BIBLE says, "But God shows his love for us in that while we were still sinners, Christ died for us." *Romans 5:8, ESV*

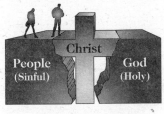

4. RECEIVE GOD'S SON—LORD AND SAVIOR

You cross the bridge into God's family when you ask Christ to come into your life.

The BIBLE says, "But to all who did receive him, who believed in his name, he gave the right to become children of God." *John 1:12, ESV*

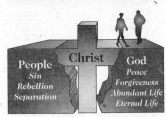

THE INVITATION IS TO:

REPENT (turn from your sins), ASK for God's forgiveness, and by faith RECEIVE Jesus Christ into your heart and life and follow Him in obedience as your Lord and Savior.

PRAYER OF COMMITMENT

"Dear God, I know that I am a sinner. I want to turn from my sins, and I ask for Your forgiveness. I believe that Jesus Christ is Your Son. I believe He died for my sins and that You raised Him to life. I want Him to come into my heart and to take control of my life. I want to trust Jesus as my Savior and follow Him as my Lord from this day forward. In Jesus' Name, amen."

If you are committing your life to Christ, please let us know!

Billy Graham Evangelistic Association
1 Billy Graham Parkway, Charlotte, NC 28201-0001
1-877-2GRAHAM (1-877-247-2426)
BillyGraham.org/commitment